BREAD
&
HENNA

My time with the women of a
Yemeni mountain town

First published in the UK in April 2023 by Journey Books, an imprint of
Bradt Guides Ltd 31a High Street, Chesham, Buckinghamshire, HP5
1BW, England
www.bradtguides.com

Text copyright © 2023 Ianthe Mary Maclagan
Edited by Samantha Cook
Cover design by Ian Spick
Layout and typesetting by Ian Spick
Production managed by Sue Cooper, Bradt & Page Bros

ISBN: 9781784779757

British Library Cataloguing in Publication Data
A catalogue record for this book is available from the British Library
Digital conversion by www.dataworks.co.in
Printed in the UK by Page Bros

To find out more about our Journey Books imprint,
visit www.bradtguides.com/journeybooks

FOREWORD

Yemen, at the moment, is racked by war and hunger. This book is not about that catastrophe. It is about one small part of Yemen that I knew, a window on to a world that has gone.

I did social anthropology fieldwork, together with Tim Morris, in al-Safaqayn in what was then North Yemen, for a year and a half in 1981–83. We were looking at the effects of high male out-migration for work to Saudi Arabia and the Gulf on the community the men left behind, and I was focusing on the lives of the women of that community. We both subsequently wrote our Ph.D theses on this research.

Safaqayn, in the western highlands of Yemen, then had a population of somewhere around a thousand people. It lies at 2,200 metres, nestling in rugged mountains. The journey from the capital, Sana'a, took about eight hours. It is hard, now, to remember how isolated one could be in those days when mobile phones, emails and the internet did not yet exist. The town had one telephone and a weekly post out and in, somewhat erratic and infinitely precious, our only regular means of communication with our friends and families.

Great changes were happening while we were there. It was a time of prosperity compared to what came later, with remittance money flooding in. The influx of new consumer goods and cash came to a community where local infrastructure, medical care and education were still undeveloped. Teachers and health workers came from other Arab countries.

My descriptions concern a particular time and place, and are not to be taken as typical or representative of anywhere else. I have drawn on my field notes, made soon after the events and conversations described. I have changed names, and rearranged some events, but I have not invented anything.

People spoke a dialect of Arabic with many non-standard features. Adjectives did not take feminine agreement, and there were characteristic past tense suffixes. I have transliterated the language with a view to making it easy to read rather than aiming for consistency. For example, the Arabic 'q' was pronounced 'g'; I have written qat, as a term becoming familiar in English, although it was pronounced gat; but *gahwa* for the word from which our 'coffee' derives. I have used 'j' for the Arabic letter *jim*, although local pronunciation was only sometimes 'j', and often 'g', 'gy', or something in between. A glossary at the end of the book lists words that are not explained in the text.

At the time of my stay there were 8 riyals to the pound sterling. Pound equivalents given are 1982 prices; it should be borne in mind that UK prices have more than trebled since then.

I can only hope for a better future for Yemen, and that one day I and others will be able to travel there again.

ACKNOWLEDGEMENTS

I would like to thank: Tim Morris, my companion in this adventure as in many others; Ben Morris, my first reader, for insight and encouragement, technical backup and processing images; Laila Morris and Fergus Morris for reading drafts and general support; Tim Mackintosh-Smith, for his enthusiastic reading; Elisabeth Hallett, for reading drafts and help throughout; Janet Watson, for transliteration advice, with apologies for not taking it all; Shelagh Weir for advice before fieldwork, and support and friendship ever since; Nancy Lindisfarne, for her insights when I was working on my thesis; Philip Bray, for invaluable contributions; and Lynn McAlpine, Christine Hogg, Claudia Cooper, Ian Macdonald, Josephine Reynell, Yvonne Lyon, Helen Newdick and Claire Hicks for reading drafts. Thanks to the staff of Journey Books for bringing this book about, and to Samantha Cook for meticulous editing.

I am grateful to the Central Research Fund of the University of London and the Emslie Horniman Scholarship Fund for grants towards the cost of fieldwork and equipment.

And of course, my deepest debt is to the people of Safaqayn, especially to those who took the trouble to explain things, and to my hosts on my return visits.

CONTENTS

I
EARLY DAYS

Come in

'*Itfaddalu 'andinna*, come in, come in to us, welcome, come and drink *shahi*!'

Faces appear at the windows of the stone houses and women's arms stretch out, beckoning, with a downward movement of the fingers.

The air is thin and sharp but the sun feels warm. We are at 2,200 metres. Each step up the steep, dusty road that rises through Safaqayn costs us a puffing effort.

We are passing a low house at the head of an alleyway. The women are calling us in from ground level. We hesitate. They press us: 'Come in, come in!'

Tim and I have been on the back of a four-wheel-drive Toyota Hilux pick-up truck, climbing for hours on impossibly rough roads, jolted, flung from side to side, clinging on as the car almost stopped to inch its way over huge rocks, up what seemed like nearly vertical inclines. We had hitchhiked the first four hours along the main road from the capital, Sana'a, to the turn-off. Then we had to find vehicles going our way for paying lifts, bumping along the lush flowing river valley of Wadi Sari' for a couple of hours, then leaving the luxuriant wadi vegetation behind for hillsides smelling of herbs warmed by the sun. It was another two hours or more up the dangerous mountain track. The driver juggled a foot between the brake and the accelerator and swivelled round the sharp-angled bends over sheer drops, seeming to scorn the handbrake. Maybe, I thought, no handbrake was reliable enough.

I am exhausted from the journey but curious about the place we've arrived at, a possible site for our fieldwork. We are glad to go into the house, kicking off our shoes and bending under a low doorway to emerge into a small, dark room with grubby furnishings, a television covered with a cloth, and all along the walls mattresses for sitting on and cushions to lean against. The walls are hung with guns and with faded tapestries of lions and peacocks. A roomful of women, headscarfed, in coloured dresses – red, green, purple – with full skirts that fall below the knee and flared trousers underneath, sit around the walls chewing qat leaves. They welcome us in, sit us down on the cloth-covered mattresses, arrange us in comfortable positions, pushing and pulling on my arms and saying, in language easy to guess from their gestures: 'Sit here. Lean on this cushion.'

I'm happy to be pushed and pulled, enjoying the welcome and the women's interest in us, encouraging for our project. I would like to get to know and understand them better.

I pull my skirt as far down as I can. I'm not wearing any trousers underneath it, because my luggage got mislaid by the airline and I have none. I don't yet realise how much this matters.

They pour us tea from a thermos into little glasses. It's very sweet, and tastes of spices. More women immediately come in to see us. One of them hands me something, a sprig of a plant. It smells familiar, herbal and spicy: basil, though it's much twiggier and bushier than the basil I'm used to and just one sprig makes a bunch. She shows me what to do with it: tuck it into my headscarf so it hangs down by my cheek, and I can enjoy the smell.

The women are all talking to each other and trying to talk to us. I desperately wish I could understand more. They have questions they want to ask us. Although it's an all-female gathering, they talk quite freely to Tim. They are speaking a dialect of Arabic I can't understand. With fingers bunched up together and rocking movements they mime something little, a baby – have we got any children?

We say we haven't.

Because I understand so little, I don't know if they mention now what one of them, Warda, will tease me about forever after.

'You were *kashif*! Exposed!' she reminds me when she sees me again, after we've come to live in Safaqayn.

When I return nineteen years later she still reminds me: 'You were *kashif*! Your legs were visible.'

Twenty-eight years after that first meeting, as we sit together in a room in a suburb of Sanaʿa, she will tell me again.

A mountain town

The town straggles up the hillside. Above the road the houses, built of large hewn stone blocks, four or five storeys high, form an interwoven mass with tiny twisting alleyways running steep in between. The grey stone façades are decorated in whitewash, some of which covers whole buildings, some individual storeys, some window surrounds. High above the town black crows with short tails play endlessly in the air, wheel, tumble, recover, as if they are showing off for fun.

Beyond the town are the most sensational views I've ever seen. Deep valleys divide irregular mountains. Little white houses cluster near the peaks, along the ridges, and on promontories. Paths and tracks connect the groups of houses, up and down and round. Steep terraces of crops cover the slopes, everywhere, precisely parallel, striping the landscape as if a comb had run horizontally along the mountainsides. It's extraordinary to see a landscape so marked everywhere, top to bottom, by labour on an unimaginable scale, maintained against the damage done by time and rainwater; whole flanks of mountain transformed by human hand, perhaps over centuries, almost into works of art.

Then the view is blotted out as mist and clouds come up and swirl around the town.

A trail of children follows us through the streets, shouting and calling. One little girl, perhaps about seven, sober and helpful, takes my hand and leads me. Others fetch the town's best English speaker, Ahmed Ali, an ebullient young man who has spent time in the US and who is to become our helper and fixer when we move to the town. We return to the capital, Sana'a, to make a final decision on where to settle to do our fieldwork and to apply for the necessary permits. We are attracted by this mountaintop of sweeping views and friendly, interested people, this town of creeping mists and tumbling crows.

We find out later that Safaqayn was once walled, with gates that were closed at night. A couple of gateways still remain, and the old houses on either side of them form an unbroken line, like a fortress. These tall, old houses have small windows on the lower floors. On the top floor a row of much taller windows with shutters and ornamental half-moon windows on top marks the *mafraj*, the men's guest sitting room. One house catches the eye: large, prominent, neatly built with well-fitting, square-finished stone blocks, obviously new, with a water tank on the roof and fine, expensive bought-in window frames. The family that built it own the generator and the town's electricity supply. It cranks into noisy action at dusk and when it is turned off at 11pm the silence of the night is total.

At the top of the town the house of the sheikh, on the highest point, rises above the rest. From its roof Safaqayn can be seen as a maze of interconnecting flat roofs at different heights, where women spread washing out to dry and tend roof gardens in collections of old containers. Tins of bushy herbs – basil, mint, oregano – are crammed on to ledges below the windows, splashes of green in the grey façades.

The flat roofs are surrounded by parapets so women have privacy for putting out washing, sitting and chatting, and observing what goes on. On the lower side of the road that climbs through the town is the old Jewish quarter, whose inhabitants left for Israel in 1950. They did all the welding and blacksmithing, we are told. Now the same mix of families live here as in the upper town. Outside the upper town a hill with a cluster of government and military buildings – an old fort from the Ottoman occupation, a prison – overlooks a flat plain. A little beyond, the town spills out: the plain outside the old boundaries is filling up with a new style of house, lower and wider.

Although at first Safaqayn in many ways seems to me like a large village, it does have all the trappings of a town: an alleyway of permanent shops as well as a weekly market; government buildings with officials; a prefect appointed by the government from outside the area who uses the old fort with his small garrison; a head of security; soldiers. It's the *merkez*, the administrative centre for the mountain, for twenty thousand people. The population of the town must be somewhere around a thousand, perhaps a little more.

The motor road has been here only about six years. Before 1975, when the road was built, people tell us, when one of the four big merchants in the town came back from Hodeida on the coast they would bring a hundred camels at a time laden with goods up from Bajil, the trading town at the foot of the mountain. The procession would stretch for nearly a kilometre round the mountain track and people would come to gape.

We are living up with the clouds. Some days the mist lies flat, like a white sea, between promontories of hillsides, below the level of the town. Peaks become islands in the mist, spurs of land become headlands. The sunset colours the sea of mist pink. Or the entire valley between us and the next mountain, Milhan, fills with white; the very top ridge of Milhan shows above it. Sometimes the cloud swirls up in wisps and surges, not level but welling up, surrounding, swallowing villages in the middle distance, even immersing the town so that we are living inside the cloud.

After rain, in the new, clear air, we gaze at the views and take photos of successive mountain peaks fading into blue distance. Nearer slopes, all terraced, are green after the rainy seasons and brown the rest of the time, thickly scattered with villages and hamlets of white stone houses.

The black birds, which I later identify as fan-tailed ravens, display their skill in the air over the town, and three kinds of vultures fly in for market day on Thursdays, when sheep and cattle are slaughtered in the open. On other days vultures, hardly more than specks in the sky, circle high over the hillsides. I wonder how many minutes it would take them to glide to the next mountain, where the distant houses can just be seen; for people, it is a gruelling ten-hour journey by four-wheel-drive – five hours down by dreadful roads and five up again – or about the same on foot for fit mountain dwellers leaping down the short-cut paths. Not many people in this town have visited the neighbouring mountain that they see every day, and some say it is full of witches.

When the electricity generator is switched off, the night is dramatic. I had not realised the stars were so many layers deep, stars behind stars, fading away like the mountains in the day. They give an impression of depth in the night sky that I've never seen. At home in England the night sky seems flat, patterned with only a scattering of stars; here there are added dimensions, fainter stars behind the foremost, all brilliant, more than I had ever imagined there to be. The Milky Way is splashed across the sky.

First lodgings

The tiled floor is sloshed wet, but not above the level of our flip-flops. This *beit el ma*, house of water – bathroom and latrine – is quite clean and doesn't smell too much.

'Don't put the scoop on the floor. The scooping tin goes into the clean water, the floor is dirty! Put it on the stone, like this.'

Fatima – the confident, bossy woman of the house, mother of seven living children of all ages from married daughters to a small boy, and, I'm told, ten dead – is scolding me. I'm glad to learn the rules of hygiene; perhaps I was assuming there weren't any. The bathroom, luxuriously, has an enamelled squat toilet fitting. A flat-topped stone rises above the wet floor, to put the water scoop on. The pipe from the toilet goes out to the hillside and empties on to the steep slope below, which is covered with cactuses and plastic bags of different pastel colours. Water, scooped with an old, clean tin from a large barrel, washes around the toilet and the soles of the user's flip-flops; of course it's dirty to put the scoop down on the wet floor, rather than on the stone platform provided for it, or back floating in the water barrel.

For a shower, we heat half a kettle of water and mix it with cold. You can wash well in the water poured from a small kettle, though hair-washing is more of a problem.

Ahmed Ali, the bouncy, extremely helpful English speaker, found us this room to rent with his brother's family, when we came back from the long wait in Sana'a, having at last got our permits to live and research here. He took us to present our papers to the local chief of police and the *mudir*, the prefect, the local representative of central government, who sat in his office in the government buildings on a carpet in front of a low table. Ahmed put us up for the first night – as on our earlier visit, the local children took us to him when we asked where we could put up our tent – and the next day found us this room.

It's their *mafraj*, the room where men look out over the view, relaxing with their guests. It's high-ceilinged, about two metres wide and six metres long – a gathering of men could sit all along the walls and easily talk across the middle as well as to those next to them. The tall windows along one long wall come down almost to floor level: to the level of a man sitting on cushions on the floor. Above the tall windows are semicircular windows with a pattern in coloured glass, blue and green and yellow. These are the half-moon windows that mark the *mafraj* so distinctively from outside a house. The room is furnished with rugs along the floor next to the walls for sitting on, and the three kinds of cushions vital to a Yemeni sitting room: fat ones along the wall to cushion your back, foam pillows on top of them to rest your head against, and little hard oblong *matka*s to lean your elbow on. A hanging patterned like a carpet covers the far wall, and below it we have a foam mattress for our bed, covered with a cloth and cushions in the daytime.

From our room I've watched the Toyota we borrowed reappear outside the town on the long stretch of road framed in the windows, reach the crest of a hill, and go out of sight again, to follow the rough four-wheel-drive track that zigzags down to the wadi by terrifying hairpin bends. Tim is returning it to Sana'a. I am here, feeling the excitement and uncertainty and newness of it, mixed inextricably with the slightly light-headed feeling that comes from the altitude, and the almost dizzy exhilaration of the view from our windows. I can see so wide and so far. The road out to the east runs right across the middle distance, through undulating, neatly terraced slopes, up a hill to where a tree and a village, a line of houses, stand silhouetted on the skyline. Behind the slopes that the road cuts through are further mountainsides, terraced from top to bottom, falling away for one or two thousand metres, with a scattering of white cubes of houses, which at night show as little clusters of light here and there. Often, cloud and mist sit on the mountains so it's like a view from the window of an aeroplane, looking over the fluffy, lumpy surface.

A bird flies right past the window, one I've never seen before, white with a yellow head and a fierce beak, an eagle or a vulture.

We don't have to go out looking for company. Katiba, the young daughter of the family, and her brothers, her friends and relatives, gaggles of grubby children, bringing smaller snotty-nosed children they're looking after, come and sit in our room and stare at us and our things. Katiba has a stolid face, friendly and practical. She becomes my guide and tutor.

We are glad to practise our language with the children. At this point I can't understand the women at all. Arabic studied in London, even sessions with a teacher of specifically Yemeni Arabic, hasn't prepared me for this obscure dialect. Men, more widely travelled and used to other and more standard kinds of Arabic, and schoolchildren taught by Egyptian teachers, are easier to talk to.

'How old are you?' we ask Katiba. She shrugs. She doesn't know. Later we hear her two older brothers arguing about how old the younger one is.

'I'm seventeen,' says the younger brother.

'No, you're fifteen, and Katiba's about ten.'

Almost nobody, it turns out, knows how old they are.

I don't know why they don't – a lack of literacy or the habit of writing things down, a clash of calendars where the Muslim one doesn't keep in step with the seasons to help remember? As time goes on the question seems to me to be more why is it that we in our culture do; or rather, why do we make such a big thing of people's ages? When I return to the UK, I will keep noticing how every news item, however trivial, always gives the age of the people concerned, as if they were tagged with it, as if it was the most important thing about them. It was a liberation for me to have my thirtieth birthday where nobody knew what it was, and has taken the sting out of age as marked by birthdays ever since.

Now there's a knock and Katiba puts her head round the door to our room. She looks with interest at our things, and our foam-mattress bed arrangement at one end.

'Can you show me how you make tea?'

The tiny lobby to the *mafraj* has become our kitchen, with our three-burner gas ring, which runs off a large, heavy gas cylinder, installed on a tabletop, and a set of metal shelves and a plastic-covered clothes cupboard crammed in. There's also a twenty-litre plastic jerrycan, one of two which the family are giving us daily, full of water, as part of the deal. They can get it relatively easily because they have a four-wheel-drive pick-up and fetch water from a spring down the mountain as they need it.

In Sana'a we bought a brass-yellow kettle, made in China, like everyone has. Katiba fills it with water from the filter we have set up and puts in four handfuls of sugar, four cardamom pods and five cloves, boils it, and adds three Lipton teabags. We sip the very sweet, spicy brew. It tastes right, like the tea I've been given here, the local mix of spices.

Katiba throws the used teabags out of the window; all the rubbish goes out to fall past the sheer rock face to a tip far below, where a few stray dogs sniff about. The teabags with their stiff cardboard tags twirl down, circling and spinning like little parachutes.

Market

The second son, Ali, a gangly youth, knocks on my door.

'Come and see the market.'

I follow him through angled alleyways to the main road down between Safaqayn on the right, rising up the slope above the road, and Meruwagha, the former Jewish settlement, on the left, huddling down the mountainside below. I can hear the hubbub of the weekly market before we get there. Men stand in the street and cluster round the stalls, greeting each other, catching up on news, talking, shouting, bargaining, gesticulating with wide emphatic gestures. They wear full-gathered *futas*, skirts, down to their shins or ankles, coloured grey, brown, sky-blue, pastel pink; a few wear a different type in coloured checks, wrapped more closely like a sarong in folds round the waist. With their skirts they wear shirts and tweedy or striped jackets that look incongruously like half of an English suit. Most have their heads covered with a cloth wound into a turban, sometimes around a skullcap or a small straw-woven hat. Just one or two wear the red- or black-checked headscarf familiar from other Arab countries.

Each man carries a long, wide cloth, embroidered at the ends, over one shoulder. These are either folded empty or, later, as they walk away from the market, filled with a bundle of goods and held behind the shoulder, the two ends grasped in front with one hand. Every man wears a jambiya, the curved dagger of Yemen, prominent in the centre front of the waist, on a wide embroidered belt that holds up their skirts. The polished horn handle of the dagger, ornamented with gold-coloured medallions like coins, sticks out from the scabbard and reaches to mid-chest. The sheath, covered in bands of green leather, hangs below the belt and curves sharply to the right, even more sharply than the polished curved blade it holds.

Some of the men have tucked their *futa*s up over their daggers for easier walking. Wiry men with muscled calves on bony legs, they wear flip-flops or plastic slip-on shoes, and have the long, springy stride of mountain people. They chat in groups, bend over boxes and sacks of goods laid out in the street: potatoes, tomatoes, onions, garlic, bananas, imported apples, Nefertiti oranges from Egypt, eggs – almost unbelievably, but it's what the boxes say – from Canada.

I love the bustle and the colour. I look intently to see what food is on sale, what there will be for us to cook.

The hubbub is at its most intense around the meat stalls. A row of ten butchers' tripods lines the street, each one made of poles taller than a man fixed together at the top, holding a pulley arrangement of chains and hooks. Here each butcher drags cattle and sheep, one by one, sharpens his butcher's knife, cuts the animal's throat, lets it bleed on the ground, then hauls it up to hang on the tripod. He quickly skins it, takes out the innards, winding out the intestines like yarn over his hands held out wide, with his knife in his mouth, and then cuts off the meat.

A press of men surround him, shouting and arguing with the butcher, competing for the best cuts since they're all the same price, £8 a kilo – shockingly expensive to us after English prices, but everything is expensive, vegetables, bread and rice as well. Later, women will say to me that I should get Tim to buy the meat, not buy it myself. 'It needs a man to say, "Not that bit, that one."'

The butcher weighs the meat out on handheld scales and gives the customers their portion in a plastic bag. The smell of blood and fresh meat mingles with the smells of the dust of the road and truck fumes. The butchers pile the meat on scraps of cardboard in front of them, and kneel to chop it smaller on a wooden block. Stray dogs, scavengers not pets, watch and wait for scraps at a distance out of reach of kicks and stones. Vultures wait further away.

The main street up through the town is lined with four-wheel-drive pick-up trucks. Some have unloaded their goods, some are selling from the back of the vehicle. They are mostly Toyotas – other makes don't have the clearance for the rocky roads. There are vehicles piled high with sacks of grain and cartons of groceries – sugar, tins of fruit and tinned Kraft cheese and tomato paste, Nido milk powder, Rothmans or Marlboro cigarettes – others with piles of women's dresses, red and black *saramiya* head coverings, men's white Saudi-style robes. A pick-up truck has a row of dresses in sparkly and bright-patterned fabrics draped over a rail in the back, and a pile of men's skirts and jackets. Others hold televisions and occasional luxury goods from Saudi Arabia: a microwave oven (a thing I haven't yet seen in England), a washing machine.

Stalls are laid out on the ground on the side of the road, a display of goods: raisins, large flat brown leaves of *tumbak* tobacco for water pipes, sticky lumps of dates that attract buzzing and crawling flies, folded foam mattresses covered in brightly patterned fabrics, smaller fabric-covered blocks of foam for cushions, plastic buckets, shiny new silver-metal water barrels. There are Indian tin trunks, red or blue or green, painted with designs of bulbous domes. Later I see trunks like these used to carry brides' trousseaux and kept padlocked under women's beds.

I look at aluminium kitchenware, shiny brass-coloured kettles lined up like families in different sizes, big rough wooden yokes for ploughing with animals, fluffy nylon blankets in plastic cases, carpets hanging up, bales of cloth. A couple of stalls sell guns and ammunition. Outside the old wooden doors of the shops, the shopkeepers too have put their goods out on display for the market. Up a side alley, a few donkeys wait while men from outlying villages load them up with piles of sacks. The ground is littered with rubbish, large and small pieces of cardboard boxes and coloured plastic bags.

There are almost no women. Local women don't go to the market. One or two, outsiders up from the wadi, sit behind pottery dishes or a headload of charcoal; they have flatter, browner faces than the local women, and wear pointed wide-brimmed straw hats. On the fringes of the market bustle, small girls and boys hang around, young girls in headscarves and still smaller girls in pointed hoods. As I will later find out, they make themselves useful, running errands for women sitting in their houses, and taking back news and information and the price of everything. A boy, perhaps eight years old, sits on a cloth on the ground with a small stall laid out in front of him: a crate of Sinalco orange drink bottles, a few cartons of cigarette packets, some odds and ends in a box, and a round of foil-packed cheese triangles. Two small boys in tatty clothes keep a tiny stall selling hard-boiled eggs from a wheelbarrow. They do their trade with none of the swagger and giggle of children playing, acting an adult role, but matter-of-factly. Childhood, I will see more and more, is very different here. Children are active agents in the life of the town.

I don't see any qat, the leaf people chew in the afternoons. People must buy it directly from the growers, or, in this rich qat-producing region, have access to their own supply. Ali buys meat and vegetables – potatoes and *bay'ah*, onion greens like thin, flat leek leaves.

In Tim's absence, the family invite me for lunch. We all, father and mother, three sons, Katiba and I, sit on the floor, round a large plastic cloth, where the dishes of food are laid out ready. The youngest son brings a pot of water around the circle so we can each wash our hands in turn. We all say *bismillah*, in the name of God, before starting. First we eat from a wide, round metal tray of *shfut*, a dish of *lehuh*, a pancake-bread made from sorghum, soaked in buttermilk (bought, I find out later, from a relative who has a cow). Dotted with quarters of tomato and onion, and little heaps of a spicy relish, *zahaweq*, it's spongy, with a slightly stretchy, rubbery feel as you pull a piece off the main round, and has a sour taste.

Next Fatima brings in the *helba*, the whole dish named for its fenugreek froth, which covers a broth of meat stock, vegetables and rice. It is still bubbling in the earthenware dish as she carries it in and puts it on a metal tray in the centre of the plastic cloth, within reach of everyone. Her husband, the man of the house, stirs some *zahaweq* into it. We each tear our round of *khobz*, freshly baked wheat flat bread with little black aromatic seeds, and dip it into the dish, soaking up the meat juice and folding it round bits of potato and vegetables in the soupy stew. The taste is permeated with fenugreek, spicy and bitter, mingled with rich meat stock.

After that we eat orange and apple quarters. Katiba and her mother clear away the serving dishes and gather up and take out the plastic cloth with the remaining bits and mess in it. Then we drink glasses of spicy, sweet, hot *gahwa*. I know it's made from coffee husks, traditionally kept and used by Yemenis while they exported the coffee beans. It doesn't taste much of coffee, more of cinnamon.

I go back to our room and work on arranging our stuff. At about 3.30pm a call to prayer sounds from loudspeakers attached to the town's mosque: it must be *'asr*, the afternoon prayer time. A little after, Ahmed, the eldest son of the house, knocks on the door.

'Come, I'll take you to see some women.'

Henna

The women he takes me to see are spending the afternoon decorating their hands and feet. I don't know, this time, if it's for a special occasion, or just for fun.

A pungent herbal-and-something-else smell comes from a bowl in which the hostess, Nuriya, is stirring a thick, smooth brownish paste. Several other women are already sitting on the long mattress against the wall. A blanket, tucked in along the row of women, covers their legs and arms.

'It's henna! Decoration!' they say in explanation.

'Has it got cow dung in?' I ask, curious. (With Arabic I've learnt previously, I can say more than I can understand.) That's just what it looks like, and even the smell, while not exactly of dung, is not completely different either. I get the gist of her reply:

'No no, just powdered henna leaves, but you can put tea in, or a little paraffin, so it comes out nice.'

First they rub a yellow paste on me: *hurud*, turmeric, pounded from the fresh whole roots. They show me some; they look like small yellow ginger roots. The paste gives off a spicy, nostril-tickling smell.

'Put it on your hands, it'll make the henna go on well. And all up your arms, it's good for the skin, it keeps it smooth, that's how we keep our skin nice. In the old days, women used to put it on their faces.'

'Do it on her!'

'Like this,' and they draw a wide, curving yellow line on each side of my face, from the forehead round the cheeks to the chin. They laugh, pleased, I think, at the old-fashioned effect on me.

Nuriya takes a lump of the wet henna paste in her hands and shapes it and plasters it in a band round the tips of my fingers, where it feels cold and damp, and another piece round my thumb. She carefully makes neat edges. She puts a lump in my palm, and curls my fingers down to hold it in place. She wraps a piece of old cloth around that hand, then does my other hand. On my feet she covers the soles with paste and pats it over my toes and a couple of centimetres up all around the sides. She wraps each foot in a plastic bag and props them up clear of the ground. The women under the blanket make space for me and Nuriya tucks the blanket carefully around my feet and hands.

'You have to keep it warm, or it doesn't take properly.' Then she uses her right hand to do her own left hand. 'I'll do the other one later.'

We all huddle under the blanket. I can feel the henna getting warmer, and then drier. The blanket is rough and tickly. I can't move much for fear of spoiling the neat rim on my feet. Soon the base of my spine begins to feel numb, and I shift slightly, failing to find a position that's comfortable for long. Then I feel a distinctive tickle, and realise a flea, no, two or three, have got into my trousers and are roaming at will. My hands are bundled up and I can't do anything about the fleas but put up with them. The room is kept warm, the windows are closed, a brazier full of hot charcoal is held under the blanket to help the henna. A tall water pipe, standing on the carpet in the middle of the room, bubbles: a coconut-shell belly held in brass, a waist-high stem in turned wood like a candlestick, a hose three metres long for reaching round the room to each person in turn, and a wooden mouthpiece. The smells of henna and tobacco fill the stuffy room. Nuriya passes me the water pipe mouthpiece and holds it for me to smoke, while I keep my bundled-up hands under the blanket. I'm not a smoker at home, but I accept it now and draw in. The smoke is cool and easy in my lungs.

We sit and the women chat and I try to catch any words I know in the conversation, but I can only understand when they turn to me and ask questions that are already familiar from repetition.

'Haven't you got any children?'

'How long have you been married? Six years? You should have six by now!'

I reply as best I can.

'I'd like to have children one day, *inshallah*, but not yet. Anyway I only want one or maybe two, at the most. This is *'adi*, normal, where I come from.'

'What do you do, not to have any?' they ask, with lively interest.

'I take pills.'

'Don't they give you *nazif*?'

'What's *nazif*?'

'Lots of blood,' they say, with appropriate gestures, bringing their hands down in front of their stomachs to mime a downwards flow. (I will find as time goes on that in any talk of contraceptive pills women invariably mention *nazif*, haemorrhaging.)

I ask the woman next to me, in turn, 'And you, how many children do you have?'

'Six living,' she says, 'and three dead.'

With the discomfort of sitting so long in one awkward position, and the fleas, and the frustration of not being able to understand much, time passes slowly. Nuriya lifts the blanket and looks under the cloths at my hand, peeling back a corner of the henna.

'*Aduh*, not yet. It's taking, it's coming along, it needs a bit more. Are your feet warm?'

The henna under the cloths slowly dries out and cracks. I can feel it getting stiffer. At last Nuriya declares it ready to be taken off. She pulls off the dried crusts into a bowl held underneath, looking critically at her work: this is good; here's a bit that went out of place.

The fingertips and palms of my hands are pale orange. 'The colour will get deeper,' Nuriya explains. 'Don't wash your hands, leave them overnight.' They feel dry, and crusty where bits are still sticking. My feet are not so good – paler and patchier, they weren't warm enough after all.

I thank Nuriya and go home, keeping my hands as unwashed as I can. In the morning they are distinctly deeper, rich red-orange, almost black in a few places. My nails are a deep transparent orange, a stain in the nail itself without the slippery coated feeling nail varnish gives. The colour will outlast the henna on the skin and only grow out with the nail – six weeks for fingers, at least twice as long for toenails. In the future, when I return from all-too-rare visits to Yemen, the diminishing rim of hennaed nail will measure out the time passing since I was there, the increasing distance between me and Safaqayn.

Back in our house, Fatima looks at my henna, turns my hands over to check. She didn't get hennaed today because she has a period, and it's *'aib*, shameful, not done, to henna during a period, till after the cleansing wash that follows.

I love having hennaed hands. I think the colour is beautiful, a constant source of pleasure adding a richness, an extra dimension to daily life as I catch sight of my hands and enjoy it again.

Women I meet the next day ask 'Who hennaed you?' and admire the result. '*Mabruk!*' they say, congratulations, on the henna. They teach me the reply, '*Allah yebarak*', God bless.

Our first days are a blur of invitations, roomfuls of women I can't understand, hospitality from people I can't remember clearly enough to identify later when I know who everyone is. In the gatherings of women I don't ask them any questions, because I know I won't be able to understand their answers; conversation proceeds as an interrogation of me.

In the bewilderment of these early impressions, before I have any sort of framework to fit them in, we walk around the town trying to make sense of everything. Small children take us in charge and show us round. Muna, a schoolgirl in the first elementary class, takes me gravely by the hand and leads me through the winding streets.

A man we don't know invites us:

'Come and have *gheda* with us!' The midday meal.

When we return to our new lodging and tell the man of the family about this, he says, 'No, you must eat with us today, I've told my wife to cook for you.'

We go back to the family who invited us and explain, and excuse ourselves, saying, 'We'll come another time, *inshallah*.'

'Come tomorrow!'

The next day is a Friday, and about twenty men come from the mosque. 'Like Sunday lunch after church,' I write in a letter to my mother. Lots of food is laid out ready: *shfut*, tomato and onion salad to go with it, then – eaten in between the savoury things – *bint* (or *bint es-sahn*, 'daughter of the dish'), a sweet dish of flaky pastry soaked in butter and honey; rice, potatoes, and a sauce of pounded mint; then the main course, the *helba*, bread to dip, and chunks of mutton with fruit to follow. It's all eaten at enormous speed, and then the men disperse. Looking back later, able to place most of the people in the town, I still don't know who it was who invited us that day.

More cooking

'And *gahwa*, how do you make *gahwa*?' I ask Katiba two days later.

'Have you got coffee?'

We have brought a bag full of whole, dried coffee berries, the beans with their outer coatings, from Sana'a. Katiba runs to her mother to borrow spices: quills of cinnamon and whole pieces of hard, fibrous dried ginger. She also brings a stone.

First we give the whole coffee a burst in the blender. I bought the blender in Sana'a, to do the things in Yemeni cooking that women use a grinding stone for. Then we pick out and put aside most of the beans, now separated from their husks.

'You can use them to make *bunn safi*, pure coffee, if you want to.'

We use the papery husks. Katiba squats down to put the ginger on the concrete floor and shows me how to pound it with the stone. The smell is somewhere between fresh ginger and the powdered ginger that I'm familiar with. It's surprisingly easy to use a stone as a hammer and crush the lump. The cinnamon sticks also get a light bashing.

Katiba fills a saucepan with water and puts in a handful of coffee husks and two handfuls of sugar, and the cinnamon and ginger. She brings the water to the boil and lets it simmer a few minutes with the lid half on. It smells, not of coffee, but spicy with its own distinctive flavour. We try a cup each: just right. I realise I must buy a thermos to keep it in. Rather than offering it to guests and then making it in response, women usually have *gahwa* or *shahi* already prepared in a thermos.

'Shall I show you how to cook something? You can give it to Abdullah for lunch.' Abdullah is Tim's new name. He has explained to people that Timothy means one who honours God, a bit similar to Abdullah, servant of God. I am Mariam, the Arabic for my second name, Mary, which I have often used when Ianthe has been too difficult. I like being Mariam, the sound of it, and the slightly different identity it gives me.

Katiba shows me how to make a basic meal, without meat.

'My mother will have to show you the meat, I don't know how.'

She chops onions and fries them in vegetable ghee from the tin we have bought and adds washed rice, tomato paste from a small tin, and water, and cooks the mixture until it's dry. Potatoes are done much the same way. She makes *zahaweq*, relish, to go with the rice and potatoes, in the blender. Two cloves of garlic, two chilli peppers, thyme, coriander, cumin, and two smallish tomatoes, ground to a sauce.

Helba, essential to a proper Yemeni meal, is more difficult. First we soak a heaped dessertspoon of the green fenugreek powder, the spice smell faintly familiar as an ingredient in curries, in a dish of water for a couple of hours. Then Katiba pours off the water to leave a slippery paste and shows me how to beat it up, with a hand acting as a paddle, round the dish and through the middle, round and through the middle, on and on, till eventually it froths up to several times its original volume.

'It's tiring, my hand gets tired here.' I indicate my wrist.

'No, no, you're doing it wrong, move your whole arm. Don't bend your wrist.' It still doesn't go too well. 'And add drops of clean water. And you need a pinch of *'ud el helba*, helba stick, it's a ground-up root, you can get it in the market.'

My first attempt on my own comes out wrong – I forgot to pour away the water. I also can't get the beating right. It takes twenty minutes' beating and my arm is tired. For some reason, the blender doesn't do it. Years later, I buy a *helba*-beating device in Sana'a with a handle that turns little paddles in a bowl, and the result is better, but still not perfect. I never get my *helba* as light and frothy as it should be.

Visiting with Katiba

The next day I cook the same meal under Katiba's supervision. In the afternoon Katiba appears at our door wearing a different dress for the afternoon's visiting and takes me out.

'Come with me, we'll go to the *walida*.' ('Woman who's given birth' – how clumsy it sounds in English!) 'She gave birth four days ago.'

I follow her downstairs, out into the street, round a corner between tall houses, in through a low, dark doorway, and up a cramped, winding, pitch-black stairway where Katiba takes my hand and guides me, a little too fast.

'*Dunni! Dunni!*'

I duck my head as instructed, and manage not to hit it on the low doorway and stair turnings. It's already sore from many bumps on low beams. We leave our flip-flops at the threshold and I bend double under the door lintel into a room where several women are already sitting, in clean dresses for the afternoon with their *lithma* veils pulled down below their chins to show their faces. The *walida* is lying on a high metal-framed bed, made higher with tins – large, old yellow Nido baby-milk powder tins – propping up the legs. There's a strong, nauseating smell of rue. Bunches of rue and feverfew decorate the room.

Katiba goes up to the *walida* and kisses hands with her, asks her how she is, murmurs words of blessing and congratulation, and gives her two tins of fruit. Then we go round the room and I follow Katiba as she shakes and kisses hands with the women seated against the walls. She takes each woman's hand and kisses it, then, with the hands still joined, the seated woman kisses Katiba's, back and forth three times, then they let go and each kisses her own hand. Then Katiba moves on to the next. When we finally sit down we are given *gahwa*, poured into little glasses from thermoses which the women have brought with them so that the *walida* can relax.

The *walida* stays lying on her bed, resting. Other women attend to the hospitality and pour out the *gahwa*. The baby lies next to the mother, tightly wrapped up. Nobody pays it any attention. When she picks it up to breastfeed it, it's a stiff parcel rather than a squirming baby.

'Do you swaddle babies where you come from?' they ask me, with gestures.

'No, we don't.'

'Our babies would take fright and cry if we didn't. They would move, and startle themselves.'

They ask me, 'Have you got children? How long have you been married? You should have six children by now! Why don't you have any?'

'I couldn't travel, be here, if I had children. I'll have some later, *inshallah*.'

'What do you do, not to have them?'

'I take pills.'

The *walida* says earnestly: 'Can you give me some of your medicine? Having children is *ta'ab*, exhausting, wears you out. I had one before and it died.'

'I can't, you have to go to a doctor and be checked. Could your husband take you to a doctor to get some, or get you some from Sana'a?'

'*Ma yerdi* – he wouldn't, he wouldn't agree.'

The women give me green juicy sprigs of qat from the large plastic-wrapped bundles they keep carefully by their sides.

'What's this?' I ask, pointing to the rue.

'*Shadhab*.'

I write it in my vocabulary notebook.

'Why is it here?'

'It's a *herz*, amulet, protection against *jinn*,' they say. They shrug, as if it's just a custom. '*Jinn* don't like the smell and go away.'

'I don't like it either.'

'It's like a dirty baby, baby pee and shit and not washed,' they suggest.

One woman has brought bunches of basil, some green and some purple. She gives me a large bunch to wear by my ear. Her name is Fatima Abdu. She's been to our room with Katiba, and I will often see her in social gatherings, lively, a good dancer when women dance together to music from a cassette player. She's a young married woman with no children yet, friendly to me, slightly bossy, with a good-natured face. I don't know what gives her the air of authority she wields – perhaps simply force of personality.

'*Allahumma salli 'ala Mohammed*,' the women repeat as they put the basil to their faces and breathe in; I gather that the smell is supposed to remind you of the Prophet. They teach me the word, *mishqor*, for a bunch of herbs worn for decoration, and I write it in my notebook.

Two young women sitting next to me tell me more words. They go through parts of the body, and I write them: arm, chest. Leg, thigh, groin... At this point I just catch the meaning as they joke with each other:

'We're getting near the edge!'

The women sit round the walls, take up their qat one sprig at a time, stroke it to make sure it's free of dust, pick the leaves off, put them in their mouths, chew. The chewed leaves, stored in one cheek, begin to make a bulge. The afternoon develops a hypnotic rhythm of picking and chewing. A pile of discarded tougher leaves and twigs accumulates in the middle of the room. The long hose of the *mada'a* water pipe snakes through the pile. The light from the windows filters through the smoke.

I don't have much success at following the conversation. When I don't understand something, the women repeat it louder and shriller and closer to my ear, then give up. One says: 'If you drink the water here you'll soon speak the language. The water here is light, it's heavy where you come from.'

At last the sunset call to prayer sounds, rising and falling over the town. They tell me the word for it and I write it down.

'Do you pray five times a day?' I ask them.

'Four.'

'Five,' says another woman.

They seem to argue, or perhaps they're just discussing, I can't tell.

'*Qduh maghreb*! It's *maghreb*, sunset, it's already *maghreb*!' the women say. They gather up their remaining qat, wrap it up carefully, and retie their *lithma*s, thin nylon scarves in bright green and pink and red. Each woman stretches hers out behind her head, folds it over the forehead down to the eyes, tucks it in behind the ears, pulls another fold round over the chin and up over the nose to the bottom of the eyelids, then tucks that in. Now it's tight over the face, leaving only the eyes showing, but the bottom part can be pulled down to show the nose and mouth. Then it can be pulled up again, but they still seem to need a lot of fiddling and retying.

They throw their *saramiya* cloths, black with a red stripe near the edge, over head and shoulders, pick up their thermoses and qat, wish everyone good evening and leave. We leave too and Katiba and I walk home together through the dusk. I put my sprig of basil into an old tin of water to keep fresh, and store it safely up on the ledge beneath the coloured windows. I long to grow basil in a pot like the ones I see all over the town on roofs and window ledges, but our windows don't have a suitable ledge on the outside.

I learn the local word for what we do in the afternoons: *rabakh*. It means rest, relax; but it's used for spending the afternoon visiting, or receiving guests.

Katiba and her older brothers drop in on us all the time. Like many children and young men they are easier to understand than older people, and better at understanding us. Young men travel to Saudi Arabia and encounter other varieties of Arabic. Children have Egyptian teachers in school and although Katiba doesn't go to school, she and her little brother have had Quran lessons with one of the teachers. Katiba becomes my interpreter and the expert on me, answering questions about me, when we go out for the afternoon.

We ask her second brother, Ali, about the round scar high on his forehead.

'It's a *misam*, a burn, to make you better. Because I had a fright.'

Who did it?'

'My mother. Anyone can do it. There's another here, on the back of my neck.'

'What's that one for?'

'It was done when I was a child, because I didn't seem alert.'

Katiba has one on the back of her neck too. Everybody has scars, both accidental and from curative burns. A completely unblemished face is a rarity, and when I return to England the smoothness of the faces there will be one of the things that strike me.

Katiba comes in to our room the most often, bringing friends, and smaller children that follow them, or are in their charge. Tim makes pancakes for us all, his speciality, with a filling of sugar and bananas. Katiba loves Tim's pancakes.

There is a downside to the constant company: we miss privacy. We have hardly a moment to ourselves. We're talking to people almost all the time, we get invited in when we go out for walks, the sons of the family and Katiba and other visitors keep dropping in to our room, sometimes when we don't particularly feel like it. Little girls stand and watch whatever we do. We are as if on stage all the time.

One of the visitors is Katiba's older friend Fatima Abdu. She comes round with a friend one morning, and I go out with them to buy tins of apples in the *suq*, for them to give to a *walida*, a new mother, on an afternoon visit.

We stand shouting distance away from the shops and Fatima calls to a boy to get his attention, gives him the money to get the tinned apples, and waits for him to come back.

Then Fatima takes me to her house for lunch. Nine people sit round the plastic cloth on the floor to eat; I feel one more can't be much trouble.

'Come with us this afternoon!'

I go home to change into better clothes and set off with Katiba after *'asr* to another, very similar occasion visiting a woman who's given birth. I begin to recognise familiar faces from Katiba's circle of relatives and friends.

Katiba arrives in our room in the afternoons, unbidden, to take me out. We go to different houses, for different occasions – visiting women who've given birth, women who are finishing their forty days' confinement afterwards, joining occasions at the houses of notable people in the town – a party at the sheikh's house, a gathering at the hakim's house – and going to the houses of friends and relatives all over the town. She tells people about me, answers their questions on my behalf, and tells me what to do, where to sit, how to behave. If I make a move to leave too early, she says 'Not now!' If I'm invited to a house, she comes with me. One afternoon she tells me she is *zalen*, angry, with me because I insist on going to the house of a woman who has given birth, who asked me that morning. All my protestations that she doesn't have to come with me are to no avail. There are too many people, she says. I wonder if her family are on bad terms with the woman, or her husband, but when we arrive there her mother is among the women sitting.

Katiba will leave a gathering only when I do, even if she wants to go sooner.

'Why do you wait till I leave? Is it *'aib* for me to go alone later?' *'Aib*, shameful, is a word I already know from my reading about Arab societies.

'No, my heart tells me to.' I wonder if she's under instructions from her family, and if my behaviour perhaps reflects on them.

Hosting an afternoon

I am hosting an afternoon's *rabkha* at my place – Katiba has put the word out. We plan to have a henna session, after giving the guests *gahwa* and popcorn.

This afternoon, instead of a *zenna*, the locally made style of dress with fitted bodice and full skirt, Katiba is wearing a bought factory-made dress, orange, straight, with a built-in belt and contrasting collar.

She borrows a *mada'a* water pipe from her family and gets it ready for the afternoon's smoking. She breaks up and soaks and squeezes out *tumbak*, the tobacco that's sold in the market in whole-leaf, orange-brown sheets. She lights lumps of charcoal on our gas burner, and uses tongs to pile them with some of the tobacco into the *buri*, the pottery bowl, a handspan wide, that is wedged with a twist of cloth over the upright stem of the *mada'a* like a lily on a stalk. An old tin with both ends open sits on the top of the burning tobacco.

Young women and little girls arrive in groups of friends, neighbours and relatives, women I know from going out *rabakh*ing with Katiba in the afternoons. The long, narrow room fills up. Katiba and I make popcorn and pass it round in bowls; it's greeted with cries of '*Timfash, timfash!*' (Popcorn!) and is very popular.

Women sit round the edges of the room, and little girls in the middle. The women are young, wearing bright dresses, with their hair parted far to one side and slicked in a glossy wing over the forehead, visible below a headscarf. If they are wearing a *lithma* down to their eyes you can't see their hair at all.

'We can't do henna, there are too many,' Katiba says. She puts a cassette into our tape player and we have dancing, two women at a time in turn holding hands, bending one knee to the beat and shuffling very slowly round in a circle.

It's a lively scene, about twenty women and girls. The women's dresses and *lithma*s are all different colours, red and green and purple and pink, and everyone is laughing and chatting busily. They seem to be enjoying the afternoon. It's all very relaxed. I decide to take a photo, and get my camera.

Half-rising, Fatima Abdu takes it upon herself to tell me: '*Aib! Aib!*' Shameful, not done. 'No, don't take photos!'

I'm taken aback by the quick shift of mood. Reluctantly, still surprised, I put my camera away. I know that women's faces are private, not to be shown to men outside the family, but somehow the relaxed feeling of this afternoon made me assume a photo would be all right. In the future I will photograph women only when they ask me to. It will never, it turns out, be in front of lots of others.

One of the drawbacks of where we're living is that there isn't another room, somewhere where Tim can go if I have women round. Tim has gone out to spend the afternoon with some men, but now he comes back, early, and I'm worried that it's *'aib* for him to be here with the women. But nobody objects. They welcome him in, obviously curious to see him.

'No, no, it's not *'aib* for him to be here.'

'Is that because he's not a Yemeni?' I ask Katiba. She seems to agree, but over time I see other men sitting in with groups of women, usually in their own houses, and also I notice how much propriety seems to vary with different people and families.

At *maghreb*, when we hear the call to prayer, the women get up to go, rearranging their *lithma*s and *saramiya*s, wishing us and each other good evening.

'Some foreigners had to leave Mahwit,' Katiba tells me after they've gone, 'because they took photos of schoolgirls and the photos appeared in a newspaper.' Mahwit is a bigger town three hours' drive away to the east, the province capital.

I'm sad to think I won't be able to take any pictures of the lively, colourful women's parties and gatherings in which I am spending so much of my time.

After a few weeks, we begin to think again about our lodgings.

'How much rent are you paying? That's too much!'

'Is it true that you're paying…?'

'*Haram*!' Wicked, sinful.

People exclaim about what our landlords are charging us with censure mixed, perhaps, with a little admiration.

Prices are high in general, the exchange rate for the pound is unfavourable, and we feel poor. The country is undeveloped and the poorest in the Arab world, yet there's a lot of money about, pouring in as remittances from men working as migrant labour in Saudi Arabia. This is the height of the remittance boom, a golden time, with Yemenis freely coming and going to Saudi Arabia and easily finding well-paid menial jobs, not yet facing competition from Asian workers as they will later. We are paying £40 a week including electricity and forty litres of water a day. It's on a par with London prices. We can't really afford it.

We start to look for somewhere else.

II
BEING A
HOUSEHOLD

Move

A swarm of children surround us, follow us, ask about our stuff and help us carry things as we move to our new house. They pour up the stairs and find places round the walls of the room and sit there unblinking.

Unlike our first lodgings, it's not one of the tall, fine, well-built stone houses of the town. Its blocks of stone are smaller and more roughly dressed. It looks old and slightly tumbledown. The floor shakes when I sit down. Later, when I first feel the tremors of the earthquake of December 1982, I assume it's just our house falling down.

The entrance is up a steep rocky path and some steps. Inside the metal front door, painted green with a pattern of raised metal strips, is an uneven step of big stones surfaced with earth. The staircase is dark, mud-surfaced, crumbly underfoot, and uneven, with several low beams to dodge overhead. Two unexpectedly steeper steps wrong-foot you as you climb. The stairs lead past the ground-floor rooms of our neighbours, past a *beit el ma*, 'house of water', and a storeroom on the middle floor, to our two smallish, roughly whitewashed rooms with an entrance space that will be our kitchen – less convenient than before, because there's no window to throw dirty water and rubbish out of.

To get into our rooms you step over a calf-high threshold, while ducking because the doorway is low at the top. For me, this makes the rooms feel slightly claustrophobic. The doors look antique, battered, dark wood worn to a patina, with traces of old carved decoration.

The rooms, a medium and a small one, have low ceilings, whitewashed. You can see the construction of the ceiling under the whitewash, long beams with shorter ones across. The windows look down over the street coming up through a row of shops outside. For a distant view we must go up to the roof.

Over the past couple of weeks we have negotiated the rent, the fresh coating of the walls in *goss*, gypsum whitewash, and the installation of electrical wiring and fittings, paid for by us. The man who turned his hand to installing the electrics also fixed us up a remarkable TV aerial on the roof, constructed from old tin lids. After we've moved in and paid him the price we agreed for the work, 500 riyals, he comes round to ask Tim for more money.

'I've had an expensive time, my wife has been ill and now she's given birth...'

'You can have the fixtures when we leave,' Tim says – the wiring and fittings that we have paid for.

The rent we're paying is still discussed among people we meet in afternoon gatherings, and we're still told it's too much: 'It was eight hundred riyals a year before!' – that is, £100. We didn't know that when we agreed the price. But at £20 a week, it's half what we were paying in the other place.

Our landlady is stout, bustling, un-demure and screech-voiced. She runs the restaurant at the bottom of the town, used by outsiders visiting for market day or litigation or other dealings with government offices. Her husband comes with us when we go to the *mudir*, the town prefect in the government offices, to make it all official, but she takes an active part as well.

People warn us about her. 'She poisons the customers,' one little girl tells me later. But there is animosity between them: they are next-door neighbours, and have an ongoing dispute about ownership of the strip of land between their houses.

One morning at the qat shop, in front of an audience, our landlady pounces on us. Screeching, expostulating, she says the fittings are hers.

'*Aib!*' she says, stroking her chin: shameful.

Tim strokes his chin and says '*Aib*' in return. 'Do you want our TV as well?'

Everyone joins in. Some of the bystanders start suggesting we should give her half.

After a lot of discussion we reach an agreement: she will pay us 200 riyals and the fittings will be hers, and the 200 riyals will go to our electrician, in accordance with our offer to give the fittings to him.

I don't see why we should pay our electrician any more, since we gave him the price he asked before we moved in; but I'm glad we stuck up for our ownership of the fittings. We are not sure how much we are regularly overcharged. Attempts to make us pay more than 1 riyal a piece for bread have now been discontinued, since we know the right price. I'm not sure if being ripped off is a necessary tax, part of paying our way in the town and conducive to good will, or bad for our status and for being respected.

We meet our electrician on the way back up and explain the deal to him. He looks unhappy until Tim says the man in the qat shop is a witness to our landlady promising to give us the 200 riyals; then he says, 'Ah, a witness,' and is satisfied.

We arrange our furnishings. We've bought new and splendid cushions from Sana'a to sit against, of red velvet with a wiggly stripe in the pile, and dark blue with a gold pattern. We have sponge mattresses to sit on, covered in the pattern we see everywhere, red and yellow and green and black; hard cuboid *matka*s to lean on, in red and pink patterned stripes; and flat foam pillows in Chinese pillowcases to be held with elastic against the wall at head height, to lean back against. We hang Tim's jambiya on the wall. It's a cheap, inferior one: some Yemeni men are walking around wearing jambiyas worth thousands, even tens of thousands of pounds. We stick pictures of England on the walls, green fields and English cows, as conversation starters. We put cushions along the back of the foam mattress we sleep on, so it can be used as seating during the day. Unfortunately they block part of the light from the small windows. Above these windows are tiny plain window lights, with no coloured glass this time. They are set into alcoves in the walls which form shelves where we put a couple of small pictures, and I keep *mishqor* I've been given, in a tin of water. The fine new furnishings contrast with the cramped little room, but look good against the fresh white walls. Vinyl in an orange-brown pattern covers the slightly bumpy packed-earth floor. We have a twelve-inch black-and-white TV covered with a cloth, and a car battery to run it off in the afternoon, when the electricity isn't on. Later we buy a *mada'a* and a brass tray for it to sit on.

Our downstairs neighbours are a couple in modest circumstances, a dwarf and his wife, another Nuriya. Nuriya has an open, guileless face. She wears an old dress and has her hair in the style older women still use: a centre parting, two plaits thickened and extended with black wool and hanging in a big loop on each side, ends tucked up under the headscarf. She has a necklace of big, square yellow amber beads.

'Your neighbours are weak, they won't give you any trouble,' someone says to us; an interesting reflection on how the powerful can be expected to throw their weight around.

We share the *beit el ma*, the bathroom on the middle floor. I am really pleased there is one; some houses have none. ('What do you do?' I ask a family who live on one floor of a big old house. 'We go a long way away,' they say.) This bathroom isn't tiled; the floor is earth, and the walls earth-surfaced. The fittings are roughly squared-off lumps of stone. You step over a low wall to reach the wet area. It's a long-drop latrine with the traditional system for separating liquid and solid waste. When you squat in the right place, over the hole, on a small stone platform, solids fall through the hole into a sealed chamber below, effectively a whole closed room on the ground floor. (After long enough, well-decomposed, inoffensive fertiliser can be taken out of the chamber, but we are told that nobody in the town wants to do this work any more.) Nuriya pours ash down the hole from time to time to keep it sweet: this is surprisingly effective. The angled front of the platform directs liquids forwards and out of a hole in the side of the building. Above the wet floor rise two flat-topped stone footrests where you stand or squat to wash, with another in front of you to put the water container on. A big covered metal barrel holds water, and a small tin sits on top for scooping it out.

The stairs go on up through a door out on to the roof. Here, on the flat whitewashed surface, we can sit and enjoy the sun, watch the bustle in the street below on market days, and, I hope – something I'm excited about – grow plants in old tins. We stand and breathe the air, crisp and thin with a faint tang of woodsmoke. We have a view south and west, as opposed to our northeast view from the old room: a terrific sense of space, a wide panorama with gnarled mountainsides rising into peaks, peaks behind them and more behind those, dissolving into haze; and looking downwards, terraces descending into valley clefts, and groups of white houses. A track runs along the side of the mountain, where we can see the next village, a cluster of houses across a dip and a little below us, before the road goes down the west flank of the mountain southwards to the coastal plain – a route we will not often take as it's even more bumpy, twisty and dangerous than the way down the east side.

Tiers of terraces rise above the road, and curve below it, stepped like amphitheatres, in hollows in the mountainside. Beyond this clear foreground is the distant face of Milhan, the next mountain to the west, hazy and tinged blue by the intervening air, with little settlements just visible. The view is as splendid as the one from our old room, but we don't live with its exhilaration all day as we did there, because of the small windows.

Immediately below is a market street of one-room, stone-built, flat-roofed shops, mostly closed up. On market days we can look down from our roof or peer through our windows at the bustle in the street, people we know and men who have come in from the countryside, a clamour rising up to us of shouts, greetings, transactions, arguments; a crowd of bare-legged mountain men in skirts with bundles, cloths filled with goods, slung over a shoulder. On other days, framed in the window, I can see women in dark workaday dresses, *saramiya*s over their heads and hanging down their backs, climbing laboriously up the hill with fifteen- or twenty-litre water containers on their heads.

Enormous, beautiful, powerful birds of prey soar round the mountains and glide right above our roof. Their wide wings end in feathers splayed out like fingers. They rise in thermal currents, hardly beating a wing. When my mother brings a bird book, I find they are griffon vultures. They are the same birds as the vultures that hop and sidle, poking their heads, ugly and ungainly on the ground, beyond the slaughtering at the market.

We will have to get our own water, carrying it from the cistern, or buying it from trucks at 30p for twenty litres. This is partly an advantage, I think, as we can use as much as we want, for example when we wash clothes, without arguments with our landlords. As in the old place, we boil, then filter, the water we drink. Because of the altitude it needs twenty minutes in a pressure cooker to be safe. It's so dirty that we have to scrub our ceramic filter out almost every day.

Nuriya from downstairs is friendly, comes up to say hullo, looks at all our stuff. It will soon be reported around the town how we have far too much. Her little girl, Sabah, quiet and well behaved, comes up to see us on her own and sits gravely in our room.

All day, various little girls, their faces framed in headscarves or quaint peaked hoods, come in and out, stand in the middle of our main room, sit around the edges, and stare at everything.

The electricity representative, a dignified, mature man who also works in the mosque, who walks around the town with his small daughter on his shoulder, and whom we knew as a neighbour in our first house, pays a visit to fix the monthly rate we are to pay for electricity. He's funny, a showman, acting out for us how people behave when he visits them on his rounds to collect the monthly fees: he pats all his pockets, assumes an air of surprise – no money to pay with! He's the collector for the family of low-status origin who own the electricity generator, unrelated to them, an ultra-respectable face for a business whose profitability might be resented.

He assesses our monthly payment at 95 riyals. People have told us to expect 60 or so. We protest. He counts up our light fittings, says there's also the electric blender.

'People told us it would be sixty.'

'No, it has to be ninety-five.'

We don't see what we can do. He stays very pleasant. We sit and drink tea, and make conversation. He starts to talk about Ramadan, still some five months away.

'Ramadan here is very good, not like Sana'a or Hodeida – there people eat each in their own house and don't stay up all night. People come here for Ramadan.'

This is the start of a long build-up of expectation, people talking about Ramadan and looking forward to it.

He gets up to go and wishes us good evening. A moment later he's back.

'Can you lend me a torch to see my way down the stairs?'

Our lethally sloping and irregular stairway is completely dark.

'I'll put a small light on your stairs – no extra money.'

An explosion. Terrific banging all round, another explosion. What can be going on? We climb the steep stairs and emerge on to our flat roof, into the night.

Everyone is out on their roofs. People are firing rifles and letting off firecrackers, and chanting in chorus, '*La ilah illa Allah*', there is no god but God. The smell of burning and of fireworks hangs in the air.

The moon is going, very slowly, into full eclipse.

'Come over here, our roof is higher!' It's our new neighbours, whom I already know from afternoons with Katiba, to whom they are somehow related.

Our roof leads up a step to the roof outside their kitchen window. We climb in through the window, and up through their house and out at the top. People are lighting bonfires on their roofs and banging pots and pans. The whole of the next mountain, across the valley, is dotted with the orange lights of bonfires as well as the usual sprinkling of house lights. There are firecracker explosions from all sides. Rockets light up the sky. Tim loses a patch of hair to a burning ember, which causes great merriment all round.

Finally the moon is fully eclipsed. It's glowing orange red and seems to stand out in 3D. It stays that way for several hours. The men go off to the mosque to pray.

We descend the stairs through the neighbours' house and they give us tea, sitting on cushions in their living room, and we learn that they knew about the eclipse in advance, last month. Somebody had read about it in a newspaper. It must have been in Sana'a or a big town; we never see a newspaper in Safaqayn. We wish we had the language to ask more about what we've just seen. Then we go back down over our roof to bed.

A day's exploring

Tim and I walk around together to explore the town, followed by the inevitable trail of, it seems, half the town's children, endlessly chanting our names and '*sura, sura*', picture, to ask us to photograph them. We find more houses than you see at first view, smaller houses hidden behind the big ones and down alleyways. We have to watch our feet to avoid the rubbish in the street. The tall town houses tower above us, drawing the eye up to the row of big windows on the top floor, with their coloured glass half-circles above, red, blue, yellow, green, geometric patterns in plaster. The plaster on the outside is cut in different shapes from the framework for the coloured glass inside, so that it doesn't correspond with the coloured pieces, but at night shows a broken-up pattern of colour with the light shining through. The windows of the lower floors are smaller and more irregular in their arrangement. The *mafraj* on the top floor, where men chew qat with their guests, is cleaner, more spacious, and ideally has far-reaching views over the dramatic mountains and valleys around. Women use smaller, grubbier rooms with older furnishings on lower floors, though they hold gatherings in the *mafraj* if the men aren't using it. From their windows women observe the street below and everyone who comes and goes, people and cars.

The houses run together so that sometimes rooms of one house are over rooms of another, interlocked. In this way our kitchen is over and under parts of the house of our neighbours across the roof, a house whose door faces in another direction and is a long walk round from our alley. The flat whitewashed roofs are like steps: they are not all on a level but you can often get from one to another.

Among the picturesque white-splashed old stone houses, sheds made of corrugated zinc sit incongruously, along with the occasional cuboid metal water tank. Over the town, high in the air, the fan-tailed ravens circle, play and dance with each other.

A row of one-storey, one-room shops runs around one edge of the town, most closed up or used for storage. They are built rather roughly of blocks and lumps of stone, and have battered wooden doors on forged iron hinges hooked into iron loops on the doorjambs. The doors, although they now look old and neglected, are elaborately and variously carved with geometric patterns, circles, dots and arabesques. They are locked with small, shiny Chinese-made padlocks fastening a metal bar through loops, but they also have huge, old wooden locks projecting, carved like another piece of decoration. An upright piece as big as a hand has a crosspiece fitting into it nearly as big, which bars the door shut. Inside where upright and crosspiece intersect is an arrangement of falling pegs. The key is a piece of wood with corresponding pegs which lift the ones inside the lock. It looks like a giant, sparsely bristled toothbrush. Women keep keys like this stuffed down the back of their dresses and pull them out from behind their necks.

New buildings have metal doors, decorated with more angular raised metal patterns and painted in several colours to bring out the design.

Some of the one-room buildings are open as shops, every day, not just market day. They sell tins of tomato paste, tinned cheese and mackerel and ful beans; eggs imported from Canada and Finland; plastic slip-on shoes, flip-flops from China, torches and batteries; bottles of Sinalco fizzy orange and cola drinks, and the dreaded Vimto, which hospitable people give us to drink and which I hate (it tastes like cough mixture); big cream-yellow tins of Nido and Nina baby-milk powder, cartons of Mamex infant formula; Marlboro and Kamaran cigarettes; different sizes and designs of thermoses; packets of biscuits. Stacked cartons are printed with Chinese writing. One shop sells frozen chickens from France. We eat them, but we wonder how many times they have thawed and refrozen in getting here.

The customers take their goods away in pastel-coloured plastic bags, pale pink and orange and blue with little red spots, the same that litter the countryside and look from a distance, drifted into gullies and stuck en masse in thorn bushes, like pretty coloured flowers.

One of the shops is a pharmacy, where a man known as '*doktur*' has a flourishing business, seeing patients and dispensing medicine. Tim spends some afternoons chewing qat there, while customers come in, mostly, for vitamin and hormone injections. The owner is neither a doctor nor a pharmacist: he has no formal training, though he says he has a licence after passing a test from the Ministry of Health in Sana'a. There are no trained Yemeni doctors or health workers in the town.

At the very bottom of the town we pause, fascinated, at the window workshop. Here the stages of making stained-glass windows are laid out like an exhibition. It starts with large shallow slabs of plaster, stacked leaning up against each other. A design has been scratched on them, wide curves at the top for the shape of the window, and the beginnings of the pattern it will hold. Another slab has a more deeply incised, definite outline, ready for cutting out. Others again have been cut out, with a wide rim of plaster remaining and narrower segments outlining the design: curved and geometric motifs, a stylised tulip, an eagle like the national emblem. They sit upright waiting to be filled with coloured glass or perspex, green, blue, yellow, red.

When we talk to the carpenter one day, looking at the windows finally being put in a house near his workshop, he tells us that one window costs 2,000 or 3,000 riyals. A day labourer working in the fields earns 60 riyals a day, with a midday meal and qat for the afternoon provided by his employer. Fancy windows display the wealth men have earned as migrant labourers in Saudi Arabia. They ornament a room and cast shapes of coloured light on to the walls and floor when the sun shines through. At night the rich colours and patterns, lit from inside, give a fairy-tale quality to the streets.

We make our way home to cook some lunch, fried onions with tinned ful beans. The girl from across the roof, another Fatima, appears on our landing with some bread from her mother. She uses the occasion to look at our kitchen and to watch us cooking. The bread is *jehin* with sorghum flour, dense and tasty.

Tim has afternoon visitors. Two young men, in *futa*s and jackets, jambiyas at their waists, one with his headcloth casually hung in front of his waist on his dagger as if it was a peg, have come to learn English. They both have moustaches and longish hair, combed flat on top with a side parting, frizzing wide at the sides. They relax, lounge, as men often do, with their hands on the shaft of their jambiyas.

These days everybody wears jambiyas, but this wasn't always the case. They used to indicate social status, worn by tribesmen but not butchers and other low-status men, and anyway, one man tells us, were not generally worn in this area, they're a new thing here. In the old days big men only, he says, would wear a differently styled, slimmer, silver-cased, diagonal dagger, *thumeh*. Now jambiyas are a general, and important, symbol of manhood. They are not much used for cutting, but we see people opening cola bottles with them. Some – old, with beautifully ornamented hilts, made perhaps of rhinoceros horn – are immensely valuable. The good ones need regular polishing by a polisher, a *saqqal*, an old occupation that only one man in the town still continues. Jambiyas are surrendered to authorities dealing with disputes as a token of submission to arbitration. Much later, when we're about to leave the town, a man expresses an interest in buying Tim's jambiya, one so cheap that it's seen as a sort of imitation rather than the real true thing. He has a proper, costly one, but he wants Tim's to use as a spare to wear on visits to government officials instead of his good one in case it gets taken. Then he would keep the real one for occasions, parties and celebrations.

To a Westerner familiar with Freudian concepts they look like a blatant phallic symbol. We tried this idea out on a Yemeni friend later: was a jambiya in any way a sort of symbolic penis? The idea meant nothing to him, and he didn't think so at all.

Now, we sit and chat. I offer the young men tea or *gahwa*, but I feel slightly inhospitable because I have none ready-made in a thermos in the Yemeni style.

'Which is England,' they ask, 'mountain or desert?'

We point to the pictures we have on the walls, English cows in green fields, and try to explain how a country can be neither.

They talk about bride prices, bemoaning the huge recent inflation in what the bridegroom's family have to pay.

'Here it's fifty, sixty thousand riyals [£6,000–7,500]. And the groom pays a thousand riyals "for the door", to go into the room where the bride is, a thousand "for the uncovering", to remove her veil, a thousand to sleep with her the first night. A man with five daughters will buy a house with the money from one, a car from another... it's *tijar*, commerce, business. The groom is cleaned out by the time he gets to his bride. How much does a bride cost in your country?'

We try to explain it doesn't work like that. 'There isn't bride price where we come from. The bride's father doesn't get anything. The young people have to love each other and agree between themselves.'

'So if I come to your country, and get one of these free brides, will she convert to Islam?'

'It's not as easy as that...'

We ask: 'Do girls get married when they're still young?' Several women have told me they were first married as children.

'No, people used to but now it's forbidden.'

The conversation moves on to illness.

'My mother is very sick,' one of the young men says. 'She's going to die. Her stomach is swollen up.'

'What is it?'

'It's because someone gave her *sagwa*, menstrual blood boiled up in *gahwa*.'

'Has she been to a doctor?'

'Yes, in Hodeida; he said an operation wouldn't help, it's in all her body now.'

After they've gone Nuriya from downstairs comes up with some *lehuh* pancake-bread for us, and she and little Sabah sit with us and drink the *gahwa* I made.

We ask her about what we've just heard.

'*Sagwa*, what is *sagwa*?'

She says the same thing: menstrual blood put in tea or *gahwa*. She mimes squeezing out the blood from the fabric of her trouser legs.

'Who would have done this to the woman?'

'Don't know. An enemy...'

In the evening we trudge down the hill in search of our gas cylinder. We sent it with a qat carrier down the mountain to Bajil, the large town on the plain, to be refilled. The shop in the lower town is closed. A little girl looks out of the window of the house behind.

'It's closed up, my father's gone to pray. Come in and wait.'

We go in and sit down on cushions against the wall. A young woman is there, with a long nose and several gold teeth. I know her from afternoons with Katiba; she's a daughter of the house, but married to someone up in the town. She's wearing all the gold she can: a necklace with a large medallion, earrings, a row of bracelets. She has her baby with her, and is obviously pregnant again.

'Are you living here?' I ask her, puzzled.

'I'm *haniq*, angry, I've run away from my husband.'

She looks quite calm, matter-of-fact, not tearful or desperate, and not embarrassed.

'What's wrong?'

She flicks her cheek with her fingers to mean 'bad'.

'He's not good. He's angry with me.'

'How, not good?'

'His mouth.'

'Is the gold from him?'

'No, I bought it.'

I suppose it's from her *mahr*, her own portion of the wedding payment; her insurance.

We wait a while, but there's no sign of her father, and we give up and climb up home. Well after *maghreb*, we go back down to the shop again. We have with us some photos we took of the family. The man is there, but he says, 'The gas bottle's come, but the shop is locked up for the night, you can have it tomorrow. Come in and have some supper.'

We sit round a plastic cloth on the floor and eat *lehuh* and pepper paste and a dip of tinned mackerel with the family.

'Why don't you have any children?' the father of the family asks us.

The daughters, who have heard me answer this question before, sitting in afternoon gatherings, explain to him.

'She takes pills.'

'We don't have pills like that here,' he says.

Children and photos

When we walk in the street, a rabble of children follows us, shouting and chanting our names, '*Mariam we Abdullah*'; grubby kids, in an assortment of clothes that are often torn and too big or too short in the sleeve, little girls carrying on one hip bare-bottomed children not much smaller than themselves. Adults as well are always popping in to our rooms, calling to announce themselves as they come up the stairs. Our downstairs neighbours complain.

'You shouldn't let all the children in. Shut the front door.'

We are glad to welcome children, up to a point, because of the useful language practice and information they give us on the town and people's names. We spend quite a lot of our time with them. But people are distrustful of the noisy, uncontrolled mob.

'Lock your things up, they'll take them.'

'Don't let them in, be firm with them.'

In the street the rabble comes after us like a procession, calling, '*Sura! Sura!*', picture, photo, and jumping and stretching out arms to be in the picture when we pause to take shots of the town. Our prints have hands spread out in the front, faces poking into the sides.

We take pictures of them. On principle, we take pictures of anyone who asks us, a way to give something back to the town. Men pose stiffly for us, with strikingly impassive faces.

'Why don't you smile for the photo?' we suggest to one man.

'Only women laugh,' he replies, and maintains his dignity in a solemn expression.

Little boys do military salutes. Then when our weekly post comes, and with it the possibility of developed and printed photos, we're besieged even more, high voices clamouring, 'Where's my photo?' A roomful of children scrabble over our pictures of the town.

'Look! There's Fulan's wife!'

'Where?' I ask in alarm. I'm always careful not to include women in the picture.

'There, on her roof!' A tiny figure, pinhead size, in the middle distance, which I hadn't noticed and could never have recognised.

It's not only children: adult men too come round all afternoon on post days. And as soon as we put our heads out of the door adults and children clamour for their photos.

People tell us we only have ourselves to blame, taking photos of the children.

Missing Katiba

After we move, I hardly see Katiba any more. This is a shock to me. I spent so much time under her guidance, going to other houses with her, being told what to do, that now I feel bereft. I assumed she'd still drop in, but the ten minutes' distance through the alleyways of the town seems to be too far for casual visits. I begin the long process of understanding the invisible spatial constraints on women's apparently free movements around the town. The change for me after being taken out most afternoons is a big one. I was getting fond of her, and I miss the range of houses she took me to and the language practice I gained from her dropping in during the day.

One day I see Katiba's friend Semira in the street and ask if she'll be seeing Katiba, and suggest she comes round. They do, that afternoon, dressed up for visiting, with a trail of children: Semira's little sister; the two small sons of Katiba's oldest brother, Ahmed, and his divorced first wife, who now live with his family and are looked after by Katiba and her mother; and the four girls from next door to us across the roof, who range in age from a toddler to a young woman.

The older girls are interested in my tape recorder. I demonstrate. I would like to record them talking, but they refuse to have their voices recorded on the tape.

'It's *'aib*!' Like photographing their faces?

We make popcorn. The children squabble and fidget. One little girl is particularly irritating, everyone finds her a nuisance, and Katiba scolds her: '*Ya gahba!*'

I write this down in my notebook, but they all exclaim: 'No, no, you mustn't write it, it's not good!'

So I cross it out. 'What does it mean?' I ask.

Katiba leans over one of the little boys and makes a scratching movement at his crotch.

'Now have you got it?'

I find the word later in the dictionary: whore, prostitute. After that I hear it often. It's one of the most frequent insults flung out in anger by mother to little daughter, by women to each other.

Nuriya from downstairs drops in, dressed up and wearing crimson lipstick, clearly on her way somewhere. She mutters something disapproving about lots of children, and soon leaves. Katiba and the children don't stay much longer. I realise that Katiba doesn't leave her house except when she is dressed up to go out in the afternoon; she can't really pop in as she did when we were in her house.

Another afternoon she comes round again, with Semira and the girls from next door.

'I came the other day, but you were out.'

'I'm sad without you,' I say.

'*We ana akthar* – and I am more.'

'Come round more often.'

'Come to Ahmed's wedding, there'll be lots of celebrations.'

'When will it be?' I am keen (at that point – before I've been to sixteen of them) to see a wedding.

'In a month, or eight days, or when the qat is green.' Of course, the wedding will need qat.

When we were living in their house, Katiba's brother Ahmed was frustrated with his lack of progress in getting another wife. We heard that he had divorced his previous wife after she had a fight with his mother.

'I'm angry, upset, because I haven't got a wife,' he told us. He added that Katiba didn't go to school because there was too much work in the house. She could go if he got married.

There were negotiations with another family for a bride, while we were living there, but they failed. The other family asked 100,000 riyals (£12,500), then came down to 80,000, then to 60,000. Ahmed went up from 30,000 to 40,000, but refused to go any further than that. He said to us, perhaps he'd get a bride from Egypt for 10,000 riyals. But now he is marrying a local girl who's been married once before, briefly.

Katiba tells me about a woman – we know her, she's now married to someone else – who was engaged to Ahmed, for a year, and then broke it off.

'Why?'

'She just said she didn't want to, no reason.'

'Isn't that *'aib*?'

'No, it's not *'aib* to say no.'

This is a different view from the one we more often hear, that a girl must marry the man her father chooses for her.

When Katiba goes the young woman from next door stays to watch our television, and hordes of little kids come in. They are dispersed by Tim coming back.

But after that I see Katiba seldom. The following year, a few weeks before we leave the town, someone tells me she's engaged.

'But I saw her yesterday, and she didn't say anything!'

'She wouldn't, it's not for her to tell you. She'd be shy to tell you.'

Some time after we leave the town she is married to a cousin in Sana'a, and when I return on visits in 1987 and 2000 I don't manage to see her. It will be twenty-six years before I meet her again.

We've been in the town for three months. It's February. The weather is foul. We are immersed in cloud, actually living inside it. It blows in through the window in visible wisps and leaves fine wet drops on the bed. Absolutely everything is damp. When we wash our sheets the only way we can think of to get them dry is to fold them round a hot-water bottle. People seem less friendly, less communicative, huddling at home and sitting out the cold damp. The houses don't have any heating except for charcoal braziers. Still, people drop in, we never know when they'll appear, and as ever I feel the lack of privacy.

I hit a low point. I miss the company of my sister, who visited for two weeks, a quick tour round some of the sights of Yemen and a few days in Safaqayn. I miss Katiba and being taken to afternoon social events.

When I go to Sana'a I realise, from the vantage point of the break, that it's work, hard work, being in Safaqayn – never quite understanding people, always having to worry about doing the right thing, struggling with the language, spending lots of time with people with whom I can't really relax as with friends, because I don't share enough of their background and assumptions, or language. My own identity is in abeyance, dismantled. At home, it would be reflected back to me and to friends by my London flat, by the books on my shelves. Here I can't express myself even through the clothes I wear or through articulate language. Not being able to demonstrate adult competence wears away at the sense of self. What I'm doing – research for a doctorate in social anthropology – can barely be explained to people with no knowledge of education systems; only – truthfully enough – that I'm trying to understand everything about their society.

I write to a friend:

'And the physical inconveniences – getting hold of water, carrying twenty-litre containers to the house and up the stairs, heating it for washing, carrying it down bad stairs to the bathroom, the mud floor and walls of the bathroom which come off on you just when you've got clean, if you're not careful; boiling and filtering water to drink, pouring it out of heavy containers, having nowhere to put things or throw away water in the kitchen, the dirt that gets everywhere from the stairs, which seem to be made of mud... it's none of it that bad by any means, but – rather than getting used to it – I find it all more tiresome as time goes on.'

Meeting the neighbours

It's a relief to come up out of our cramped rooms, where I have to bend to get through the low door, up the dark, lumpy staircase and out on the roof, to breathe the sharp air and feel the warmth of the sun on my face. I can see far away to distant hazy mountains, the scatter of square white houses dotting the land, the ranks of terraces, the swirl of unsealed track, and near at hand the patchwork of flat, whiteish roofs, higher and lower, irregularly stepped.

The whitewashed surface is powdery under my hands as I lower myself on to the cement and find a comfortable position with my back against the step up to the roof of the next house. Sparrows chirp. Voices, children calling, people arguing, rise up from the street below. Across the alley, in front of me, and half a level up behind me, are my neighbours' roofs. Opposite, one of the daughters of the Islamic judge, the hakim, is hanging out washing. I don't know which; she's unrecognisable in a black veil and cape and skirt, as much cover as most women use to cross the town.

Two of the neighbour girls, Na'ma and little Adiba, have come out on the roof one step up behind me. They have headscarves on with wisps of hair showing underneath, and grubby indoor dresses over trousers.

'*Ya* Mariam!' they call.

They throw something at my feet. I pick it up, breathing in an already familiar smell. It's a bunch of basil, the bushy kind they grow here in pots on ledges and roofs. They call it *rayhan* or *hamahem*. Yemenis hold it in great affection. They never use it in cooking, but women wear it regularly, as they've given it to me to wear before, tucked into their scarves and hanging by their cheeks.

I push the stalks up under the arm of my glasses into my scarf so the bunch hangs in front of my ear, and call my thanks.

'I want to grow *hamahem* in tins like you do,' I call.

'Get a tin,' they call back.

I squeeze myself back through the door and feel my way down the uneven stairs to our kitchen, where I find a largeish empty tin which held Tang orange squash powder, a ubiquitous drink offered by those who can afford it. Back on the roof I peel the label off the metal, and they tell me what to do: make holes in the bottom with a nail, banging it in with a stone off the roof. I'm already used to running up for a hand-sized stone to pound ginger in the kitchen for coffee, so it feels natural to use one as a hammer.

Now a woman on the roof across the alleyway, with a *lithma* covering her face, joins in.

'I'll give you a cutting,' she says.

Adiba disappears from the roof to fetch it.

The woman on the further roof calls again: 'I've got another tin you can have – come here, come over to our house.' She beckons, her hand pointing downwards and scooping the air towards her.

The alleyway between my house and hers means I can't go rooftop to rooftop but have to head down our stairs and across the street, and through her stone-walled courtyard to her front door. She opens the door from three floors up by pulling a string attached to the lock. This is a fine, solid old house. She meets me at the top of her spacious stairway, pulling down her *lithma* to show her face: kind, slightly anxious, inquisitive.

On the ledge around her roof she has a flourishing garden, all in old tins – square blue vegetable ghee tins, yellow and red Nido milk powder tins – and old round metal water containers and faded plastic jerrycans. Besides basil she has onions, coriander – for *zahaweq*, she says – mint, and a grey herb I can't identify. She gives me another tin filled with rich earth, and tells me where to go to get compost like it, describing the route to an old rubbish heap on one side of the town, near where we used to live. This is how I meet my neighbour Thuraya, who will become one of my closest friends, for whom I will run errands, and with whom I will stay on my first return visit, for the week I'm in the town.

Thuraya invites me into her *mafraj*, the long, narrow, grand room where men receive their guests. She has to unlock the padlocked door, which makes me wonder if the room is used much. It has old wooden doors with a carved pattern picked out in old red and yellow and dark green paint. White walls and high ceilings give a sense of dignity and space. On the floor along the walls are strips of patterned carpet, over a central strip of lino. Upright cushions sit at the sides with headrest cushions propped on top. The cushions are covered in an assortment of faded material, in prints and brocade and embroidery, and above them hang faded tapestries depicting trees and flowers, tigers in a forest, stags. Piled neatly in the corners are the elbow-cushions that would be put out at intervals for a row of sitting guests.

The tall windows come down to the level where people sitting on the carpet can look out of them easily, and above each is another arch-shaped, deep half-circle window. Instead of coloured glass, these windows let in a diffuse light through translucent panes of alabaster. A ledge below them holds brassware, coffee pots and smaller vessels. Above the alabaster windows a curved and angular pattern carved in the plaster runs right along the top of the wall. Small framed decorated Quranic texts hang between the windows. In one corner a sewing machine sits on a cushion. A brass tray in the middle of the floor holds two *mada'a*s and two brass hourglass-shaped spittoons for use when chewing qat, all brightly polished, and a vase of yellow and pink plastic hibiscus flowers.

Then she takes me one floor down the dark stairway, wider and more even than ours but, like ours, surfaced in some sort of hardened, dusty earth, and I meet and slowly work out the relationships between the occupants of the lower half of the house: Thuraya's half-sisters, who are schoolgirls in the fourth elementary class; pretty, giggly Nabila; Karima, with a direct gaze and a strong chin; and their little brother. Their mother, Khadija, firm and dignified, invites me into her *mafraj*, where we sit for a little: another long room, with foam mattress seating all round the edge, windows at sitting height that look out towards the street, carpets along the floor, lino in the centre, schoolbooks stacked in a corner, and at one end a bed raised on Nido milk-powder tins and piled with blankets. There's another pile of blankets, neatly folded concertina-style, in a corner. Again, it's all rather faded.

It's after *'asr*, the afternoon prayer, and Khadija is about to go out with the hakim's wife, who has just come round.

'Would you like to come with us?' Khadija asks. 'To the house of the dead man? People crying, mourning?'

The news came to the town by telephone last night. The dead man had gone to Saudi Arabia to earn money to finish his own half-completed house, and died in a building accident there.

'Are my clothes OK?' I'm wearing a black jumper, but I'm not sure about my brown skirt, which has sparkly threads in it. Khadija is wearing black, and she says it is because of the dead man, but she says my clothes are all right.

Khadija and the hakim's wife and I walk down the hill together, on the wide main street between the upper part of the town and Meruwagha below. Khadija carries a thermos of *gahwa*. At the last house at the bottom of the town we go into a small room crammed with women. Among them I recognise a few I know, including Fatima Abdu. Some are red-eyed. There are quite a lot of black clothes, but not only black, and the black dresses often have coloured patterns. The mourners hand out qat – I get given a lot – and glasses of *gahwa*. The atmosphere is only fairly sober; the chat level is mostly quieter than at other afternoon gatherings I've been to, but there is still some animated talking, and smiles when women greet each other. There are even jokes at some points, repeated around the room, seeming to relieve tension. At other times the mourning reaches a pitch of intensity, with the dead man's wife sobbing rhythmically and lamenting, and others crying and sniffling.

The women next to me ask me the usual questions: 'Why don't you have any children?'

'I've got four,' says the woman on my right, 'and one dead. It's good not to have any.'

More women keep crowding in to the packed, stuffy room. I squash up as best I can, folding my knees tightly, feeling large and awkward. (At 1.78 metres, I am taller than any man in the town, or on the whole mountain, let alone the women.)

The men, in another room, can be heard chanting, '*La ilah illa Allah*,' there is no god but God; some of the women join in. Later we can hear a melodious chant from the men, rising and falling like plainsong. Then a small group of five or six girls troop in. They are carrying two big Qurans. I recognise the older, pioneer schoolgirls, the few who have stayed to progress into the higher classes. The women move up to make space and the girls group round the Qurans. They read or chant – somewhere in between, a bit like singing psalms in an Anglican church, I think to myself, but less up and down. They alternate phrases with two older women, both from the sheikh's household, who are reading from Qurans. I didn't know that any women could read. Incense wafts from a burner during the chanting.

The reading is disturbed by a small boy outside, clearly audible, singing a definitely unsuitable song, in which I catch a word I have not been allowed to write down, *'unguri*, clitoris. The women exclaim '*Yu!*' and a girl goes out to deal with him.

After the reading is over there's an outbreak of laughing and chatting, and I think they are perhaps discussing shortfalls in the performance. An older woman says, 'Thank you, girls.'

When Khadija gets up to go, at about 5.30pm, half an hour before *maghreb*, she makes a quick movement of her hand to tell me to come with her, and I obediently follow. Several other women leave at the same time and we all start the climb back up the road together.

'Will the same thing happen tomorrow?' I ask one.

'Yes, for seven days.'

At the top of the road, after the steepest part of the hill, Khadija sits on a stone to rest. 'I'm tired,' she says.

Back up the hill, the hakim's wife goes into her house nearby, and I go in with Khadija to fetch the tin with the basil cutting I left there earlier. Khadija sits me down in her living room. She pours me *gahwa* and passes me the mouthpiece of a water pipe, a fine tall one with well-polished brass fittings.

'I can't sleep at night unless I smoke,' she says.

The *mada'a* makes a gargling sound as the smoke bubbles through the water in the coconut-shell body, the coals glowing red-hot; I wipe the mouthpiece with my hand, as I've seen people do, and draw in, and enjoy the cool smoke and the brief feeling of light-headedness, and the distinctive smell of burning *tumbak* tobacco.

'Come here,' Khadija says, kind and bossy and emphatic, 'come round if you want *gahwa* or to smoke a water pipe.'

'You must come and see me,' I say.

'Tomorrow morning.'

She asks me keenly about my country. 'Do you do the same for a dead person?'

'No, different, we have a funeral but not visiting in the same way.'

'What do you do with the body? Do you bury it? Is it true you burn dead bodies where you come from? You don't, do you?'

Cremation is forbidden in Islam. Khadija obviously regards it with horror. I find I just can't bring myself to admit to Khadija that we do cremate some bodies, and the lie stays on my conscience for years. Aspects of my country – women's education and independence – are attractive to her, and it seems wrong to have concealed a counterweight, a bad side.

'If you and Abdullah divorced, you wouldn't go to your father, you'd stay in your own flat and work?' she asks me one day.

I say I would.

'I'd sweep the streets to do that. It's good where you come from. Here, a divorced woman is worked hard by her family.'

Independence isn't an option. She's a pensioner of her dead husband's powerful extended family, who give her a monthly allowance for herself and her children in cash and in grain.

But these are things I find out later. For now, I go home pleased with my tin of basil. When I put it out on my roof the neighbour girls lean out of their window.

'Where did you go?'

'To the dead man's house at the bottom of the town, but I don't know his name?'

They tell me the names of the dead man and his wife, and they tell me Khadija's. This is useful: nobody ever introduces themselves.

'Will you go there with us tomorrow?' they suggest.

From all over the town, groups of neighbours will set off together to visit and mourn with the dead man's family.

The next day, in the late afternoon, I'm climbing up the hill from Meruwagha and fall in with some heavily veiled women coming from the dead man's house. They turn out to be my neighbours, Thuraya and her sisters. They say something about coming to my place, so as we get to the alleyway I invite them in.

'Do you want *gahwa*?' I ask, trying to be a proper hostess.

'We don't want it,' they say. 'Because of the qat.' They are still chewing from the afternoon.

I struggle with the conversation. Thuraya turns to me, frowning.

'I'm *zalen*,' she says – angry, upset – 'because you can't understand.'

'I just need more practice,' I say. Over time, Thuraya will put much time and effort into explaining things to me, with patience and humour.

A couple of days later, I hear a rattling sound, something on our stairs, falling. Puzzled and a little alarmed, I go up to see. It's pebbles falling down our stairwell from the opening to the roof, and when I look up I see they are being thrown by Thuraya from her roof, across the way and higher than ours. It's to get my attention. When I go out into view she calls 'We-eh, *ya* Mariam!' and throws down to me, from the roof of her tall, imposing house to the roof of our rough two-storey one, a bundle wrapped in a piece of nylon fabric. I bend to pick it up, undo the knot in the slippery cloth and inhale the smell of freshly baked bread: two rounds of *khobz*, flat bread, from her morning's baking.

Then the neighbour-across-the-roof, the mother of little Adiba, calls me over the roof from her window and she too gives me some bread.

The next day Karima comes up our stairs with more bread, 'From my mother.'

In the days that follow Thuraya gives me more earth and a rooted mint plant to grow in it, and Karima comes round again with *kak*, little shiny buns somewhere between bread and cakes, from her mother. Khadija in turn gets me out on the roof by throwing pebbles, and throws me bread. I borrow Khadija's *mada'a* – this is before we buy our own – and when I go round to return it I sit and drink *gahwa* with Khadija and Thuraya in Khadija's *mafraj*.

Khadija is polishing her brassware, picking up small handfuls of dust from the carpet and using her hand to rub the brass with dust and Brasso. The brassware sits on a tray, all newly shiny: the tray itself, circular and engraved with a pattern; ornamental coffee pots; perfume sprinklers; brass spittoons.

'It belongs to my son,' Khadija explains. 'For when he grows up.'

A few days later Thuraya lends me a cassette, music by an Egyptian singer. Khadija sends a girl round to fetch me when she has women with her for the afternoon, two or three neighbours. I'm given qat and a mint sweet to put with the qat in my cheek, to make it taste better. We watch a Jordanian soap opera on TV, then talk. They ask me questions about my country; when they ask about religion they don't make the pressing comments about me converting that I suffer in some houses.

I tell them, 'In my country, men are only allowed to have one wife at a time. It's the law.'

'Your law is good,' they say. 'Several wives means fighting and problems.'

Khadija says: 'You must come any time you aren't going anywhere. It's not good to sit alone.'

Three days later another cloth bundle lands on my roof. Inside is a round of soft bread, a patterned nylon headscarf and a small bottle of perfume. I think at first it's from Khadija, but when I go over to thank her she says it was from Thuraya. So I go upstairs and thank her.

After that Thuraya often calls me by throwing pebbles – to give me bread, *lehuh*, a headscarf; to take me on an outing or a visit; to ask me to run errands for her. She doesn't have a man in the house, and women don't go to the market or the shops.

'Where have you been? There must be a pile of stones by now,' she says when I don't respond right away.

Afternoon visit

The *'asr* call to prayer sounded from the mosque a while ago; it's mid-afternoon. Groups of women, twos and threes, are crossing the town in all directions, going to *rabakh*. They have cleared up the midday meal and washed and prayed and changed into their afternoon finery, and they are wearing outer clothes: a *saramiya* over head and shoulders, or − smarter, more expensive, worn when going further, for bigger occasions − a complete head-to-toe black three-piece *sharshaf*, with a full skirt, cape and veil right over the face. They carry a thermos in one hand, and a long bundle of wrapped-up qat under the other arm. As they go they chat, stop to greet others, ask where they're going, argue and persuade. Women call from windows to interrogate the passers-by. Where are you going? To so-and-so's house; to Fatima's lying-in; to the house of the dead man; or, evasively, 'over there' or a wave of the arm.

Some of their visits reflect obligations: attending wedding celebrations, going to the house of mourners or the sick, or of women who are staying in for the forty days after childbirth − visits to be returned next time these women in their turn are lying in. Other decisions about where to spend the afternoon are motivated by inclination, habit, where the neighbours are going today.

I'm thinking of going to Khadija across the way, when a boy appears in our doorway.

'My mother says, come to us.'

He waits to show me the way. Out in the street I follow him, watching my feet, picking my way in my flip-flops over the stone paving of the alleyway, between bits of rubbish, old cans, cardboard, dodgy-looking squishy plastic bags, which perhaps result from the expedients of those with no sanitation in the house. The path climbs between old stone houses − how old? No one seems to know. They could be any age.

We pass under a narrow archway where the houses are actually built over the street. Near the top of the town the boy leads me into a tall old house. He takes my hand to guide me up the stairs, too fast, as it's completely dark. I have a torch in my bag, but there isn't time to get it out.

'*Dunni!*'

I obediently bend down, holding one hand over my head, which I've knocked so often on low beams and doorways in houses designed for shorter people than me. The staircase twists. I feel my way in the blackness.

We reach the top floor, where the women are sitting in the *mafraj*; the men are somewhere else today. Light shows through an open door, and I hear the hubbub of women talking.

At the threshold I take off my flip-flops and add them to the pile outside the door. I see one pair of flip-flops marked with a circle burnt into each with an empty small tin, tomato-paste size, and make a mental note that I must mark mine; people sometimes take the wrong ones when they leave, accidentally or not.

I duck in through the door.

'*Ya* Mariam! *Itfaddali!*' cries Selma.

A dozen women are seated round the edges of the room. I go round greeting them, kissing hands three times with each. At the same time we murmur, '*Kef halish? Alhamdulillah*' – how are you? Thanks be to God. An older woman, in a screechy squawk, uses instead the old, local greeting, '*Mi halish al yaum?*', how are you today?

Women shuffle up and make a place for me. Selma arranges the cushions behind my back to make me comfortable, and a small pile of hard cushions for me to lean an elbow on. I take up the approved position, one knee up, one tucked under, being careful to keep the soles of my feet in and not point them at anyone. I spread my skirt decently over my knees.

The women sitting round the room have taken off their dark street-coverings and are revealed in brilliant colours and glittering gold. Their dresses are made of bright, shiny fabrics with metallic threads and embroidery and sequins. The flared trousers they wear below the dresses are also bright and glittery. Some, mostly older women, wear more sober dresses, variations on a black background dotted with little coloured flowers, their hair in wool-padded plaits looped up by their ears.

'*Askublish gahwa?*' Selma says: shall I pour you *gahwa?*

She takes a little glass from a brass tray and fills it from a thermos. I sip the sweet infusion, breathe in ginger and cinnamon. Selma rinses glasses in a bowl of water and pours out and hands round more.

After *gahwa* it's time for qat. Before I can unwrap the small supply I've brought, a woman across the room throws a sprig over, deftly, to land by my knee.

'Now you say: "*Akramish Allah*".'

'*Akramish Allah,*' I obediently repeat. I copy the gesture they show me that goes with the thanks, holding up the sprig and bowing my forehead to it.

She replies, '*Akram man akram.*'

I write the phrases in my vocabulary notebook. The women are intrigued.

'Why are you writing?'

'So I don't forget. I forget everything if I don't write it down.' This is not obvious to them, of course; they are not literate, and aren't dependent on writing in this way.

'What are you going to do with all the words in there? Are you going to teach them to girls in your country?'

What I do is try to learn them, go through the notebook in spare moments and test myself and try to get the words into my head. I hunt for the words in a dictionary of modern written Arabic, but often they aren't there, or have a different meaning.

I take the qat sprig and copy them, stroking the sprig, snapping the leaves and tender juicy stems off the tough lower stems, and stuffing the good bits into my mouth. I choose one side to chew on, and begin to store the chewed pulp in my cheek. The leaves taste acrid and produce lots of saliva. I spit out into a *matfal*, an hourglass-shaped aluminium spittoon. Selma offers me cardamom seeds to chew with the qat to offset the bitterness. The bits of chewed leaf circle my mouth and feel chokey, almost make me gag: the stuff is difficult to control. I chase the bits with my tongue and push up the wad in my cheek from outside.

'*Ad ummish bikher?*' Is your mother alive and well?

I respond, '*alhamdulillah,*' praise God, she is well. I take photos of my mother and father and sister and brothers out of my bag, and the women pass them round from hand to hand and look at them with real interest, pointing and repeating to each other. After I've put them back, more women join the gathering, each going round the room and kissing hands with everyone there.

'Show them your pictures!' the others urge. I get out and put away my photos perhaps six times altogether.

The women talk about the gold they're wearing: big medallions called *jelaleh*; little gold pendants in the shape of Arabian long-spouted coffee pots; the English word LOVE on gold chains round their necks; bracelets jingling up their arms; earrings. The pieces are obviously mass-produced in a limited number of popular designs; I see several women with coffee pots. Only a few older women still wear the beautiful, finely worked, much more varied and intricate silver jewellery which Jewish craftsmen used to make, and which cannot flash as much wealth. In previous times, wealth was measured in the *riyal fransi*, or Western riyal – also known as the Maria Theresa dollar, bearing the profile of the Empress Maria Theresa of Austria and minted continuously since the eighteenth century. The heavy silver coins, four centimetres across, were also incorporated into headpieces and necklaces and melted down to make silver jewellery. Some people still give prices in Maria Theresa dollars. Nowadays gold is an obsession and a topic of conversation. Some of the women are wearing several thousand pounds' worth. Even in workaday clothes, women will often wear a gold medallion on a string around their neck. Women and men have teeth covered in gold, one or two or more. Not to have gold is to be pitied.

'How much did that cost?' they ask each other. 'Who gave it to you?'

My mother, my father, my husband, from my *mahr* – the women's own portion of the bride-price.

'Haven't you got any gold?' they ask me. I have two rings, one of which might not be gold anyway.

'Didn't Abdullah give you any gold when you got married? Didn't you get money? Not even clothes? It should be ten dresses and ten pairs of trousers and a watch and gold. Didn't you get any gold at all?'

'Don't you find it cold here?' I'm still comfortable in flip-flops and wearing a jumper only in the evenings.

'No, it's colder where I come from.' Even half an hour's walk down the mountain the climate is warmer; they think this is a cold place. I try to describe snow.

The room smells of tobacco smoke and qat and qat chewing, a sharp, bitter crushed-leaf smell. Selma comes round with a can of perfume and sprays each woman in turn, aiming for the top of her bodice and her wrists. The fragrance, rather sickly, fills the room and stays on my clothes and hands afterwards.

The *mada'a* gurgles in the centre of the room and women pass the long hose with its mouthpiece from one to the next, each taking a few inhalations of the tobacco smoke.

I shift my position as often as I dare. Right knee up, left leg tucked under. When my left knee starts to ache too much, left knee up and right leg under. I don't want to seem to fidget.

The room is warming up, close with the smells of qat, perfume and tobacco smoke. The *mada'a* makes a soothing bubbling, and even chewing qat, I have trouble staying awake. The conversation between the women is hard to follow. I can just hear that it's interesting, gossip about people I know, without getting the details. I try to look alert and engaged.

One older woman, with a wrinkled face and one cheek already swollen with qat, asks me: 'Haven't you got any children?' She holds up a hand, fingers bunched together, the other hand round it below the tips, and shakes it, indicating something little.

I admit I haven't.

'We have a baby every year,' says another. 'It's *ta'ab*, hard.' *Ta'ab* is 'tiring', but the meaning is much stronger: exhausting, wearing out.

'I couldn't travel, be here, with children. Later, perhaps, *inshallah*. One, or two maybe.'

'Only one or two? What if they die?'

(The words stay with me, and I eventually have three children.)

The buzz of talk goes on. I wish I could understand it. Then attention focuses on one woman, talking in an angry torrent, eloquently, with rhythmic repetition, like a performance, and violent gestures. She has seized up a qat twig as a prop or illustration: sometimes she raises it and plants it down on the floor for emphasis, in time with her words, and sometimes she tears off bits of leaf.

'What's she saying?' I ask the woman next to me.

'She's angry,' she replies, getting me no further.

The centre of the room fills up with discarded, picked-over lower branches of qat. The qat bulge in my cheek is growing and now – unlike on many afternoons when I will chew token amounts for form's sake – I begin to feel a slight effect. I feel at ease with the company, benign towards everyone; the slow passing of time doesn't matter, I enjoy the colours of the dresses and the stained glass in the windows.

There's a crackle, a cough, over the mosque loudspeakers, and the evening call to prayer takes life, rises, expands into the late afternoon.

'*Gduh maghreb!*' the women exclaim. They stand up, fasten on overskirts and arrange shawls. The gaudy finery vanishes under concealing black. They exchange 'good evening's and depart in little groups to go home, spit out their qat, wash and pray, and get some supper, if anyone wants it after the afternoon's qat, which suppresses appetite. Then they will watch television as a family or with neighbours, or sit up chatting into the night, as people did before they had television.

I go home and spit out my wad of qat, a bright green crumbly ball, down the hole in the bathroom, and rinse the bits out of my mouth. I feel the strange slight after-qat feeling, almost a little shaky, empty, cold, but not really quite any of those. However I still have an appetite for some supper, and I don't have any trouble sleeping. First I take off my trousers to check carefully for fleas hiding in the seams, and type up my notes for the day.

Getting to know the neighbours better

'What are you looking at?'

It's a relatively clear morning after several days of mist. I'm on our roof, watching the wheeling vultures through binoculars. Every now and then the wide circle they glide in brings one right overhead, and I can see the splayed wing feathers, the eyes, the hooked beak.

Khadija is calling from her roof.

'I'm looking at the birds,' I call back.

'Come over here, bring your binoculars!'

I duck through the doorway down from our roof and pick my way down the dark of our stairs, out at the bottom, across the narrow alley, and into Khadija's courtyard and up her wide stairway, past the storerooms at the bottom and the living rooms above them, past Thuraya's rooms on the next floor up, and out on to the roof.

We take turns looking through the binoculars. She looks at the town and the terraces beyond, I look at the vultures.

'Do you have birds like that in your country?'

'No, we don't, that's why I want to look at them.'

'What eats the dead animals then?'

I'm stumped for a reply. 'Crows, perhaps.'

I turn my attention from the sky and look at her roof garden. There's basil, of course. I recognise the dangling sprays of *heynan*, a decorative plant related to lavender, which I've seen women wear, and mint and coriander.

'What's this?' I ask, pointing to a tin growing flowers that look like yellow daisies.

'*Munis*, you can wear it as *mishqor*, for decoration.' Like the basil bunches tucked beside the ear.

The pretty, feathery greyish leaf? It looks like a kind of artemisia.

'*Wadhare*. You can grind it and eat it for '*urug*, pains inside.'

'And this one?' It smells like marjoram or oregano.

'*Uzzab*. You can put it in tea. It's good for your stomach if it hurts, or in hot sesame oil as drops for ears.'

I recognise the white and yellow flowers of feverfew.

'For a child's stomach aches, you grind it up, put it in milk, squeeze it out and give the milk to the child. And it's a *herz*, a charm, against *jinn*, with rue for protection after childbirth.'

'What are *jinn* like?'

'They live in mountains, they make people mad. Maybe you don't have them where you come from.'

'I don't know if we have *jinn*, but we have people who have problems with their brain.'

'Then you have *jinn*.'

After we've chatted for a while, Khadija asks me: 'I want photos of Nabila and Karima – can you take some?'

'Yes, but you'll have to wait for the pictures to come back, it's not instant.' This often puts women off; they're afraid something will happen to the photos *en route*, and people, men, will see them.

'That's no good, I want to send them to their father's brother in Saudi Arabia, with someone who's going tomorrow.'

'OK, I have an instant camera.' I fetch my Polaroid, which takes poorer quality pictures and is too expensive to use much.

'I'll take some with this to be ready now, and some to be ready later.'

The girls and Thuraya spend a long time preparing themselves, putting on best dresses and gold jewellery, a coral necklace, a bunch of basil by the ear. I take pictures with veils on their faces, pictures without, pictures where they pose stagily with hands held to their mouths, showing off rings and watches and bracelets. Their brother, a tousle-haired, gap-toothed little boy in a jacket too big for him, sits in for some of the shots.

They are pleased with the Polaroids. Khadija gets out some riyal notes and tries to give them to me.

'*Aib!*' I protest, with all the vigour I can. 'Do you want money for all the bread you've given me?'

'I sent my uncle a cassette letter,' Thuraya tells me later, 'and told him Mariam from London took the photos I sent, because he would be angry if a man had taken them.'

Another day Thuraya calls me over.

'I'm making the dough for frying-pan bread; you wanted to see how.'

She puts yeast from a tin in warm water, then mixes in flour and pulls and kneads it with one hand for about fifteen minutes, then stretches and flops it around till it's smooth and seems full of air. She covers it.

'I'll cook it about noon; I'll call you.'

Before I leave a woman comes in. She's from the town, I know her slightly. She hands Thuraya some ampoules. It turns out she has come to Thuraya to be injected with antibiotics she got from the health centre, rather than be injected by the male health worker there.

'My uncle taught me to do injections,' Thuraya explains. She says she uses new throwaway needles, or she boils them. She puts the injection in the woman's forearm, just above the wrist. I'm surprised it's not all right for the health worker to inject her there.

'It's still '*aib* for a male doctor to do it,' Thuraya says.

Another time I see her inject Khadija in the buttock, with vitamin B.

'I've been ill with malaria, and tired since Nasser's birth,' Khadija says.

'It would be just as good to eat liver,' I say, struggling hopelessly against the local overvaluing of injections.

'We haven't got a man to buy it for us.'

That day I go back after lunch, afraid I've missed the cooking of the bread, but Thuraya hasn't started. She shapes small rounds of dough rolled in flour with a swift tucking-under movement, flattens them by patting from palm to palm, and fries them in deep hot oil.

'You have to put it in very carefully, the oil can splash up.'

They puff up and turn into something like doughnuts, rather than bread.

'It's called *zalabiye*.'

She leaves a couple of rounds' worth of the dough as a starter for tomorrow's *khobz*.

While I'm in her kitchen a boy comes in with a bowl of *dabbikh*, tomatoes and okra and rice with a bit of *helba* on top.

'It comes from my friend Adiba Ahmed,' Thuraya says. 'I often eat just bread and *samn* [clarified butter] or bread and milk for lunch. We eat badly, not having a man.'

On other days, I see Thuraya in turn sending out bowls of food by child messengers to her friends or to the man in the communications office, an outsider without a family in the town.

Now she says, 'I wanted some bananas, but there was nobody to go for me. I thought of asking you but I felt it was *'aib*.'

'No, no, I'll get you things, you must ask.'

'I'm looking after my friend's baby this afternoon, where are you *rabakh*ing?'

'I don't know.'

'You can sit with me, but it'll be just us.'

I say I'd like to, but on the way home I remember a woman with a new baby, Amina, who I really ought to go and see. I climb Thuraya's stairs later with some bananas.

A week later I make doughnuts, rather successfully, and take some to her.

I've just heard the *'asr* call to prayer when Khadija's daughter Karima appears on our landing.

'Thuraya says come to the *wafe'* in the sheikh's house below Meruwagha. She's there already, she had lunch there.'

I make my way down through the town. This is another house belonging to the wider family of the sheikh, not the one conspicuous at the top of the town.

This *wafe'* – the completion of confinement after childbirth – is to celebrate three women coming out of their confinement. They have finished their forty days of staying at home, they have washed and become ritually pure and available to their husbands again, and they have hennaed their hands and feet.

The three women are Thuraya's friend, a daughter of the house, who has one child and one dead; Nuriya Ahmed, a woman I know from Meruwagha (three, and two dead); and another woman I don't know, whose baby died straight away. The celebration is not about the babies.

This is a huge party. I count seventy to eighty women, and about twenty little girls. The large room, in a spacious house just outside the town, is crammed and hot and smoky and smells of incense from a pottery burner and of qat, which is provided for the guests. Everyone is dressed up in new, bright, shiny dresses and wearing quantities of gold: earrings, rings, chains, medallions and rows of gold bangles. Many have new deep-red henna and extra decoration painted in black arabesques on the backs of their hands and up their arms.

A small space is cleared in the middle of the room, and two women at a time get up to dance to music with a strong drumbeat, played on a cassette player. They do the usual dance, side by side, with downcast eyes, holding hands, taking small steps to the music, bending the knees, and slowly moving round. I wonder if there are subtleties to it that I'm failing to grasp. Other women ululate in appreciation, part covering their mouths with a hand.

It's hard to talk against the general noise. I manage a brief conversation with the woman next to me.

'Don't you have any children at all? What do you do?'

'I take pills. You have to take them every day.'

'Every day?' She seems to think that's very hard.

One day, visiting Khadija, I find a heap of cow dung between the entrance door and the storage rooms on the ground floor.

'What's that for?'

'To replaster the stairs, mixed with earth and water.'

'Where did you get it?'

'From someone with a cow.'

'Isn't it dirty?' I ask, interested to know how she sees it.

'It's unclean, it's shit after all. You have to wash afterwards.'

The surface of the stairs in our house is worn and powdery, and I can see how it needs renewing from time to time. I go up to Thuraya's and wait; she's asked me to go out with her. The little boy from downstairs in our house is in her *mafraj*, saying, 'My father wants qat.' She gives him a few sprigs.

It's a Thursday, market day, and I've gone across the alleyway to ask if I can get Khadija and Thuraya anything.

'In the market, if you see that woman who sells charcoal, bring her to me.'

The charcoal seller is very obviously a woman from somewhere else, lower down: she has a broad, brown face and wears a pointed straw hat, like those worn by women on the coastal plain.

'The *naqib*'s daughter wants to see you.' This is how Thuraya is always referred to. The *naqib*, leader, chief, was her father, Khadija's dead husband. I take the charcoal seller to Thuraya's house. Thuraya seems to be befriending her, and stocking up on charcoal.

Thuraya gives me some flour, ground at the mill from wheat. 'The *wakil*, our family agent, gives me a sack every two months, and two hundred riyals, but three hundred last month because I had to entertain guests when the *muhafidh*, the province governor, came.'

'How do you get the sack from the mill?'

'It's difficult – Nabila and Karima carry it bit by bit. It's hard not having a man.'

After that, sometimes Tim carries sacks for them. Thuraya is involved in endless shifts to make do in her circumstances, ties and obligations and exchanges established with other women, with traders in the market, with children who run errands, and with us.

Nuriya, our downstairs neighbour, has said she'll show me how to mix henna. The colour from the first time faded long ago, and was refreshed by Katiba and her mother in our old lodging. When my sister was visiting we both got hennaed together. Now time has passed and that has faded too.

In the early afternoon I go downstairs. Nuriya, as I find out gradually, has three children living (four died), from different marriages, but the elder two stayed with her earlier husbands, as happens when women remarry. Only Sabah, the daughter of her current marriage, is with her, the self-possessed little girl who comes up to visit us. There's also a boy in the household, her husband's son from a previous marriage.

Mixing the henna is simple: she stirs hot water into it till it's a thick paste, and leaves it to sit. Then we put *hurud*, turmeric, on our hands, feet and faces. She uses a mixture of dried and fresh (*akhdar*, green) turmeric roots. It comes from Milhan.

She brings a special grinding stone out of her kitchen to use in the space outside the front door and squats to grind the dried and fresh turmeric together, bending her body in time with her two hands on the smooth, round upper stone as she pushes to and fro over the slight hollow in the heavy base stone.

'Where do you get the stone from?'

'When men are building a house – they chip it flat. The one upstairs in the bathroom is only for grinding *zahaweq*. If I used the same stone for *hurud*, the chilli would make it sting.'

Then we go upstairs to our rooms and she hennas my hands and feet. She does a slightly different pattern, keeping my hands open and covering the palms as well as the fingertips with a solid mass of paste. There isn't enough left for her – the bag of Sudanese henna I bought in Sana'a has less in it than the sort I got before.

'I'll give you more later.'

'I want the same sort, it's good, look, it's coloured my hands already.'

She and her little daughter sit with me to keep me company while the henna dries.

'We don't have any money,' Nuriya tells me, 'because no one has given the Qadi any money to read the Quran.'

She always refers to her husband as the Qadi, though we don't hear others according him this respect for status and learning.

'How much do they give him?'

'Ten riyals, fifty riyals if someone is ill, for him to read it. Two hundred to read the whole Quran.'

'How long does that take him?'

'A long time. He gets tired, his back hurts.'

'Does he read it in the mosque?'

'No, at home.'

As time goes on, Sabah comes up often in the early afternoon to ask for qat for her parents. She uses a formulaic request, always in the same words: 'My mother wants some qat from you.'

When we hand over some of what we've bought, she says gravely, 'That's enough, keep some for yourselves.'

According to her mother, she's three.

Women come to our place

We have been watching for water all morning, but we have only seen a truck returning with a load of already full *dabba*s – plastic jerrycans – belonging to people who've sent them to be filled at the spring down the mountain. Then I see a group of four or five women carrying full round tins and *dabba*s on their heads.

'Where did you get the water from?' I ask.

'*Ba'id*, far.' They point. 'It's for the plants,' they say, indicating the tins of herbs on the window ledge of the house they're going into, a large, tall house opposite us.

'Come in!' they urge me.

I go in with them, up to the second floor, a fine, large room with a collection of polished brassware arranged on a tray in the middle. We sit and drink *gahwa* and they tell me about the house.

'We're five families, one on each floor, five brothers. Stay and have lunch with us!'

'Thank you, but I must go and cook for my husband.' This is an excuse they can easily understand.

'Another time, *inshallah*.' They say they will come and visit me tomorrow after lunch.

When I get into our house, Karima from over the way comes in to bring me some bread from her mother. I go out again and across the alley to invite her to come tomorrow too.

The next day I go to the five-family house to confirm about the afternoon.

'We have guests, we'll come tomorrow, you come to us today.'

'But I already invited my neighbour.'

'We'll tell her.'

At their house I spend a long, hard afternoon, saying and understanding next to nothing. I get sprayed with perfume. Several women give me qat, and after a few refusals I accept. They reassure me I'll learn the language soon, saying again, as I've heard before, that it depends on the water: 'The water of Yemen is light, it frees the tongue.'

The next day I tidy our larger room and arrange the cushions and make the bed up into a sitting space with an extra cloth over it. This is what we have furnished the room for: inviting guests. I make *gahwa* in advance and put it in a thermos, and wait.

At 4pm women start arriving. They bring a *mada'a*, borrowed from Khadija, ready loaded with a bowl full of tobacco on the top. Khadija comes with her daughters and Thuraya, and seven women from the house opposite with some of their children, a couple of women from houses I don't know, and a girl in a *sharshaf*, full cover-up, who never takes her veil off, so I have no idea who she is.

They kiss hands, greet each other, sit down round our room, and I offer and pour out *gahwa*. The first thing they ask is: 'Where's Abdullah?'

Tim is sitting discreetly in our other, small room. Again, I was afraid it would be *'aib* for him to come in, and this time we have another space he can sit in. But they want to see him. They call him, 'Come in! Come in!'

Tim sits and spends the afternoon with us. Nobody puts on extra veiling for him. He joins in the conversation. The women tell me, to my annoyance: 'He understands better than you!'

We put on our television, running it from the car battery, and we all watch an Egyptian soap opera.

'Can you understand the Egyptian dialect?' I ask the women.

'We understand all the programmes, from Egypt, Syria, Kuwait, wherever.'

However Tim reckons Karima, whose teacher is Egyptian, is doing some translating for the older women.

We have bought qat for the occasion, and the women between them already have a lot. The twigs pile up on the floor. They have brought a cassette of music which they play on our machine.

'How much are you paying for your electricity?' they demand.

'Ninety-five.'

'That's too much, it should be sixty.'

'What can we do?' we ask, more or less resigned to paying a premium.

'A meter is better. But the *mudir el kahraba*, the electricity manager, still increases ours over the amount on the meter,' Khadija says.

When they ask me the usual questions about children, and whether I can give them contraceptive pills, I ask them, 'Which is better, girls or boys?'

'One of each!'

'Which are people more pleased with?'

'They're both from Allah.' Then they add, 'Men want boys.'

'Why?'

'Girls are weak, pitiable.'

'Which do women want?'

'Girls.'

'Why?'

There's no answer, so I suggest, 'To help in the house?'

'Yes! But everyone loves their child anyway.'

They ask about everything in our room, the pictures of England we have on the walls, and where we come from.

'Where is London? Is it behind Hodeida?' Hodeida is the biggest city on the coast.

'How much does a sheep cost where you come from?'

I admit, embarrassed, that I don't know.

'How much does a bride cost? Here it's fifty, sixty thousand... [£6,250 to £7,500]' We know already that bride-price inflation is a huge concern and a constant topic of discussion.

'With us the man doesn't pay anything. But the woman has to love him, and agree.'

'If it was like that here, the men would marry one every month!'

'And you can't have more than one wife, it's forbidden by law.' This meets with approval all round.

'Your law is good!'

The *maghreb* call to prayer signals the end of the afternoon and the women get up to go.

My mother visits

'*Itfaddalu*, come in, come in!'

I'm walking round the town with my mother. I can hardly believe this myself, two separate worlds brought together. She's in her early sixties, it's game of her to brave the discomforts of paying me a visit, and I will be grateful forever after. We hired a car and fetched her from Sana'a, and she's spending four days in the town as well as visiting some of the highlights of Yemen.

I'm conscious of things I've forgotten to notice myself any more: the unevenness of the steep streets, the rubbish and filth everywhere, small children relieving themselves in the alleyways, the flies, the scrawny chickens pecking at pools of infant diarrhoea, the gaggle of children running after us shouting. My mother has already noted the dirtiness of the towns we've come through on our way here, but now, in Safaqayn, she is wowed by the views and by the hospitality.

She has brought me a small gold locket into which she has put tiny photos of her, my father and me as a baby, to add to my inadequate gold. Women I show it to later find it mildly interesting, when I open it and show the pictures, but it's still not much gold compared to theirs. They like the picture of me as a baby – 'You were nice and fat then,' I'm told more than once.

My mother is a subject of great interest. When we brought her up the steep rocky path to our door, and up our uneven stairs, warning her about the low beams overhead, and gave her a rare chair to sit on so she could be comfortable in our room, about thirty children flooded in to look at her. They sat quietly on the cushions round the room, coming and going, perhaps fifteen at a time, a handful of boys and a greater number of girls, from toddlers to the older, black-veiled schoolgirls. They all sat and stared at my mother.

The older girl from across the roof came round immediately with a thermos full of tea. All our neighbours gave us extra bread, and they, or the children who delivered the bread, took the opportunity to come in and have a good look.

Now, everywhere we go, women are calling out, inviting us in. We pay visits to four of my friends. Each gives us tea or *gahwa*, and the last one a snack of *lehuh* soaked in meat juice with mutton, and little cakes. Each time we go up twisting earth-surfaced staircases in the dark, trying not to hit our heads. Each woman sprays us liberally with cologne, the sickly smell mingling with the last one, shakes and kisses hands with me and with my mother, and gazes at her.

I invite everybody to our house for the next afternoon. About twenty women come, some of whom I invited, and some I haven't directly asked. Late in the afternoon Thuraya arrives. She wants to take my mother away for a bit, to her house or her friend's house.

'We can't leave, we have guests here.'

Thuraya is insistent; she's the centre of attention for about fifteen minutes. I think people are perhaps taking sides. The neighbour girl Fatima, next to me, tells us not to go. We stick to our principles; to us it seems rude to leave the guests we've invited.

'We'll come later, or tomorrow.'

Eventually she leaves. I'm not sure how far an uncomfortable atmosphere remains. One woman says, 'There are a lot of women here,' as if this is bad. I'm puzzled: it's no more crowded than many gatherings I've been in. Later I think perhaps this means the wrong kind of women, and I have mixed people who don't get on or who disapprove of each other or who don't usually socialise together. I also wonder if Thuraya wanted to take my mother away because she felt it wasn't a suitable gathering for her, Thuraya, to stay in; I only realise much later how few houses in the town she *rabakh*s in, the sheikh's and the sheikh's daughter's and perhaps one other. After *maghreb*, when the women all leave, my mother and I visit Thuraya, and she takes us to see her friend, still in confinement, with a new baby covered up in a cradle slung under her high bed.

When we get back from taking my mother to Sana'a for her flight home I look at her slept-in bed and can hardly believe she has really been here. It seems a mixing of worlds so disparate – England and my family, and my life here – that I would almost have thought they couldn't coexist without one turning the other into unreality. I feel quite homesick and sort of left-alone-again.

Her visit to the town lasted four days, but has a disproportionate impact. For a long time women remember her, ask each other if they saw her, ask me how she is.

Language

My downstairs neighbour Nuriya is gossiping in Khadija's yard, as Khadija sits sorting sorghum grains in a big, round metal tray, and I'm standing by wishing I could follow what they say to each other. It's definitely about people they know. I just catch some discussion about whose children have snotty noses.

As Khadija shakes the tray and picks out the bad grains they tell me the word for this kind of yellow sorghum, from Mahwit: something like *akhsha'a*. I say it wrong. Nuriya laughs at me, mocking my pronunciation. Khadija defends me: 'We can't speak a word of her language.'

Nuriya isn't the only one who laughs at me. One afternoon recently, when a child who couldn't yet talk was babbling, the women said she was talking like me. Thuraya's friend, the one we took my mother to see, mimics and mocks me by addressing me in baby talk. Others that I try to have a conversation with shrug and give up. Everyone thinks I'm slow to learn, slow to understand. The only foreigners they have encountered are Egyptian and Sudanese teachers and health workers, who speak dialects very different from anything Yemeni, but still Arabic. Women are highly aware of linguistic differences – words used here, in the next town, in the capital, in Egypt – and they think I must use Egyptian words. Again and again they say things like:

'We say *ma* [water], but you call it *moya*, don't you?'

'You say *akhuya* where you come from, don't you?' (The Egyptian form of 'my brother', where a Yemeni would say *akhi*.)

'You say *sheikh*, don't you, not *sheiba*?'

'No, we say "old man". In my language every single word is different from Arabic.'

They turn to each other. 'Did you hear that? Every single word in her language is different!'

Women are interested in dialects and words in other areas, and collect examples of different usages. The dialect changes over even a few kilometres: we find different words for wish, breakfast and morning in a small town seven kilometres away as the crow flies but separated by a wadi between steep cliffs; and a different word for the midday meal in a large village an hour's walk down the mountain.

'We call it *ghaweth* here, not *gheda* like in Safaqayn. Here, *gheda* is in the morning,' the villagers say, as if consciously differentiating themselves. And of course there are much bigger divergences in more widely separated areas. These differences are noted, perhaps even cultivated, as part of local identity.

A woman I visit, Amina, has spent time in Saudi Arabia with her son who works there. One afternoon as we're sitting *rabakh*ing, the conversation turns to different words for 'roof'. Amina tells the group of women the Saudi word.

'What do you call it?' they ask me.

'Roof.'

Amina sums up: 'In Sana'a they call it *jebi*', here *reym*, in Saudi Arabia *sut'h*, and where you come from, *roof*.'

Another time, another woman lists differences between pronunciation in Sana'a and here. 'They say my name as Sayide in Sana'a, and Siyde here. They say *ma tishti* for "what do you want?" in Sana'a and *mi en tishti* here; they say *tafrita* for sitting relaxing in the afternoon, we say *rabkha*.'

Women find it frustrating that I can't talk to them, and most give up. The most patient, those with a knack of explaining, those who take the trouble to try, become my friends. All the women I end up seeking out and spending time with are those who will make this effort. My debt to them is unending.

After about eight months I find I have a feeling of ease, of swimming in the language, and understand much more.

'This is crazy. This is a completely new dialect.'

Much later, in our last two weeks in the town, a German dialectologist, Peter Behnstedt, has come to visit. He's sitting in our room with Tim's friend Yahya, checking on verb forms. Unfortunately, we are getting his insights only when it's almost too late for us.

I knew it was different. Listening to the news on Yemeni TV in standard Arabic hasn't helped with understanding people here. Now I can understand when people speak to me, though not when they speak quickly to each other and don't want me to catch what they say. And paradoxically, when I can understand what someone says, I can't at the same time analyse or capture how they said it, what grammatical forms they used, or even if they used 'g' or 'j' or something in between. It's as if I'm too busy getting the meaning, or as if it requires a different part of my brain that can't be engaged simultaneously.

Behnstedt's dialect atlas of Yemen, published in 1985, shows some of the local peculiarities, for example the way feminine adjectives don't agree as they do in standard Arabic – *hiya zalen*, not *zalena* for 'she is upset' – and the distinctive verb endings, like the use of -k for the first person past tense, which may hark back to a much older non-Arabic language.

Baking bread

Flames leap up from Khadija's oven. The smell of burning wood fills the kitchen, the *beit en nar*, the house of fire, as people call an old-style kitchen. More modern ones with gas burners are called the standard Arabic word *matbakh*. The *tannur* oven is nearly as high as her waist, a smooth fired-clay cylinder, open at the top and perhaps half a metre across, embedded in a hump of earth smoothed on the outside. The fire can be seen through a round hole near the base. At the top, on a support of two crossed strips of metal, a blackened kettle sits encircled by the flames. Next to the oven a ledge or work surface runs along the wall, made of the same smooth-faced earth. Rising from this surface is another cylindrical structure, with a large, round pottery hotplate set into the top, to be heated by coals underneath. When not in use, as now, it's protected by a basket-weave cover. This is where Khadija makes *lehuh*, the sourish spongy bread that uses a fermented liquid batter of sorghum flour, and which used to be the staple before people had much wheat. People say that in the old days rounds of wheat bread were only eaten on special occasions like 'Id. I suppose they mean the days of the Imams, before 1962.

The whole of the kitchen – ovens, ledge, floor, walls – is surfaced in a layer of earth or clay, like a whitewash but pale brown. This is *summakh*, a special earth which women fetch from one particular place in the mountain to coat their kitchens with. The walls are smoke-blackened towards the top, where a row of small square holes let in a dim light, and let some of the smoke out. There is no decoration; everything is functional and arranged for work. It's all soft, lumpy curves in the clay, with no hard edges.

Between the oven and the hotplate sit two thermoses, bright red with a tartan pattern, almost incongruous in the kitchen of earthen white-brown and dull metal pots and dishes. There are tongs, of the kind blacksmiths make from a strip of metal bent and hammered together near the middle to give a pincer and a loop to hang it up by. Tucked down beside the oven is a piece of sacking for covering the oven when it's not being used, and a small box of Tide washing powder, used to wash pans as well as clothes. There are two large metal barrels of water with square wooden lids and an old tin for a scoop sitting on the top, and an assortment of aluminium pots, dishes, trays and lids. Dishes on the floor hold used, dirty water. There's a charcoal brazier on the floor full of hot coals, where Khadija puts the kettle now that the flames have died down, leaving ashes and hot coals at the bottom of the oven. She pours *gahwa* from the kettle into the thermos, holding the kettle handle with a cloth.

Khadija sits on the floor, one knee up and one tucked under, to shape the balls of soft, elastic dough that lie in a dish, coated with flour. Her dress, black with a small pattern, is tucked up just above her knees for work, into the waist of the purple flared trousers she has on underneath. She shapes the balls in the flour. Then she takes up one and stands to pat it from hand to hand, so that it becomes a wider and flatter circle. She takes up her *makhbaza*, the bread applicator. It looks like a mushroom two handspans across, coiled like a basket, with a basketwork stalk or handle, and cloth sewn over the dome. Khadija pats the round of dough on to it and stretches the edges to fit the edge of the dome. She bends over the *tannur*, and with one swift practised movement plunges her hand into the searing hot oven and sticks the round of dough to the inside wall.

The round sits on the side of the oven, near the top. The smell of baking bread fills the kitchen. Khadija waits a few minutes and then reaches in a hand to feel the edges, gives a corner a little pull to see if it's ready, waits a little, then reaches in again and flicks it off the side and safely out. It's *khobz*, the ordinary, everyday wheat bread. The outside is browned and crusty; opened out it's soft and absorbent, good for dipping in sauce. She puts it on a basketwork tray.

This seems difficult enough, but I know that women also make larger rounds, *guram*, and *meluj*, where instead of forming the dough into a round they paste it directly with the fingers on the oven side, giving a wider, flatter, harder-crusted bread with finger indentations still on it. *Guram* is unleavened, with sorghum flour and buttermilk. *Jehin*, another of the many kinds of bread, is made with millet, sorghum or barley flour. *Gafu'a* has oil and eggs in. Leftover bread is made into *dafi*, heated up and stirred almost to a porridge in milk and butter. Some kind of bread, either the rounds from the *tannur*, or the *lehuh* pancakes made on the flat hotplate, is eaten at every meal.

'Do you want to try?'

I stretch the round of dough over the *makhbaza*, using my right hand to touch the dough as a matter of course, and holding the *makhbaza* in my left. Still holding it in my left hand, I go to put it in the oven.

'No, not that one! *Baraka*, blessing, is in the right hand – which hand do you eat with?'

Chastened, I transfer the stalk to my right hand. Choking smoke fills my nose. Flames lick up from the bottom of the *tannur*. I reach in to apply the round of bread to the side, but my courage fails: the intensity of the heat shocks me, my arm will burn! I drop the bread and the *makhbaza* in the ash on the bottom. Laughing, Khadija reaches into the hot coals and retrieves them.

'Look, I don't have any hairs on my right arm, the oven singes them off. And look, these are burn scars from cooking.'

I never learn to bake bread. We can buy it from our landlady in her restaurant for visitors to the town, though it's not cheap and we tend to feel we're giving her enough money as it is, in rent. But neighbours often give it to us. Women are always giving bread to each other too: hands reach out from window to window, across corners, to adjoining houses, bundles wrapped in scarves are thrown from roof to roof, children are sent with fresh-smelling rounds to their mothers' friends. In the early mornings, plumes of smoke rise from all over the town and the air has the smell of woodsmoke. Women bake on different days from their neighbours and swap on the others. Anyway, you can't throw away spare bread: that would be wicked, *haram*. Coming back from *rabakh*ing one afternoon with a group of women, I see them pick up a part-round in the street, exclaiming, and tuck it into a crack between stones in a wall where scavenging dogs won't get it.

The school

The elementary school is under a tree. Chairs and tables are spread around. There are no Yemeni teachers here; a huge Egyptian in a long pale robe is in charge, pointing at a blackboard with a cane. Tall and thick-limbed, he looks like a different species from the small, wiry Yemenis. The older pupils sit on chairs at tables, against the wall of the old school building and in the shade of the tree. The younger ones sit on the ground, scruffy children in dusty clothes, school bags and books balanced on their knees. Ten or twelve little girls, wearing either headscarves tied under the chin and part-covering their hair, or *lithma*s down over their foreheads, sit together in a cluster among the boys. The boys are at least twice as many.

There are plenty of girls in the first elementary class, but as the classes progress their numbers tail off. Their families worry about their daughters going to school, what might happen to them; or keep them at home to help, or take them out of school to be married. There are only three or four girls in the second and third elementary class, and six in the fourth. The girls in the three intermediate classes, one to four in each class, who sit inside the classroom with the older boys, are a select group of pioneers. They include girls from leading families, the sheikh's and the hakim's daughters. They're noticeable as they go through the town, a group of girls together more veiled than others, wearing black *sharshaf* overskirt, cape and head-covering and coloured *lithma*s tight over their faces up to, and down to, the eyes. (Soon the sheikh's eldest daughter will teach the younger girls, before she leaves to be married to the son of a sheikh in another area.)

A new school is being built, and by the end of our stay in Safaqayn the class is no longer held in the open air. Also by then there are three Yemeni teachers.

'I'm going to study in the afternoons with my mother,' my friend Amina's daughter Hasiba tells me, a year into our stay. I'm excited to learn that a school for girls and women has opened in the afternoons. Three of the schoolgirls from the highest intermediate class are the teachers, older girls with eight or nine years of education. One of them tells me they're paid a salary of 700 riyals a month, and that the three of them each teach two days in turn.

One afternoon on my way to *rabakh* I go by the school to have a look; one of the schoolgirl teachers opens the door briefly, and I can see her holding a big stick and hear the sound of chanting repetition in chorus coming from inside. I walk back at the end of the afternoon with Khadija, and we see some girls coming out.

'It's a literacy school for girls and women,' Khadija says, 'but there are no women, only girls. Women want to sit and smoke and relax in the afternoons.' It does seem that an afternoon school is in competition with a vital part of women's lives, all the enjoyment and social connection of *rabkha*.

My neighbour Thuraya wants to study. She has half-sisters in Sana'a who, in contrast to her, are educated. But she can't just go, she needs permission, since her father is dead, from her father's brother –

and he won't agree. He says it would be *'aib* for her to go. She is asking another uncle, who is in Saudi Arabia, but while she waits for an answer it becomes too late to join this year's class.

A few months later I'm *rabakh*ing at the house of a *walida*. Several women have brought their children, so it's a fidgeting, squabbling afternoon as the bored children whine and the mothers try to keep them quiet:

'Mariam, have you got a knife in your bag? Scissors? We'll cut his *zebb* off!' threatens one.

'Why don't you let your daughter study in the mornings?' one woman asks another.

'I go out in the morning getting grass for fodder.' That means the daughter is needed to look after the younger children.

'Do you have a cow?' I ask.

'Not any more, she died. I sell the hay to men from outside the town. I get one hundred riyals for fifty twists of hay. I can get ten in a morning if I work till noon.' The daughter goes to afternoon school, and her aunt, her mother's sister, is there too.

Another girl says, 'I went, but I left because I got hit by the teacher. There were twenty-eight in the class and there are seven left now.' A sad end to what seemed like a brilliant idea.

Amina's kitchen

'Come tomorrow, I'll show you how to make *gafu'a*,' Amina said to me yesterday.

Amina has emphatic movements which seem to me to contain a kind of intensity, pent-up energy and intelligence. Now she stands in her makeshift kitchen, a corrugated zinc shed at the side of her one-storey house on the edge of the town.

'He should be building me a proper kitchen, but he's helping his brother build his house instead,' she tells me. She avoids referring to her husband by name.

In the shed she has a three-ring gas burner, a *tannur* bread oven, a clay hotplate for *lehuh*, a large water container, and a ceramic squat toilet pan let into the floor, where she throws away dirty washing-up water.

She's already made the dough. It's a rich yellow colour. 'I made it by putting yeast like this' – she shows me about a teaspoon in her palm – 'in a jar with the same of sugar, and hot water. You leave it till it froths, mix it with flour, eggs, a tea glass full of oil, salt water, not too hot or too cold, bit by bit, kneading. Then you leave it till it's risen. It's for the *gafu'a* and the *bint* as well.'

Now she wipes a non-stick frying pan with vegetable ghee from a tin, and puts in a flat round of dough. She cooks it for a longish time, turning it once, when it has brown spots on the underside.

She's also made plain, creamy-white dough for *khobz*. The kitchen fills with smoke from the lit *tannur*. There's nowhere for Amina to put things down; she has to improvise all the time. She's making *bint es-sahn*, layered pastry to be soaked in honey for the first course of the meal, on the gas ring. The underside of the *bint* is cooked, and now she turns a round metal tray upside down over the top, takes red-hot glowing wood coals out of the bottom of the *tannur* with tongs, and places them on the top of the tray to finish the cooking. When she drops a red-hot coal, she picks it up with her fingers and juggles it from hand to hand to put it where she wants it, never touching it long enough with either hand to get burnt. She has a big pile of wood in her kitchen.

'How much did that cost?' Everyone always asks how much things cost, of us and of each other, so I reckon I can too.

'One hundred riyals.'

'How long will it last?'

'A month or more, depending on whether I bake every day.'

She has a girl helping her cook, her husband's sister's daughter. They work hard, in this difficult kitchen, pound and grind and cut and cook and bake in the smoke, alternate pans on the gas rings, beat up *helba* froth. This is a meal for guests. *Bint*; *lehuh* with *ra'ib*, buttermilk; rice with *zahaweq* relish pounded from tomatoes and chillies and spices; and a meat and potato stew bubbling up through a layer of *helba* on the top.

'Stay and eat with us. Fuad, go and fetch Abdullah.' Her eldest child sets briskly off up the town on the errand, and comes back after twenty minutes with Tim.

There are three other guests, senior men of Amina's husband's family. The meal is served in the house, where we gather round a plastic cloth on the floor, and, as always, is eaten quickly and with no talking. After lunch the men go off to chew qat in other houses, and I sit and chat with Amina and an older woman, her mother's sister, and a neighbour or two.

'Haven't you got any children?' the older woman asks me, inevitably.

'I've had six children,' Amina tells me. 'Two died, a girl and a boy. The girl was called Fatin, like my new baby now. The boy was fat, he was beautiful.'

'What did he die of?'

'People's eyes, looking at him, he was so plump.'

She tells me about her early life.

'I've been married to my husband for ten years, since I was about fifteen. Before that I was married twice, at seven and eight, but I refused to stay. I ran away, cried, slept outside.'

These marriages weren't consummated, the older woman confirms, pushing a finger between two on her other hand and shaking her head.

'My father only wanted money, he didn't care about my happiness. When a girl's ten, people start looking at her, so she's married to avoid problems.'

'Will your daughter be married so young?' She must be about eight now.

'No, she'll study.'

For now, she's busy in the house, sweeping, helping cook, minding the baby.

Amina takes a little container of *kohl*, a fine-ground, bluish-black, faintly glittery powder, dips in a thin, smooth stick, and puts some on my inner eyelids, right next to the eyeball. I flinch. She laughs: 'You're worse than the baby!' Like every baby I see, Fatin has *kohl* smeared thickly around her eyes. 'It will help your sight.' I can't deny that my sight needs help, because I'm wearing glasses. Hardly anyone here has them; one or two men, and one old woman.

'Which is better?' the women ask me. 'Here or Sana'a?'

'I prefer it here, it's beautiful and people are good. Which do you think is better?'

'Here except for water,' Amina says. 'Sana'a is better for that, it's *ta'ab* here, hard work, getting water.'

'Why don't they have a pipe from the spring down the mountain?'

'Money. The officials eat the money from the government, the government gave a million riyals for water.'

'Who ate it? Government people?'

'Yes.'

'Is it true,' they ask me, 'that Abdullah and you take turns with the housework, him one day and you the next?'

'Yes, and in London we both go out to work and both do the housework.'

'That's good, it's nice him doing the housework.' The other women agree.

I stay till we hear the *maghreb* call to prayer.

'Will you spit out your qat before you pray?' I ask Amina.

'Yes, to be pure for praying.'

'Some men don't.' Others, we know, store the chewed wad in a corner of their headcloth to put back in afterwards.

'We say the woman is polluted, and the man is pure,' she says. I think the implication is that women have to make an extra effort to be purified, an effort that is not so necessary for men.

Dressmaking

Selma, bright-eyed and swift-moving, puts the folded fabric to her teeth and tears a hole in the middle. Then she tears the hole to size by hand and lines it with facing to make a neat neckline. She measures out the other pieces for the dress in handspans and tears them off.

Selma has four children, and none dead as far as I know. Whenever I see her she's always busy, with her house, her kitchen, sewing; she never seems to sit still. She's very chatty and friendly, so I often drop in, hoping to find her free to talk. She makes dresses for private customers and in quantity for a merchant in the market. Now she's sitting on the floor behind her heavy black-and-gold manual sewing machine, one leg folded up and one tucked under, in the middle of a pile of work. A heap of half-finished dresses in bright colours is behind her. The skirts are full and the bodices are close-fitting, but three seams at each side hold extra fabric, to be let out when the customer is next pregnant.

Selma's husband is away in Saudi Arabia; she says he will be back in a year or two. 'It's *ta'ab* without him, but when he comes back I get pregnant. I take pills while he's here.'

'Are pills *haram*?'

'Who told you it was *haram*? It's *haram* to take them if your husband doesn't agree, but mine loves me so he agrees, because it's *ta'ab* for me without him. He gets them from Saudi Arabia.'

She asks me about adultery in my country. 'Women whose husbands are away in Saudi Arabia have a *sadiq*, a lover, nobody knows.'

'What would the husband do if he finds out? Would he kill her?'

'No, divorce her.'

'What if she gets pregnant while her husband is away?'

'The *sadiq*, if he loves her very much, will go to the doctor secretly in the night and pay lots of money for an injection to make her abort. If he doesn't love her, he will just go away.'

She asks me my age, but she doesn't know hers, not even approximately.

'Do you wash all over, and your head and hair, like we do, after sex?'

'Not the hair.'

'With us, the man and the woman both wash all over.'

This time she's making a dress for me. I bought the material from a market stall. I chose a stall where I know the boy who runs it: some time ago I photographed him, and gave him the print. It's relatively plain, gauzy bright red nylon with a pattern of silver thread and sequins, and cost 35 riyals, which seems cheap. Selma charges 20 riyals for the sewing.

Selma measures me up in spans. There are two kinds: *shibr*, thumb to spread little finger, and *she'z*, thumb to index finger. She measures my arm length and my shoulder to my waist with her thumb and index finger. I'm three and a bit spans, she says, where Yemeni women are three. She folds the fabric and measures it with her hand before she tears off the piece that will make the bodice.

'Shall I make seams in the sides for you to let out?' I'm not planning to get pregnant, but I might get fatter, so I say yes.

She looks, disapproving, at the smock from England I'm wearing over my trousers. 'Women here would use a dress like that to sleep in.'

This seems a good reason to get a proper *zenna*, something they'll approve of, for wearing on afternoon visits.

But when it's finished and I wear it to *rabakh*, it too gets critical looks. 'You should have a red lining under that dress.'

I didn't get a lining made. I thought one layer of thin nylon that I could wear over a cotton shirt and skirt would be more comfortable.

'Is it *'aib* like this?' I need to know if it's actually indecent.

'No, it needs a lining to look nice.'

It seems I've got it wrong again.

Afternoon in Meruwagha

Another afternoon, I'm down in Meruwagha, where the Jewish town used to be. To me it now seems like part of the town, divided only by the road, though it has its own mosque. I set off aiming to visit Amina, but her daughter says she's gone to a house nearby for the afternoon. I start to make my way there, but a small girl waylays me.

'Come to my mother!'

She's asked me before, when I was already committed somewhere else, so this time I go with her. In the room where she takes me several women are sitting, some of whom I know. I go round kissing hands, and take a place against the wall. There's no qat available in the town at the moment, because of the time of year or lack of rain to make it grow. This afternoon everyone is cracking and eating pumpkin seeds and spitting out the husks, as if to give their hands and mouths something to fiddle with instead.

The room smells of incense. The hostess is passing round a *mabkhara*, an incense burner, a rough terracotta bowl with a stand in which grains of frankincense resin smoulder on charcoal. Women take it in turn, wave the smoke towards them, inhale the smell, and lift their skirts and waft it underneath to perfume their clothes.

I am sitting next to bright, lively Warda, whom we met on our first visit to the town. She has distinctive greenish-brown eyes that slant downwards to the outer edge; she's one of the few women I can recognise by the eyes when her face is veiled. She's spirited and outgoing, and always particularly friendly to me. Now, I can't follow the conversation, and Warda, a rare, kind explainer, asks me, 'Do you understand what we're talking about? About diseases caused by *jinn*. See this? Feel it!' She has an amulet, a little cloth bag, under her left arm, on a chain over her right shoulder. 'I wear it day and night. It's for illness, it comes from a man who opens the book.'

'Opens the book?' I ask, puzzled.

'These men make amulets and they also cure people by writing on a piece of paper. They wash the writing off in water, and give the sick person the water to drink. They cure mad people.'

'What about the madman here, who wanders the streets and shouts?'

'He's been mad for too long, his brain is sick and dried up.'

They use a word, *dhara'*, which I don't understand at all.

'If you're angry with someone,' Warda explains, 'and you say "A *jinni* take you!" and they get ill, have aches and pains, you take a *shanbal*, a flip-flop, and circle it round their head, counting. You go seven times in one direction, seven in the other, to send the *jinn* away, then throw the flip-flop behind their head where they can't see it. Or they can do it themselves. It's as good as a doctor.'

'A *jinni* take you! A *jinni* snatch you to the bottom of the cistern!' are standard phrases we often hear people say when they're angry with someone. Later a man tells us that men circle a jambiya, rather than a flip-flop, to perform *dhara'*.

'*Ad ummish bikher*? Is your mother alive and well?' one of the women asks me, someone I don't know, with a wedge-shaped, yellowish face.

'Didn't you see her? She came here,' says another.

'How many children have you got?'

'None yet. Anyway I only want two.'

She says to the other women: 'She's looking after her–'

'*Aib*! *Aib*! *La tursudi*! Don't write! Don't write!' they all chorus.

I have my vocabulary notebook poised. They all know I write down words in it. Women who already know me explain this to those who haven't met me before. Sometimes, on learning about the words I put in the notebook, they ask, 'What about the rude words?'

When the conversation gets bawdy, they warn each other, 'Mariam'll write it down!' I feel a huge shift in attitude from groups of women cheerfully repeating rude words, to collective anxiety at any idea of writing them. Now they say: 'Promise you won't write it?'

'All right.'

'It tears each time you give birth, you know,' the woman continues. (She has, I learn later, four children, and four dead.) 'Ours get big from so many children.'

'What do you call it where you come from?' they ask me.

I regret the lack of a good word in English, one that women own and use comfortably. I have a mental picture of roomfuls of Yemeni women chanting 'Cunt! Cunt!' at the next English visitor.

'Vagina,' I say cautiously. They repeat it carefully.

At *maghreb* Warda and I leave the house together. As we pass Warda's house she invites me in. Her brothers and their wives live there. Warda is married but her husband is away working in Saudia Arabia most of the time. He comes back every year or so.

'Do you miss him?'

'It's nicer with him away, *efthin*, I'm tranquil, comfortable. But I'd like a child, I haven't got one, I had one but it died. I live in my brother's house, my husband pays money for me.'

'And what do you do when your husband comes back?'

'I go to his house, but I don't get on with his sister.'

She adds: 'He's coming back in Ramadan, I hope I'll get pregnant.'

We eat supper, sour *lehuh* with fried-up eggs and tomatoes.

'There's a wedding starting tonight,' Warda says, 'of Fatima, the divorced wife of Ahmed in the house you were in. I'll take you after *maghreb*.'

'Will Abdullah be angry when you don't go back?' asks Warda's brother's wife.

I say he won't. Warda repeats Tim's explanation to ease these concerns: 'Abdullah said there was *amana* here' – trust, honesty. The phrase *hina amana*, here there is trust, seems to make it all right for me to be out.

'Ahmed might be married soon too,' Warda says. 'To a woman from here, who's been married before, but just for a short time. He didn't get the one from Mahwit.'

'Does the bride have to agree to the marriage?' I ask Warda.

Other people have emphasised to me, 'Marriage with us is with the consent of the girl and the boy,' but Warda says: 'A girl must marry the man her father tells her to, even if he's horrible. If she doesn't like him, she'll refuse to sleep with him and he'll divorce her.'

When I write this up in my notes I comment, 'Hard to tell when Warda's being serious'. I am wrong to be dismissive. I think then that no one ever gives me neat, abstracted summaries of customs and how things work. As time goes on, I realise that this was one, a rare one. Yet, striving though I was to understand and extract general patterns, I didn't recognise it.

Warda's statement is also an indication of the point in her life, to me unexpected, at which a woman may have most scope to make a choice: not before the marriage, but after.

Weddings

At the house of the bride's father Warda and I press up the stairs together with a crowd of other women. Warda hasn't put on extra finery, just her ordinary afternoon clothes, the clean bright dress which she was already wearing and one gold medallion on a chain round her neck.

'Are there men in another room?'

'Not tonight.' Other stages of the wedding will have parallel celebrations, the men together somewhere else, but this, the evening of the *ma'shara*, the tray, is a women's event.

People greet me warmly and welcome me in; they seem pleased to see me. We reach the room where the round trays are laid out. In the darkish room the eye is immediately drawn to the burning lights. One tray has thick cotton wicks flaming in oil; another holds sweets and biscuits with candles sticking up between them. Two small girls with hennaed hands, one with a leopard-skin pattern headscarf and one, slightly older, with a *lithma* over her face, are carrying a bundle each of lit candles, bunched together with blue-green sprays of rue and bright orange French marigold flowers. I can smell the rue, at once bitter and unpleasantly sweet, like something dead. Someone dips a bit of rue in the oil and shoves it down the front of another woman's dress, against her protest, and another does the same thing to someone else.

'Why are you doing that?' I ask.

'She's pregnant, it's to protect the baby.'

The bride is wearing a bright red dress, large amounts of gold – necklaces, pendants, medallions – and also a heavy, traditional silver headdress. Massive finely worked panels of silver circle her forehead, while chains and little balls and coins hang down in great clusters over the ears.

The crowd shuffles and reorganises into a procession, down the dark stairs and out into the dark streets, with women drumming and singing. People carry torches. The bride holds hands on either side with women, her friends taking turns, and for a while she holds mine. Two women carry on their heads the trays with the burning lights. The women ululate, shrill whooping trills, tongues moving fast behind their hands. I try to do it, and they're pleased at my efforts.

The procession, points of flame, a crowd pressed together, the sound of ululating and drumming and singing and the smell of rue, pushes through the streets, up an alleyway, and into a house I don't know – not the bride's or the bridegroom's. The procession crowds up the dark stairs and into a large room where we all sit down. *Gahwa* is handed round in little glasses. The bride sits in the far corner flanked by two friends. One is the woman who Warda told me is perhaps going to be married to Ahmed, the bride's ex-husband; the other a pretty young woman I've often seen at afternoon gatherings, who seems to be popular. Katiba is there, sitting next to her brother's potential bride, Selma. Katiba seems on friendly terms with his ex-wife, who is anyway her cousin, despite the breach, a row with the whole family, that led to the divorce.

As I try to make sense of it all I think to myself: when I've been here longer, I will know why each person is here, what their connection is to the bride. And this is true, and I later notice that I mostly recognise the women at these occasions as a mix of neighbours from the nearest houses, and relatives from near and far.

The bride starts to cry, and hides her face in her friend's shoulder. The friend cries too.

'Is it necessary for the bride to cry?' I ask Warda.

'Didn't you cry at yours?' she answers.

Two older women are beating drums and singing, with words I can't follow. The drumbeat is regular and hypnotic, the singing rises and falls in repeated verses. Two young women stand up and dance to the beat of the drums, side by side, hand in hand, bending at the knees, taking small steps, rotating slowly. Then the bride stands up and dances with Selma, the woman who will soon succeed her as Ahmed's wife, first with a veil over her face, and then without. Ululating bursts out, and again.

My neighbours from across the roof are there and Fatima says she'll take me home.

'I don't need to be taken home, I can go by myself.'

'Aren't you afraid? There are dogs!'

Warda says goodbye. On the way up through Fatima's house I'm pressed to stay for a little, and sit with some men and her mother; then

I leave through their kitchen, out of the window on to our roof, and down our stairs home.

The next day is a Wednesday. The wedding will culminate on Thursday, market day, when there's meat to be bought. It's windy, cloudy, a foul day with the wet mist creeping up around the town. After *'asr* I set off to go to the wedding party. On the way I fall in with a large group of women going there too. It's happening in a different place from last night's celebration, and without going into a house or upstairs we enter a large room that reminds me of a barn, with a high ceiling and straw on the floor. The electricity is on, evidently by special arrangement. The room is filled with women in rows, sitting on makeshift seating, planks laid on barrels, large tins that women have brought with them. There are some adults, but the great bulk of the audience is made up of little and adolescent girls. People are more dressed up, in newer, shinier dresses and wearing more gold, than they were last night. Some have brought qat. There's a clearing in the middle of the room where two women at a time dance to the drumming and singing of a female musician. The bride sits up at one end of the room, wearing a red dress, looking solemn and impassive, with a companion on either side. The room is hot and crowded, fidgety, and noisy with little girls shrilling and squabbling and falling off the rickety piled seating. It's impossible to have a conversation. I'm relieved when the party ends at *maghreb*.

The next day there's another similar celebration in the same room, still with a large proportion of little girls, but more crowded. As the gathering breaks up at *maghreb*, the bride and cheerful, bossy Fatima Abdu ask me to go home with them. Their fathers are brothers and live in the same house.

At the bride's house, there's a lot of sitting around with the bride, her older sister, who is married to a brother of the man of the house we first lived in but lives with her baby at her father's while her husband works in Saudi Arabia, and her younger sister, still a little girl. The family invites me to supper, for which they all crowd round in the kitchen. There's rice with lumps of meat, and spongy *lehuh* to dip into rich meat stock. After supper is finished there's a feeling of waiting around. Then two men arrive. They are men I know well, more brothers of the man of the house we lived in. They are, it's explained to me, the bride's maternal uncles. They escort the bride, one on each side, as we all leave the house. A crowd of women gather, women I saw in the afternoon reappear, there's ululating, and a procession winds through the streets to the home of the bridegroom. Painted tin trunks like I've seen in the market are carried on women's heads. I follow into the bridegroom's house and up the stairs, to a room where the bride sits on cushions and guests file in to give her money in turn.

I find myself next to a woman I know, whose baby I photographed a few days ago.

'How much should I give?'

'As much as you like.'

'How much are you giving?'

'Ten riyals.'

So I give 10. A woman standing behind the bride takes it from me to pass it to her. She's announcing all the gifts: 'From Selma, daughter of Ali So-and-so; from the wife of So-and-so.' When she hands mine over she starts, 'From the wife of...' and the announcement trails off.

I see the bride's ex-mother-in-law, briefly sitting in the group nearest her, and the girls from my neighbours-across-the-roof. Most people don't stay long. Fatima Abdu, before she leaves, gives the bride an encouraging hug.

By about 10pm most people have gone, leaving me and one old woman and a younger one, and neighbours popping in and out with a thermos and *kak*, little glossy buns. The bride is still chewing qat. It's all rather low-key, with a feeling of the festivities petering out.

Then a man comes in, one of the maternal uncles who flanked the bride in the procession. The bride stands up and walks to one of the brightly painted tin trunks that were carried over on women's heads. She takes out a bundle wrapped up in a nylon scarf. She unwraps it. It's the money given by the guests.

The uncle counts it for her: I can see a lot of 100- and 50-riyal notes. She follows the counting intently. It comes to 5,000 or 6,000. She looks glum.

'*Galil*,' she says. Little.

She tries to give him some of it. He refuses, resists. A long struggle ensues. The bride is trying to foist it on to him, push it into his hand, tuck it into his clothing, thrust it down the neck of his shirt, and the old woman who's been sitting with her is helping her. The uncle keeps protesting and refusing, and eventually he succeeds.

My neighbour-across-the-roof says her family want to lock up, and that's my obvious route home, so I say goodbye and leave. The bridegroom, Tim tells me, is sitting with a gathering of men, which he leaves about forty-five minutes later, quietly, without any escort, to go to his bride.

The next day, Thursday, Karima across the way waves to me from the roof, and signals to me – an urgent beckoning movement with all the fingers of her downturned hand – to come over. I find a terrific baking in progress, the women of the house slapping in and taking out from the circular oven round after round of fresh, fragrant bread for dinner at the bridal house. There are also trays of *bint*, honey-drenched pastry. I wonder if they're helping with the cooking because they're neighbours; they aren't relatives. Thuraya makes the *bint*; unlike most women she has a gas oven, and it's easier to cook *bint* in that, because it needs heat all round. She sends one dish to a neighbour and gives us one to take home, sweet and buttery and delicious.

A week later, Ahmed from our old house and his new bride are married.

'Aren't you going to Ahmed's house to see the wedding preparations?' says Fatima from across the roof. It's seven in the evening, I've just got back from *rabakh*ing in a house below the town, tired from scrambling up a rough path. But I hurry over to the house we used to live in, and ask where Katiba is.

'Come, I'll take you.' Ahmed shows me, along a narrow alley and round several corners, to the house of his bride.

'*Itfaddali, itfaddali, ya* Mariam!' Come in! call the women from within.

In the upstairs room, the smell of henna meets me. The bride is sitting in a corner, and Katiba, her sister-in-law to be, is starting to take off her henna paste.

'Did you henna her?' I ask Katiba. It's not the ordinary solid-coloured design. The bride has elaborate patterns on her feet and on the back and palm of her left hand, rows and rows of tiny V shapes.

'No, not me, the *muzayyina* did it.' I know who she is now: the wedding attendant, organiser, mistress of ceremonies, decorator of the bride, singer, and player of the drum.

Women come crowding in to the room, one after another, in groups of friends and neighbours, perhaps eight different lots of women. This time it's Katiba who has prepared the trays, and now she puts them on the floor. One has several candles in it, held in cement, with rue sprinkled over, and the other a mixture of biscuits and wrapped sweets, with thick cotton wicks alight in the centre.

The room is very crowded. As well as being small, it has one end shut off by a curtain. The *muzayyina*, who has a bony, sharp-nosed face and an authority that comes through in her beat, sings and plays a small drum in a complicated rhythm. Her strong voice rises over the pattern of the drumbeats, joined by another woman, singing a twisting melody in long lines and answering phrases; each final note is drawn out long, then ends abruptly. The bride stands up and dances in a space in the centre, with a veil over her face, a slow, knee-bending, small-stepping dance to the beat of the drum. Then, to a changed tempo, different drumbeats and a different song, she dances with another woman, hand in hand, side by side, moving in unison. Sitting down again, the bride cries briefly.

There's no procession this evening, and the wedding tomorrow will last one day only. Both bride and groom have been married before, so a briefer celebration is in order.

'Ahmed didn't want more. But we had a celebration last night, when the bride was hennaed – we sat up till eight at night.'

That would be about 2am, I calculate. There is a different system here for counting the hours. Their time (*'Arabi*) has sunrise and sunset at twelve, so it's about six hours off ours, which they call *zaweli*.

After an hour or so of crowd and music most of the women take their leave, wishing everyone good evening.

'Sit, stay a bit,' the bride urges me. I sit for a while, together with an old woman, whose name and connection with the family I fail to grasp. A man, the bride's father, comes in groaning loudly, and lies down on the bed. The women cover him with blankets.

'He's been like this, ill, for four years, we took him to doctors in Sana'a and Ta'izz but it was no use.'

Someone brings in a watermelon. A little later the bridegroom's married older sister Selma, who lives in a house nearby, pops in with half a melon for him.

The old woman gets up to go. 'I'll accompany you home,' she says to me.

'Stay a bit longer!' the bride presses me. I'm not sure if I should or not.

Before I can decide, a voice sounds outside, coming up the stairs. '*Allah! Allah!*'

It's the usual warning to the women in a house that a man is approaching. The bride dives behind the curtain at the end of the room. The man is Ahmed, her bridegroom.

He has an argument with the bride's father, who is still lying on the bed. I can understand only that there's a problem; the explanations of the old woman next to me about the bride's brother in Sana'a and a telephone call don't really help. Then he leaves again. Shortly afterwards Katiba comes back. There's a disagreement. Some last-minute glitch, some negotiation about – of course – money. At one point she shrugs, she's just a child messenger, she doesn't know. Eventually the sick man hands her a 100-riyal note, and she goes away.

When I finally get up to leave, the bride says to me, 'Come back in the morning. Come early, very early, come at three – my mother will henna you.'

I leave my henna with her to be mixed ready in the morning. The next morning I arrive at the bride's house at 9am.

'*Inti behin*! You're early!'

Have I got the time wrong? I recalculate. If their watches are set to dawn, I suppose they'd now, in February, be more than six hours different from ours.

The bride's mother and two younger sisters, unmarried girls, are there. The bride's eldest sister lives not far away, married in Meruwagha, but she has a baby and can't come to the wedding; she hasn't completed her forty-day confinement. The bridegroom's older sister from nearby keeps coming in and out.

They set sweet, spicy *shahi* in front of me, and then *gahwa*, and a flap of sour *lehuh* to eat. The bride hennas my feet, then my hands. The *muzayyina* arrives and starts to put henna on the bride. She goes carefully along the lines of yesterday's pattern, little V shapes up the fingers. She shapes each tiny sausage of henna, half of a V, in her mouth and puts it on the bride's hand with a matchstick. A couple of young women, Fatima Abdu and another, help her. It's a long, laborious process: the whole hennaing takes over an hour. The bride's feet are covered with cloths and a *mabkhara*, an earthenware pot with incense burning on hot coals, is put near her feet under the cloths.

After the henna the bride puts on *shedher*. It looks like wet cement. 'What is it?' I ask.

'From fire,' they say. Can it be ashes mixed to a paste with water? There must be something else: it has a strong ammoniac smell. The *muzayyina* slathers it all over the bride's hands and feet and wraps them in plastic bags. When she takes it off some time later, all the henna has gone black. The *shedher* has only stained where the henna was; the elaborate V pattern still shows, but now in black. I suppose it makes a stronger contrast with the uncoloured skin, but I miss the rich red colour that the henna was before.

We hear heavy steps on the stairs. Puffing with effort, the bridegroom's youngest brother brings in a suitcase on his shoulder and plumps it down in the middle of the room. The bride and her mother and sisters open it and examine the contents minutely.

There are eight *zenna* dresses, of the type that's made locally on sewing machines, in different colours. Six pairs of trousers, also in various colours. A pair of fancy sandals, with high heels and silvery uppers. A pack of six Western-style panties (as against the more traditional white machine-sewn shorts worn under women's trousers). Two *saramiya*s, thin headcloths for outdoor covering. Several nylon headscarves in different colours and patterns. A bottle of perfume.

The bride's disappointment is obvious from her face and the dismissive gestures of her hands. After a while she cries a little.

I make an attempt to cheer her up: 'In my country the bridegroom doesn't give any clothes at all.' Everyone says this is very bad.

Later Katiba appears again, carrying on her head an Indian tin trunk, a green one with domed buildings painted on the lid. This holds two more pairs of trousers and a scarf, but hardly anything else, and the bride cries again. The bride and her family seem not to like the suitcase; they transfer everything to the metal trunk. It's the kind women keep their possessions in, padlocked, often under the bed.

The bridegroom's little brother brings in a bunch of herbs, aromatic *'uzzab* like oregano, and *heynan*, which hardly smells but has pretty trailing flower bracts.

'They're from my sister Nuriya.'

'Where is Nuriya?' the bride demands, as if she should be here.

'In her village.'

She's married out of the town. Last night they were complaining that the bridegroom's other married sister hadn't come.

The bridegroom's father, the man of the house we lived in, comes in, a portly, dignified man in late middle age. To my surprise, nobody runs to hide. He starts speaking, firmly, emphatically. I can understand that he's defending the contents of the suitcase and listing how much it all cost.

After he's gone again, emboldened by all the discussions of costs, I ask the bride how much the bridegroom is paying in bride price.

'Twenty thousand,' she says. That would be about £2,500.

'Thirty thousand,' says her sister.

'Thirty thousand,' the bride says.

'Why did you get divorced from your first husband?'

'He wasn't good.'

'How?'

'I didn't like him. I was married for four years, but I lived here, not in the town where he was. My father paid him fifteen thousand to divorce me.'

'How much did he pay to marry you?'

'Twelve thousand.'

My right hand is de-hennaed so I can eat some lunch, and a little later my left hand and my feet, which haven't taken very well; I was given the incense burner too late to keep them warm enough.

'Come back in your *zenna*! Not the red one,' says the bride.

I wonder what's wrong with the red one, and if this is because I didn't have an underdress made for it. I dress as instructed, putting on another nylon Yemeni-style *zenna* I've had made, multicoloured and more opaque than the red one, and return to the bride's house at about 4pm our time. There's a bustle of getting ready. Then the bride leaves her house in procession with drums and singing from the *muzayyina*, down through the top of the town to the same huge, high-ceilinged room as the last wedding, where there's already a packed gathering, and women are arriving with barrels to sit on. There's a crush, lots of noise, women all talking to each other; familiar faces of women I know, and once again a great number of little girls. The *muzayyina* drums and sings. I slip out and nip back home to get my tape recorder. Back in the big room again, I catch the eye of the *muzayyina* as she pauses between songs, and tap my cassette recorder, taking out and waving the cassette to show it's not a camera, and she nods agreement. I tape the drumming and singing when the bride gets up to dance.

I leave at *maghreb* when everyone else does. Later, after seven in the evening, Tim and I go out and find the men's procession outside the mosque. The men are all holding hands and singing, powerfully, in unison, something like a chant. They go in procession to the bridegroom's house.

I double back to the bride's house to see her leaving, again, in a procession with the *muzayyina* drumming and singing, brisk and joyful.

In the bridegroom's house the men sit in the *mafraj*, the room we once rented, and the bride and the women sit in another room, where I join them. Men and women come in and give the bride money, 5- and 10- and 20-riyal notes, handing it to the *muzayyina*. She announces each donation, waving the note and calling out who it's from. I give 50 this time, because of our connection with the house, and the *muzayyina* announces it: 'From Mariam the tourist!'

The family invite me to go upstairs to eat dinner. There's rice, salad in the rice as a garnish, meat. Then I head back down and sit with the bride and the other women for a bit. The bridegroom's married sisters are all there this time. The bride asks me for a copy of my recording of the wedding music, and I promise to bring it over. The bridegroom comes in and out, and this time there's no rush to veil or hide. Later we all move to the room Tim and I used to live in, now with hangings on the walls and a cluster of *mada'a*s in the middle. Men and women are together, and the bridegroom sits next to the bride. They look quite relaxed together. Some people get up to go, and I stand up, but the bride presses me: 'Stay longer, *ya* Mariam, it's still early, sit with us a bit!' We watch an episode of a soap opera, and when it ends at nearly 11pm, I finally leave.

The next day the bridegroom's father invites Tim and me to the house for lunch. There's *bint es-sahn*, drenched in *samn* and honey; rice, bread cooked up with eggs (*susi*), then a bowl of boiling *helba*, and piles of meat in chunks. The bridegroom's father, our old host, gives me lumps of meat, presses them on me, more than I want, before I've managed to finish the last one. I am still chewing away on a mouthful of meat while trying to eat the orange and apple quarters that end the meal. The same women are there as were sitting with the bride last night. The bride is busy helping with the cooking. The bride and bridegroom seem happy and at ease.

This bride stays with Ahmed, but not, or not for long anyway, under the direction of her mother-in-law. They move out into two rooms in another house, where I pay her a visit after she has had a baby. She's not very happy with her husband.

'He gets angry a lot, for example if I go out. But it's nice being in these rooms, I'm glad we left his father's house. I quarrelled with Katiba, and Ahmed had a row with his mother because he hit Katiba.'

'Did you leave because of a row with your mother-in-law?'

'No, but I was worked hard, all the work fell to me. Now I'm *murtah*, at ease, I can get up and go to bed when I want.'

When I visit the town four years later, they're living in a small house at the bottom of the town with three or four children.

'I was twenty-five when I got married, I didn't want to before,' my neighbour says one day, telling me about her life.

'Did you want to then?'

She shrugs. '*Nasib*.' Fate, lot in life.

'We're all married far away, Sana'a, Khabt,' says the sister of another bride, as the wedding procession leaves from the tall house near us with five families in. The bride is going to Bajil at the bottom of the mountain on the coastal plain, some three hours' drive away, the town from where most of the town's supplies are brought.

'Why?' I ask.

'Fate is from Allah.'

At first I think they're saying marriage relations, in-laws, are from God. But though similar to the word for a man's brother-in-law, the word is different, with a different S sound, and means share, lot, fate. It comes to the same thing for women: their marriage is their fate.

An afternoon's entertainment

The *walida*, plump, no longer young, with three children living and two dead, lies back on a high bed in her house down in Meruwagha. Perhaps ten women are sitting in the room, visiting her. Among them are her husband's mother and their neighbour, my friend Amina. The new baby lies next to the *walida*. Her small child, the next one up from the baby, grizzles until someone lifts her up on to the high bed. The baby is covered with a light cloth.

'To keep off flies,' someone says when I ask. I wonder if it might also be to protect the baby from people looking at it, but nobody says so.

The room has old, assorted, grimy cushions, and small, high windows; the sort of room women sit in, not as clean and spacious as a men's *mafraj* reception room. A ledge on the wall is crammed with pots of plastic flowers and plastic oranges. In the corner there's a *dulab*, a set of free-standing metal shelves, found in nearly every sitting room. It holds the television, a small black-and-white one, covered in a cloth; a tray holding little *gahwa* glasses; a spray can of cologne, another of air freshener; some plastic pots of brightly coloured plastic flowers. The room smells of rue and milk. I've given the *walida* two tins of fruit, kissed hands with everybody, and taken a place sitting against the wall. One woman circulates with the inevitable cologne spray, dousing our fronts. The *walida*'s sister comes in to give her some blackish liquid in an old tin.

'What's that?' I ask her.

'*Gatera*, from burnt herbs, it's sold in a bottle, it comes from wadis. You put it on the wall,' she draws a cross shape in the air, 'after a birth, and the same on the baby's forehead, and on its fingernails and toenails – it's a *herz*, an amulet, protection.'

The conversation has ranged over illnesses and operations and childbirth horror stories, joking, gossip, people's movements, which men have gone to work in Saudi Arabia, who has come back, quarrels, prices. Now Fatima, an older woman, large and jolly (despite her tally of six children alive and nine dead, cited as extreme even by local women), entertains us all with tales of her journey to Saudi Arabia on the Hajj.

'It was the first time I'd been anywhere – my first time in a car at all. I was so terrified, I put a scarf over my face.' She laughs at her own naivety, and mimes how she covered her face.

Some of her listeners have never been in a car. Another who has concurs. 'Yes, I kept my face covered all the way to Mahwit.'

'When I first saw the flat, hard tarmac road, I said it was a roof! When they put petrol in the car, I said the hose was the intestines of the car coming out!'

The audience is loving it. Everybody is in fits of laughter and one woman claps.

We chew qat. The men have taken the household's hourglass-shaped spittoons to use in the *mafraj* upstairs, and we are handed old tins to spit in, with a handful of twigs in the top to hide the green liquid beneath.

I give the others some of the qat I've brought.

'Give them only one sprig each, and keep the rest for yourself,' says the *walida*'s mother-in-law, Nuriya, an oldish woman with a brown wrinkled face. She makes a lively play of instructing me. 'ONE!' she says, very clearly, raising her voice for my benefit, holding up one sprig to demonstrate, 'ONE!'

'She'll write it down!' says Fatima, who has *rabakh*ed with me before. Everyone knows I'm always writing words in my notebook, it's a standing joke: 'Look! She's going to take out her book and write it down!'

The old woman Nuriya snatches my bag to tease me.

'You'll have to write the words for me,' I joke in return. She delves in my bag for the pen and notebook and pretends to write, going left to right.

I ask about the bag one little girl is wearing on a string over her shoulder, sewn up and about ten centimetres square.

'It has the Quran in it, with *hiltit* and *merr*.'

'What's that?'

'Incense.' Asafoetida and myrrh. 'So the *jinn* don't take the baby. It's a *herz*.' A protective charm, an amulet. They also say something about *bedat*, witches. But later someone tells me it's not against *jinn*, but the eye; the evil eye, as we would call it. I get the impression that the eye is a threat that is less often and less lightly mentioned, but more seriously feared.

Then we watch a serial, on a television powered from a car battery, since it's not yet time for the town's electricity to be switched on. Everybody has been watching these Egyptian and Jordanian serials, talking about them in the afternoons, naming their new babies after the characters. You could probably date the point when TV came to the town, about six years ago, by the influx of a much wider variety of new names – Fadia, Faten, Ashwaq – instead of the old Selma, Fatima, Amina, Nuriya, Adiba, Katiba. The older names were much repeated: over a quarter of the women I know, or know of, are called either Fatima or Nuriya, and another sixth Amina or Selma. I can count thirty-four Fatimas and twenty-six Nuriyas. There's a household where the women, two wives of brothers and a sister, are all called Selma. To distinguish between people, their father's name is often added: Selma Mohammed, Fatima Ahmed.

The women watch the serial intently, asking each other when they can't follow the plot or are puzzled by the Egyptian Arabic. The plot of this one, which the whole town is following, revolves around identity concealed at birth, with a climax of reunion ('Father! Father!'), and of course love and courtship. Some show modern Arab urban life. ('Did you leave a note on the table for Abdullah,' one woman asks me when I go on an outing with her, 'like they do on the television?' People say our marriage is 'like on the television'.

And a man asks Tim, 'Is life in your country really like that, always chasing each other in cars?')

Afterwards we see the Yemeni TV news. The female announcer has her head uncovered.

'Isn't it *'aib*?' I ask. Even when they aren't veiled, all the women in the town, down to small girls, have their heads covered. Even babies wear little pointed hoods.

'She's a Sana'ani woman.'

'So is it OK in Sana'a?'

'She's educated, she has a job.'

'And if you went like that?'

'It would be *'aib* for us, but not for an educated woman with employment.'

Then my friend Amina repeats to them what I've told her about marriage where I come from.

'There's no bride money, they marry for love. And it's forbidden to have a second wife.'

I take the opportunity to ask, 'Which is better? A man being allowed to have two wives, or not?'

There's no ambivalence in the reply, a chorus in heartfelt agreement: 'Not!'

'Doesn't anyone want a *tabina*, a co-wife?' I press.

The proportion of men in the town with more than one wife is actually small. I know of five men in and around the town with two, and the sheikh's father has three. For most women – unless their husbands are rich, powerful or capricious, or have property in different areas, or if they don't have children – it's reasonably unlikely to happen. But the possibility hangs over them. They say, emphatically: 'We fear it till we die.'

The afternoon's talk is interrupted by the small daughter of one of the neighbour women, rushing in and announcing with maximum drama: 'Hamali's wife has died in Sana'a!'

At *maghreb*, the women who were there relay the news to everyone they pass as we walk up the main road home. You can almost see it spreading through the town.

Water

At dawn we hear voices, chatting and laughing, as women and girls set off in groups to fetch water. For the houses near ours, it's a twenty-five-minute round trip. At the bottom of the town, nestled into a swirl of the terraces, is a large cement-lined cistern, about twenty by thirty metres, which collects run-off rainwater from the hillside above. The whole cistern is widely stepped in a spiral down to the flat bottom. Shallower runs of steps join up the tiers and lead down to the water, a dark expanse covered in green duckweed. All day women descend the steps with ten- and twenty-litre plastic jerrycans and ten-litre metal cylinders, stoop to clear the surface of the water with a sweep of their container, fill it, then straighten up to settle it on the crown of the head, on a ring of twisted rag, helped perhaps by the women next to them. Then they toil up the hill through the town towards home, straight-backed, straight-necked, brushing the drips from their foreheads, sometimes briefly steadying their loads with a hand, chatting as they go, pausing to greet women coming the other way. Arriving at their houses they enter the doorways with one graceful swooping movement, sinking at the knees, right down so that the containers on their heads clear the low doorways, and then straightening up again inside.

Khadija's daughters go to the cistern after the dawn prayer, to and fro, getting three or four ten-litre metal cans – *barmils* – each, most days. 'We go to the cistern early so there's no sun,' they tell me. The family don't drink the water from the cistern. 'It has *duud* and *jerathim* in, worms and germs,' their mother says. 'Even boiled and filtered you can't drink it.' They also go to the spring further away at Hasib for drinking water every day, at 7 or 8 Yemeni time, that is 1 or 2 in the afternoon, after they come back from school. They rest before they come back with the water or while they're waiting their turn to fill up.

When there's no water in the cistern, before the rains fill it up again, pick-up trucks with one-thousand-litre-capacity tanks bolted on bring water from the *seil*, a spring in the side of the mountain that forms a pool an hour's walk below the town. They sell it by the *dabba*, plastic jerrycan, at 30p for twenty litres. We buy it when we can. Getting water has become a huge preoccupation for us. There are far fewer trucks selling water than we had thought when we first moved to become an independent household. So we have to keep a constant lookout, rushing to the window or the roof whenever we hear a car pass, watching for water for whole mornings. Then, when it comes, we have to lug the *dabba*s back to the house from the end of the street where the trucks stop. I slowly get stronger, till I can carry twenty litres in my right hand and ten litres in my left and only stop to rest twice.

In late March I go down to look at the cistern: I've heard it's empty. The weather is miserable, mist that almost amounts to fine rain, and cold. An old woman from Meruwagha sees me going to the cistern and comes down to show me. There's no water left at all, just damp clayey mud on one side. A neat half of the empty cemented basin has had all the mud scooped out, and piled up outside the rim at the top.

'That was done by the country men, by Meruwagha and Mesqif, that village up there. The other half is Safaqayn's share, but the townsmen just sit and bubble away, *yegargaru*, smoking their *mada'a*s...' She does a very funny mime of the men, their indolence, the sitting back, the gargling sound they make.

She shows me where the water comes in, with a small pit to catch the mud before it flows into the main basin.

'Some years it doesn't dry up. Once, when it was very full, two girls fell in, they were drinking from it, they were fished out, drowned, with a hook.'

Later, in April, dark clouds have been gathering for days. Mists come up every afternoon, frothing up the slopes, so the gap between the mountains looks like a bay or inlet; up over hamlets that sit on rocky outcrops, till the town stands alone like an island in a sea of cloud stretching below us. People have been anxiously watching the sky. Now, in the clearer morning, we can see that rain is falling over the next mountain.

'Do you think it's going to rain?' we ask people.

'*Allah karim,*' God is generous, they reply.

'Does it usually rain more by this time? Did it rain more last year?'

'*Allah karim.*'

Finally the rain falls. Children dance in the streets. Everyone says, '*Allah karim.*'

Now it's pouring, really heavy rain, drumming on the paving stones of the street and on the flat roofs. The young woman from the house we reach across our roof is standing on the shop roof below our house, scooping up the water held by its rimmed edge, her clothes soaked through, laughing as the rain falls on her. Triumphant, she gets nine *dabba*s: 180 litres.

Three weeks after rain, when the qat sprouts, all the cars are busy, heaped high with packaged bundles, taking it down the mountain west to Bajil or east to Sana'a. At the peak of the season, we're told, twelve or thirteen cars a day make the trip from the town itself, not counting other collection points. For days on end no cars bring water, since they're all busy with this trade, and we have to eke out our supply and wait to wash our hair and clothes.

We look out for water opportunities wherever we go. One day we see a procession of girls going along the edge of the town with empty containers, plastic *dabba*s and cylindrical metal *barmil*s, and returning carrying them, full, on their heads. There are young girls with tins that hold ten litres, and a woman I know, young and strong and supple, carrying a twenty-litre *dabba* on her head although she's at least eight and a half months pregnant. We follow them with a *dabba* of our own to see where the water is. A small cistern on the outskirts of the town, a few metres wide, which we have only ever seen empty, has filled with rainwater and run-off from the terraces round it. Tim carries our *dabba* back, and we bring two more. I fill them up, helped by little girls. Tim is the only man carrying water, but the women we pass don't disapprove.

'You're tired, let Abdullah do it!' says one. Another says: 'Carry one each!'

Cool, sweet drinking water is essential to the pleasure of chewing qat. Men with means use bottled water, or offer guests cola-flavoured fizzy drinks – the alternative flavour, orange, is said not to go (*'ma yesloh'*) with qat. Women don't use bottled water, and all agree that the best drinking water is from Hasib, the spring twenty minutes' walk from the bottom of the town. When it is flowing, after rain, women and girls come and go along the path all day. When it dwindles to a trickle, they sit waiting their turn to fill up, for an hour or two, passing the time in lively chat.

It's all in the neck, I find. I can't carry twenty litres on my head. Little girls start at the age of about three with water in a small, empty fruit tin, on their heads, accompanying their mothers. They build up gradually to twenty-litre loads.

'Call me next time you go to Hasib, and we'll go together,' Warda said to me a few days ago. Now I'm on my way to get some drinking water (which we will still boil and filter before we actually drink it). Tim has gone on ahead; he ends up getting lifts both ways. I stop at Warda's brother's house, and Warda and I set off together.

'Should I say congratulations or not?' Warda asks a young woman we meet along the way. I ask Warda what she means. Warda explains that she has just got divorced from her husband.

'She ran away from him, she was taking refuge at her uncle's. Her father is dead. She was glad to get divorced.'

I am carrying a small plastic *dabba*, ten litres, to fill at the spring. We descend the rest of the hill from Warda's brother's house and leave the town behind us as we walk out on the road below. Here it's easy going, a four-wheel-drive track, smooth and nearly level as it skirts the mountain, firm and slightly dusty under our feet with the odd small pebble that I feel beneath my flip-flops. The morning is fine, clear and sunny and fresh. Loose, woolly clouds hide parts of the next mountain. Birds are singing all along the way. The expedition feels fun, a jaunt, a pleasant outing together. Warda will remind me of it many times over the years.

We meet and exchange greetings with other women along the way.

'She's fasting,' Warda tells me, as we leave one young woman behind. I ask why.

'It's for when she had her period, last Ramadan.'

'*Last* Ramadan?' Next Ramadan starts in a month.

Warda explains. Women who missed days fasting last year when they weren't ritually pure need to catch up on their fast days before next Ramadan starts.

Before the road curls round towards the next village, al-'Atanah, we take a track leading upwards off the road, which takes us to Hasib. The spring comes out into a concreted bowl in a lush green hollow alive with birdsong. It's a beautiful place. Pomegranate bushes flaunt bright vermilion blossoms. Tiny sunbirds with long curved beaks and metallic blue-green breasts flit in and out. There are other small birds, partly pinkish beige, not in my bird book.

A small crowd of young girls wait with empty *dabba*s, laughing and talking together. For them too, perhaps, it's an enjoyable excursion.

Warda fills her big *dabba* and I my little one from where the water comes out of the rock. Today it is gushing freely. For the return I put my *dabba* on my head. It's not easy to carry it. The water sloshes about inside, making it hard to balance the load, even if I support it with my hand. Most women carry twenty litres with ease, using their hands only to wipe away drips.

With the *dabba* on my head, I find it hard to see the path.

'It's because you're holding your head wrong,' says Warda. She demonstrates. It's more my neck that's wrong, perhaps. Warda says it's wobbling. We stop to see what I'm doing wrong, and Warda tries my *dabba* on her head.

'It's not just your neck, it's the *dabba*. You should get a *barmil*. A small one.'

They are available in the weekly market on Thursdays. I can see how the cylindrical shape might be easier to carry.

I help Warda load her twenty-litre *dabba* on to a ring of twisted rag on the crown of her head, further back on the head than I would have thought. We head off more slowly, back towards the town. At her house, she unloads her *dabba* in the kitchen. Then we sit for a while drinking *gahwa*.

On market day I invest 20 riyals in a metal cylinder that holds ten litres.

'Come with us,' says my neighbour Khadija the next day. 'We're going for a *dowra* to Hasib.'

'Are you getting water?'

'No, just a *dowra*, to *etneffes*, relax and enjoy ourselves and look around. Bring your binoculars!'

I fetch my new *barmil* so I can bring back some water, and we set off. Khadija and the hakim's younger wife from the house nearby are veiled up completely in *sharshaf*s, unlike most women going for water who just wear a thin *saramiya* cloth over their head and shoulders. This is an outing, not work, and they are women with a position to maintain, the wife and widow of important men. We set out down the steep street through the town and out along the flat, powdery road. We chat as we walk.

'You and Mariam seem friendly, you visit each other?' I ask the hakim's wife, about her co-wife. They live in different rooms in the big house next to us.

'Yes, we don't get on badly, but it's still hard, being one of two wives.'

We stop to look at the view through my binoculars. The distant terraced slopes fade into blue haze. Small black-and-white birds, wheatears, perch on stones on the hillside and take off as we approach. I see birds flying across the valley, the size of starlings, with orange-red wings that look, spread out in flight, like stained-glass windows with the light shining red through them. They are Tristam's grackles, and I'm always pleased when I see them. My bird book, in a moment of poetry, says their call is 'wild and weirdly melancholy', a description I can't improve on.

We see Warda sitting on a rock by the road, taking a break on her return with her load of water. We all exchange greetings, and we leave her sitting and go on towards Hasib. A car overtakes us, a pick-up truck with men standing in the back, who call out greetings to me. I know them, and would like to reply, but Khadija hurries me on, 'Pay no attention, don't listen to them!' Whenever I'm out with other women they always prevent me from returning men's greetings.

We arrive at Hasib and I enjoy the beauty of the place, the vivid green grass and orange pomegranate flowers and all the birds singing. A hose carries water from the spring to the nearest village, on the road between Hasib and the town. I feel envious of their supply.

The water is coming out slowly, so I only half fill my *barmil*. I settle it on the top of my head, on a piece of cloth I've twisted into a ring, and we turn to go back along the road. We haven't gone far when I turn my head to look at a bird too sharply, the *barmil* falls, the water is lost and to my surprise the cylinder cracks around the seam at the bottom.

On the way back, we meet a succession of women coming towards us on their way to get water. I have to explain to every one of them, all the way.

'What happened to your *barmil*?'

'I dropped it and it broke.'

'*Beridu*, forget it, you can't carry it.'

'I didn't know it would break so easily,' I say.

'Oh yes, they always break.'

'You must stick to *dabba*s, much easier.'

My friend Amina tries to console me: 'My daughter broke two, one after the other.'

Tim and I take to carrying water from Hasib in *dabba*s in rucksacks. After some months, Tim cements over our roof and installs a pipe leading from one corner, down through the window below and into a barrel in the storeroom next to the bathroom. The barrel rests on top of an old *tannur* oven embedded in earth. Our neighbours across the roof are unhappy.

'Look, it's only earth, it could all crumble, it could fall through the floor, and our rooms are underneath,' they complain. I can see their point, but Tim is sure their fears are groundless. As it turns out, the barrel stays firm. On one day in April, when the afternoon brings very heavy rain, we collect 120 litres from this arrangement. When we get water from the roof, we give some to our downstairs neighbours.

Khadija drinks the water that collects on a small roof above her kitchen. 'It's not dirty, nobody goes on the kitchen roof.' To get it she climbs up a level from her roof, the one that has the plants, on a ladder made of a single pole with footholds sticking out each side. The ladder is old and the footholds slip out; once, she tells me, she fell and hurt herself and was ill for two months. The small walls round the roof have regular swirling patterns in the plaster; Khadija asks us if it is writing. We fix a hose to bring the water down from her roof, like ours.

One April day we are tramping home, stiff and weary after two days away. Every muscle aches. We walked for most of these two days, to another town and back, but so much down and up that we see, to my astonishment, when we look at the map, that we only covered about seven kilometres as the crow flies. Nevertheless, it felt like another area: there were different words and the women wore quite different clothes, *gamis* smocks with zip fronts, tucked up for work into striped trousers.

As we come in at the bottom of Meruwagha we see Abdu Ali the truck driver, and we order 40 riyals' worth of water, four hundred litres. This is a mistake: when we get home we find our big storeroom barrel is two-thirds full. There has been rain here, and Tim's personal small water project has worked well. We put aside our fatigue and hastily use some water up by washing clothes. Washing and rinsing clothes always takes a disproportionate amount, compared to washing ourselves, and has given me a new appreciation of the women's nylon dresses, which absorb so little and need only one quick rinse.

The truck arrives at the top of the town, a narrow street and an alleyway away from our house. What are we to do with all this expensive water? We bring every container we've got, from twenty-litre *dabba*s down to food bowls. We offer water to our neighbours across the alley, but Khadija says, 'I've got seven *dabba*s full from my kitchen roof.'

We give some water to Na'ma and Fatima who I often *rabakh* with, to another woman who lives in the same house as them, and to our downstairs neighbour Nuriya. The next afternoon, when I'm sitting *rabakh*ing in Na'ma's house, they tell me: 'The water you gave to our neighbour is *ajr* for you, reward in heaven; she'd had none in the house.'

We stand by the tank on the back of the car dispensing water, getting soaked with the sloshing, facing a barrage of demands from the gathering crowd. They bring their buckets and *dabba*s, take them away full, and come back for more, jostling and competing. By the time we have just enough left to fill our own containers, we are besieged by other women asking. Our downstairs neighbour hands us a yellow bucket, and we fill it, realising too late that she's passing off the bucket of one of the disappointed women as her own. Later I challenge her with this, and her excuse is, 'She told me to!'

I ask Na'ma and Fatima to bring a jerrycan for a very old woman who lives alone near them who we've got into the habit of giving water to, but it comes too late, although they themselves have had plenty by then. Khadija lends us a couple of barrels and some bowls to put water in for ourselves. Her daughter fills up a blue bucket, saying it's hers, then takes it to her friends in the hakim's house.

It's all a hassle. I stumble back to the house exhausted and upset, thinking how horrid people are. Next time, I resolve, we'll fill our own buckets first, and only then give water away; this'll give no one time to come many more times than anyone else, as well.

By the second year of our stay, we are tired of filling our *dabba*s from trucks, carrying them in rucksacks or dragging them full from the cistern or from Hasib, obsessing about rain, watching for cars, always worrying how we are going to get water. We use perhaps eighteen litres of water each a day, profligate by local standards. One by one, families in the town are buying sheet-metal tanks and now cars don't so often bring water to sell by the *dabba*.

'You should get a *khazzan*,' our neighbour Thuraya says. She has two tanks outside a storeroom in the street a little way from her house near us, and gets them filled from cars. She drags *dabba*s of water from there to her house under cover of darkness. Her father was an important man and she has a certain status: she doesn't want to be seen carrying water. In the past a neighbour's daughter lived with her and fetched water for her, but this girl is married now, and Thuraya has to make shift. Her younger half-sisters in the house help her, giving her water from Hasib once a week.

One market day Thuraya calls me, pebbles rattling down on to the roof, to ask me to get some tomatoes for her. When I return with them, I sit and watch her: she is lighting incense, little lumps of Arabian frankincense mixed with sugar, in a small clay burner.

'It's special incense for perfuming water. I bought it ready like that, it comes from Sana'a.'

The smoking incense gives off a smell we'd associate in England with church. She upturns an earthenware water-pot over it, and leaves it for the incense to infuse the pot. She explains: 'The earthenware pot keeps the water cool.'

If she has to drink the water from the tank, she says, she brings it to the boil first. 'Otherwise it makes me tired, gives me illnesses, hurts in the stomach. It's heavy.'

She says, 'It's *ta'ab*, hard work, here because of water.'

'Couldn't there be a pipe from the *seil*?' I ask.

'There's not enough.'

We would like a tank, but we can't see how it would work. 'There's nowhere near the house we can put it, where it can be filled from a car.'

'You can put it just outside my storeroom on the street, next to mine,' Thuraya says.

This offer makes all the difference. We buy a four-hundred-litre tank for 350 riyals, a bit more than £40, a big investment for us. We can always sell it when we leave and recoup some of the cost. We will still have to fetch the water from the storeroom on the street, but it's not as far as the 'head of the market' where the trucks stop.

But our troubles are not over. We order and pay 40 riyals, £5, for half a truckload of water, and when it comes we fill the tank from the truck by hose. But as soon as we have filled it up, it leaks. Helpful children run off and get chewing gum to plug it for us, but we are afraid other less helpful children might pull it off, so we laboriously empty the whole tank, *dabba* by *dabba*, into Thuraya's tank. Her sister Karima helps us. The empty tank is too heavy to carry. We wait for a car to take it to be repaired at the car workshop at the bottom of the town. When we get it back, we pay another 40 riyals for a load of water to fill it again. It leaks again, this time from higher up. I buy a tube of liquid metal from a shop and spend two hours trying to fix the leak with a patch. I have at least reduced the flow when I'm interrupted.

'*Ya* Mariam! There's a letter for you!'

I hurry away to collect my precious post. As I come back I'm met by children jostling for my attention.

'He did it! *Ibn* Mohammed Yahya! That one!'

My patch has been pulled off. The children are pointing at a very small boy. Tim finds out who his father is and has a talk to him in his shop, but I suspect that a child too small to be held responsible has been picked to carry the blame.

We empty the tank again to below the leak, putting the water into the tank of other friends this time. I apply another patch and we attempt to siphon our water back in from the other tank. It doesn't work. We are laughing stocks again.

Now we have to try and get it filled once more. We go round possible drivers. One says he'll get a load to divide with us. But later he tells us it has all spilt. Then we find another who says he'll get a whole carload. This is more than we can fit, so we ask the first driver if he would like to buy some, but his tank is mysteriously full after all. Finally the too-big load of water arrives. We fill our tank and all our jerrycans just as heavy rain starts. We get very wet, fill everything, *dabba*s for our next-door neighbours, a bit in their tank, some for a boy who helped us with the filling, some for our neighbour downstairs. Then our neighbour Khadija says she saw the driver filling ten jerrycans from out of the load we paid for, before he brought it to us.

'*Beridu*, leave it,' she says. We take her advice. We are exhausted. We put the kettle on and enjoy hot washes, and I wash my hair for the first time in thirteen days.

Our tank problems become a story that people tell about us, fodder for gossiping afternoons.

Getting water is hard not only for us. For most women of the town it's the hardest physical work they still have to do. I look at how the people I know manage, sorting and juggling the various sources and qualities of water and the different things they use it for, seeking out seasonal opportunities and ways to get by. Every household has different strategies.

When the cistern below the town is full, I sit beside it to see how many women use it in a day. I want to know this both for myself and as part of research into water use for the German development company we're doing some work for. The sheikh is dismissive.

'If you ask the women, they'll say they go twenty times a day.' He seems to see them perhaps as chronic complainers, and untrustworthy. He tells Tim, *rabakh*ing with him one afternoon, that Mariam is not to believe what women say about water use. All the women in Safaqayn are liars, he says, they can't be trusted. However nobody I ask says they go twenty times a day. They say they go perhaps four times, or a few more.

There is a generally agreed hierarchy of different kinds of water. 'Hasib water is *khafif*, light,' women say. The water from the *seil* is *thagil*, heavy, in the stomach' – a downward gesture with the hands explains what the 'heavy' *seil* water feels like in the stomach – 'but it's better than the cistern water.' Some say you can sometimes drink the cistern water, when it isn't muddy after rain. Nobody besides Amina and Khadija mentions germs; everyone else talks about the water being muddy or heavy.

After rain a pond forms in a rocky outcrop a little outside the town, near some of the newer houses. It has worms in, the women nearby say, but it can be used for a first rinse of dirty baby clothes, and for gardens, and for mixing cement for building.

Before the road to the *seil* was made, women used to carry water up from the *seil*, an hour's walk down the mountain. Or they went to several springs further away, 'lots of different places,' they say. I imagine these women in the past, searching out the different sources of water around the countryside, walking long distances to various springs and back with their loads. Carrying water used to be an opportunity for poor women to earn money. A widow with no property to support her would get money for fetching water from Hasib, but this is an opportunity that has gone, as people tell us: 'Not now, everybody has tanks.'

For us, in the UK, water is something uniform that comes out of a tap, always from the same source and consistently the same. In this place the women are constantly dividing water into different sorts, with different uses, using shifting strategies at different seasons, and spending time and hard work to get enough of it. Different households sort the water differently, but everyone is making distinctions, and everyone has to think about getting hold of enough. And I, even when I've returned to England and reverted to profligate use of water, will always remember what it is to have to carry to the house every drop you use.

A German visitor

I have acquired a sudden, unexpected reputation for outstanding virtue.

It starts when I'm sitting with Selma Yahya, the busy seamstress who sewed my red dress, in her house just outside the old town. We're in her living room, square, low-ceilinged, furnished in the same way as the old town houses with mattresses for seating round the walls, cushions and a set of metal shelves holding a TV covered with a cloth and little pots of plastic flowers. Another woman is with her, her father's wife, so that Selma isn't alone. Selma's husband is still away working in Saudi Arabia, and her husband's brother who also lives in the house has taken his wife to have medical treatment in Sana'a. When Tim's away, as he is now, people ask me who's sleeping with me to keep me company. A neighbour's little girl, perhaps? We say, *hina amana*, there's trust here, and that seems to be an acceptable response.

Selma has just shown me round the new first floor of her house. Before, it was one low storey, in the out-of-town style: the painted metal door, decorated with a pattern in strips of metal, opens on to a wide passage with two rooms off each side. On the right-hand side live Selma and her husband and their children, and on the left his brother, his wife Lutfiya and their children.

'It's finished now except for the windows and doors, and the *goss* paint. It was *lots* of work for me – cooking *gheda* and making tea for the workers, and carrying up the water for the cement. I'll have two more rooms on the new floor, and my husband's brother will have two.'

Selma has poured me a glass of *gahwa* and I'm sipping it gratefully, glad of the refreshment.

Then comes impossible news: '*Ya* Mariam, *ya* Mariam, your brother is here!'

It seems that every child in the town always knows where to find me. My neighbour's daughter Karima has come running to Selma's house. I look up at her standing in the doorway. I'm enjoying sitting with Selma, who is often too busy to chat. She has invited me to lunch with her as Tim is away, and I would like to stay. I know both my brothers are in England. They are hardly likely to drop in on me in Safaqayn without warning.

'It can't be my brother, that's not possible.'

But Karima is so insistent that reluctantly I take my leave and go to see who it is.

The visitor is a German I've never met before, a young man with an open, intelligent face. He is sitting in the house of a man we know, who invited him after the visitor gave him a lift up the mountain. He is an employee of the development agency Tim and I have been doing some work for, and has come to check out the area. I explain my dilemma.

'I don't know what to do. My husband isn't here. I'd like to ask you in to our house, but I'm not sure it would be proper.'

He agrees I can't ask him in with my husband away, and goes for a walk around the town. I fervently hope Tim will be back some time today. I feel inhospitable, and sorry for Klaus who is tired and hot and thirsty, and I'm worried about what to do if Tim doesn't get back by tonight. I feel conflicted between the desire to be hospitable, reinforced by the local norms I've been absorbing, and the need to preserve my respectability, again according to local norms, norms which seem, in this matter, to be complicated and variable. I need to be able to stay in the town, and to be accepted by people, so I can't just do what I feel like.

'Where's your brother?' my downstairs neighbour Nuriya asks when I get back to our house.

'He's not my brother, he's not even from my country, he's a German, he's gone for a walk till Abdullah gets back.'

Women in the town have probably met no Europeans before us, and have very little idea of European countries, or indeed of how big the world is, so it's perhaps natural to think every non-Arab is in some way connected to us.

I go back to Selma for *gheda*, feeling guilty that I'm not making lunch for Klaus.

'You did the right thing,' she says. 'If your mother or sister had been there it would have been right to ask him in.'

We sit and chat and she tells me about her husband.

'I married him when I was about twenty – he's my father's brother's son but I didn't know him, I'd been living in another town where my father was employed. He'd been married before and divorced his wife. Life is tiring when he's here, and tiring when he's away... When we first got married he was employed here, as a soldier.'

'Why did he go to Saudi Arabia?'

'All his friends went, and told him how wonderful it was.'

'Would you go with him?'

'They don't let you, it's hard to get a visa.'

'Would you go there on Hajj?'

'That's for old women, afterwards you have to be good and not speak bad of people, or curse them.'

On my way to Selma's and back I have to explain to everyone I see, because they've all heard my brother is here. They all say I did the right thing. Tim comes back at *maghreb*, to my great relief. He is introduced to Klaus on the way to our house, and brings him back for the night. Klaus has excellent English and, starved of conversation in our own language, we talk and talk. He makes plans to explore some villages the next day, and look at potential for small water projects. After that, we don't see him again.

For the next three weeks or more, men praise my virtue to Tim. They come up to him in the market to congratulate him. They re-enact a scene where I forcibly and indignantly order Klaus from my door with a pointing, flung-out arm – 'Mariam said "Go!"'

Women commend me too, even thank me, almost, I feel, as if I've upheld the honour of the women of the town with my own. The reaction seems so exaggerated that I wonder if my fears were really necessary, or if I overdid it. But I decide it's best to have erred on the side of caution.

Post, and an enemy

The post comes weekly. I'm amazed that it comes at all. A letter reaches me from a friend who's teaching English in a provincial town in China, and another from a colleague doing fieldwork in Indonesia; from those places to this remote Yemeni mountain, it seems like a miracle of communication. On our increasingly infrequent trips to Sana'a we pick up precious piles of the *Guardian Weekly* to fill out what news we get from the radio. The news is weird, almost surreal, and for the rest of my life I will feel strangely disconnected from the Falklands conflict. We wait hopefully every Wednesday for letters from family and friends. I had written labels with the address in Arabic for them to photocopy.

Sometimes the post is delayed, and sometimes lost altogether. When we get nothing for two weeks running, we become suspicious. Two men, it seems, are vying for the job of controlling it. One has been our friend from early days. The other, Abdul Mughni, sleek and well built, is from another area. We mistrust him. We can't think why he should be our enemy; perhaps he just likes to throw his weight around and demonstrate his power. Perhaps it has something to do with Tim's denial that we had any supplies of whisky when he came round to our house and asked for some. Sometimes he's affable, other times he denies all knowledge of missing post and we don't believe him. Sometimes it mysteriously turns up later, sometimes never. I feel sorry for his young, struggling wife, isolated in the town and homesick. Slight and nervous, with dark eyes in a pale face and heavy black eyebrows, she looks very young and seems to be not quite coping. Her furnishings seem even grimier than other people's, her rooms have more flies. She also comes from another area; she's an outsider with no close friends in the town. She doesn't look happy, and as we know, her husband is a bully. Also he is one of three men that both men and women, separately naming the same three, have told us prowl round the town at night, going to other women.

I go to their house and take seventeen pictures of his children, out of sympathy for her rather than to ingratiate ourselves with him. Then she's worried that he will be angry because her hand and part of her arm appear in three of the photos, holding a child. But when I take them the prints, both are pleased with them. She gives me some bread.

The women I'm *rabakh*ing with one afternoon tell me, 'She's crying for her mother. She came to visit her, but she couldn't stay long, she had to go back to her children at home and her cow. There was no time for them to talk. It's hard for women married *ghurbe*, far away, it's not good to marry a daughter or take a wife from far away.'

'Hasn't she got any friends here?'

'She can't confide in women here about problems with her husband, they'd talk, word would get around that there are problems between them. A mother is the safe person for a woman to unload her heart to, if she's sad, if she has a problem with her husband or anything.'

Naʿma, whose room we're sitting in, adds: 'I only have my brother here. If I had problems with Mehelli'–she uses her husband's surname – 'I would go to him, I would cry, he would cry.'

I visit Abdul Mughni's wife once with my neighbour Khadija, on our way out on a *dowra* for Khadija to warm up in the sunshine. On Abdul Mughni's door is a big brass ring that has worn a groove in the wood underneath. Khadija knocks. There's no answer. Undeterred, she pushes open the door and leads me up the stairs, and indeed Abdul Mughni's wife is there. Khadija pulls out a round of *lehuh* for her from under her *sharshaf*. She refuses pressure to come and sit and have *gahwa*.

'I want to go and get warm while there's still sun.'

At the last minute, as we are going down the stairs, Abdul Mughni's wife somehow finally persuades her to come back and drink a quick *gahwa*. We go upstairs and sit down. Khadija gives advice about the rooms, how to manage better: 'Leave the best room, use it less to save trouble.'

'My husband wouldn't agree.'

Her husband is from a powerful family; even if distrusted, he has status in the town. His wife has to work hard cooking for his guests. Once, when preparations were under way to entertain the *muhafidh*, the province governor from Mahwit, and she had been busy cooking all day, I thought I heard her mutter under her breath, 'A *jinni* take the *muhafidh*.'

A friend of ours, Hamid, a teacher from Sudan, is almost in tears as he tells us what happened on the examination inspection committee. There were four men on it, none of them from the area. Our enemy Abdul Mughni had come trying to do something about his younger brother's exam paper. It was for the certificate at the end of six years of elementary schooling; the papers were to go to Sana'a. The committee refused his request, and the papers were put in an envelope and tied up officially. The next day Abdul Mughni came back with a rewritten, correct paper. Three of the committee said no, but the chairman said all right, opened the packet, and substituted the good paper. Apparently he is from the same area as Abdul Mughni's family.

'What's the point?' says Hamid. 'Why do I bother? It's pointless being here, trying to teach, if that's how it works.'

Tim and the boy

The problem of the children is getting worse and worse. They follow us in the street in a chanting, mocking rabble; they swarm up the stairs and invade us. Our neighbours complain and everybody says we should take a stand, control them.

'Hit them! Like Abdullah hit our Khalid!' say the women in the sheikh's house. Perhaps he was one of the children Tim dealt with on a previous occasion, one afternoon when photos arrived and there was chaos at our house and he decided to try and be more Yemeni, losing his temper and grabbing them by the scruffs of their necks.

'Get the child's name, and bring his father to me,' says the sheikh as a general directive. One day we hear a scuffling and whispering and trying of our outside door and Tim, at the end of his tether, flings it open and chases a fleeing crowd. One of the smallest boys slips and falls, and Tim catches him. He doesn't hit him, just shouts at him and lets him go.

The boy's mother is round in minutes, throwing a large, heavy stone at our locked door. We can hear and feel the juddering impact from inside; it's like being under siege. When we go out she shouts: 'I'm going to the *mudir*,' the government prefect.

I remember, anxiously, how often disputes between adults, between neighbour women, seem to have started with problems with or between children.

Bystanders, neighbours, have gathered and try to calm her down. No one actually seems to take her side. Our neighbours suggest we go ourselves to the prefect and ask for a general edict for the children of the town not to bother us.

The next morning I feel upset and vulnerable and paranoid. I hear loud intense talking between our neighbours up on their roofs. When one of them rattles the door at the top of our stairs as she talks, I run up and unlock it. Fatima, the girl from across the roof, was rattling the door. Khadija across the way is joining in the conversation from her roof.

'What do you want?' I ask.

'Lock it, keep it locked.'

It was unlocked the night before because neighbour girls came up asking to be let out on our roof to see a wedding procession. I wonder if that was really what they were saying before I came up.

Fatima from across the roof says, 'Mariam's been crying.'

'We've had lots of problems with the children.' I add, 'And Mohammed, he's insulted me in the street,' then regret it, because I meant to tell Khadija privately that I'd had an incident with her son.

'Mohammed who? My son?' asks Khadija sharply.

'Yes.'

'What did he say?'

'Something bad in English.'

I still wish I knew what they were saying before I came out on the roof.

Sabah, our neighbours' little girl, climbs our stairs with effort and hands us some bread. 'From my mother.' Her mother usually gives us bread just after we've done something for her, most often giving her water or qat. This time it feels like a gesture of support. I go down to thank her.

'The *naqib*'s wife says go and see her, for bread.' She refers to Khadija by her late husband's position and not by her name or her father's name. I mount Khadija's staircase and she too gives me a round, freshly baked and smelling delicious. She asks me: 'What did my son say?'

'He said "I want to fuck you" in English. Obviously a bigger boy taught him.'

She makes an angry, throat-grabbing gesture, and says, I think, that she'll strangle him. He isn't back from school yet. In the meantime she asks me, curious, 'Say it in English, how do you say it?'

When the boy comes in, a bright-eyed gap-toothed scamp, she scolds him very severely in front of me. I'm impressed with the scolding: I thought she indulged her son, a swaggering little man of six or seven (perhaps partly because he won't take his medicine, she says, where I assume an English mother would make him take it). It looks something like a ritual curse or threat; she points to her eyes and then at him.

'What did you say to Mariam?'

'I've forgotten.'

'Who taught you?'

He names an older boy. Khadija mutters something about what she'll do to him.

'Apologise to Mariam.'

He hides behind her, grinning, showing the new front teeth he's just growing. 'I didn't know what it meant.'

'Well, he knew it was something not good,' I say.

Khadija pushes a round of special *jehin* bread into my hands, as well as the wheat *khobz*.

'People here are bad,' she says.

Later, when I'm back in our house, Thuraya throws stones down my roof well, and I go out to see what it's about. She throws me some wrapped-up bread; now we have a real glut.

'Come and *rabakh* at our house!'

At Thuraya's I find a roomful of women in her *mafraj*, a celebration for the sheikh's wife coming out of confinement. They are all talking animatedly. I feel vulnerable and suspicious: I can't quite tell if it's about me.

'What are they talking about?' I ask Thuraya.

'About Na'ma,' she says. I feel this is a cover-up till it emerges that this is the name of the woman, Mohammed Khowlani's wife, who threw the stones at our door. Thuraya relays what I've said about having lots of problems with children. Later in the conversation I catch our names, spoken down the other end of the long room, and ask what they're saying about us.

'The young people want marriage like yours, the woman getting a salary,' Thuraya says. My paranoid feelings are allayed; I did catch the words 'he will cook', so it fits. I wish I could understand more.

Certainly the incident is being discussed, and perhaps magnified, in afternoon gatherings.

'Why did Abdullah hit the boy?' one woman asks me, aggressively, when I'm out visiting.

I explain.

'You must take the child to their parents, and they hit them.'

'The children really bother us.'

'Yes, it's true,' they agree.

And the next afternoon a woman asks me,

'Has Abdullah been put in prison by Mohammed Khowlani's wife yet?'

A couple of weeks later I'm visiting in a house and a woman downstairs beckons me in. It's Na'ma, the mother of the boy Tim caught.

'Do you recognise her?' her neighbours ask me. '*Majnuna*! Crazy woman!'

'The children came and told me Abdullah was killing my son, I thought he was dead. '*Inti ma lish she*,' she says to me, *you're* all right, I have nothing against you.

'We've had so much bother...' I explain, and it's all quite friendly.

Twenty-six years later Tim is visiting Safaqayn. He calls me on Skype.

'Guess who I'm sitting with!'

'Who?'

'It's the boy whose mother threw rocks at our door, the small boy I caught!'

They are relaxing together, spending an afternoon chewing qat, remembering old times. His mother died a few months ago. He says that before she died she forgave Tim.

Ramadan

Something feels different in the night. The electricity has stayed on right through, and there are sounds of people – talking, moving around, merry groups of girls going to get water before dawn. It's finally Ramadan. People have been talking about it for months, looking forward to it, like the build-up to Christmas in the UK. Men who work in Sana'a and Saudi Arabia are coming back. Houses have been repainted inside with new white *goss* gypsum or *nura* whitewash and the old stone houses have new splashes of white on their outside walls, around the windows. Our downstairs neighbour Nuriya has spring-cleaned, swept, taken out her carpets to shake outside the front door.

'Are you fasting already?' I ask her that first morning.

'I had a bit of bread, but the Qadi,' her husband, the Quran-reader, 'went straight into fasting without anything to eat in the night.'

By mid-afternoon there's a sense of activity in the town. Men are visiting the shops, all carrying away the same ingredients in their plastic bags. Custard powder, a vinegar substitute called Vinegarine, little yellow bottles of banana flavouring. They cluster round the butcher's corrugated zinc shed.

'We-e-eh *ya* Mariam!'

Amina is calling me into her house. 'Come and *efter*, break the fast with me at *maghreb*!'

And, when she learns Tim is away, 'Come and sit with me till dawn!'

Before *maghreb*, Amina's son Fuad turns up at our house to get me. He stands in our kitchen-cum-lobby space, a well-grown ten-year-old lad with an air of quiet responsibility.

'Can we borrow six spoons to eat the *muhallabia* with?'

I find six spoons, and we go down together through the town, quiet now, to his house. I give Amina a new tin of Tang orange juice powder from Sana'a, which I know she likes, and a lettuce from my roof garden. I assume she knows and likes lettuce, though I haven't seen it on sale here, because she's asked me for seeds. As soon as it's *maghreb*, with the call to prayer sounding through the lower town, we eat *feter*. This is the meal that breaks the fast. *Helba hamudh*, sour fenugreek: the same soaked fenugreek powder beaten to a green froth that is served on stew at normal midday meals, but now cold and mixed with sugar and Vinegarine. We dip radish leaves into it; it's sweet and sour and refreshing. There are none of the big white radishes that should go with it. 'They haven't grown,' Amina says. 'And there ought to be *shuraba*, but I don't have any.'

'What is this *shuraba*?'

'From a tin.'

I know the word from other Arab countries as 'soup'. I ask more questions, but I can't work out what it can possibly be.

We eat spaghetti cooked with milk; *dafi*, bread heated with milk and *samn*; rice with *zahaweq* relish. *Muhallabia* is not the milk pudding I expected, but something made with Bird's custard powder, cardamom and banana flavouring. It is bright yellow, translucent, sloppy, and tastes of artificial banana.

'It relaxes your body to eat after fasting,' Amina says.

Then we drink lots of *gahwa* and, later, tea. We settle back on the cushions of Amina's room to pass the time. Like everyone else, she extols the pleasures of Ramadan and compares it to Ramadan in other times and places.

'Ramadan's not so good in Sana'a, people don't stay up so late,' she says.

Amina keeps translating from Arabic time, with sunset and dawn as twelve, to our, noon-and-midnight-at-twelve, time. She sets her watch to ours, six hours different. When she tells the time, as the night passes, I notice she counts round from one rather than recognising the numbers on her watch.

We watch television. Extra programmes, a special serial, are on for Ramadan. Some time in the middle of the night we set off to Hasib to get drinking water, Amina and I and the daughter of one of her neighbours. She leaves her older children, about ten and eight, to look after the five-year-old and the baby. I carry one very small *dabba* for Amina. We take torches. The June night is warm and pleasant, and all the villages on the mountain slopes around are lit up. The side of the next mountain, Milhan, shows distant twinkles of light.

'It'll be better halfway through the month, with the full moon,' Amina says.

No one is at the spring and the cemented basin where the water collects is fairly full. Amina washes the bottom of the *dabba* carefully with handfuls of water before she puts it into the basin. We walk back with our water along the road, shining our torches ahead on the rough, dusty surface. The warm June night surrounds us, the points of light scattered around the mountains showing people awake everywhere.

Amina doesn't get round to her prayers, for *maghreb* and the later evening *'asha*, till we come back from Hasib. Then she washes and puts on her prayer robe and performs the prayers, bending and prostrating and murmuring. Afterwards she explains that women group some of the five daily prayers of Islam together: 'Women always pray in three goes, with noon and *'asr* together, and *maghreb* and *'asha* together.'

We settle down again in Amina's living room. I haven't managed to buy any qat. Amina is chewing small amounts.

'Come and spend every night with me. I can't go out, because of the children.'

Amina's husband has been away working in the east of Yemen. Now she expects him back. Every time we hear a car, she rouses Fuad from his doze and sends him out to check. There are many cars in the night.

In the middle of the night we have a snack of *dafi* and *khobz* flat bread and *lehuh* and hot *helba* on a tomato base, and some more *bagl*, radish greens. The younger children sleep. The elder boy drops off, but gets woken up for tasks.

At 3.30am we eat *gheda*: more *dafi* and remains of *helba* and rice. Amina gives her five-month-old baby the breast. She also offers her bits of the food she's eating, a small bit of rice, but the baby always turns her head away. 'It's best to breastfeed babies,' she says.

At about 4am I leave. 'Start fasting now!' Amina instructs me.

The dawn call to prayer sounds out at 4.20am. I sleep and don't wake up till 11am. I go out for a *dowra* and walk around in the sun, which makes me thirsty. Invitations come from all sides.

'Why didn't you come to me? Come about two tonight!'

'Come and *efter* with us!'

'Come again and *semer*, sit up chatting, tonight; my husband still isn't back,' says Amina.

I have more invitations than I know what to do with. I try to juggle them, eating *feter* and *seme*ring parts of the night in several different houses.

Everyone asks if I'm fasting. I'm not, because I sneak drinks of boiled and filtered water at home before I leave for *feter*, so as to avoid the risks of unboiled water in people's houses; but I try not to eat or drink for the rest of the day because everyone is inviting me to feasts where the point is that they're breaking their fast. Invitations come even more than at other times. The food is varied and always special, something extra, sustaining, refreshing, different from the everyday. *Lehuh* and buttermilk, dates, small figs, chopped tomato and onion, sweet-and-sour *helba hamudh*.

'It's good to change food in Ramadan,' Amina says.

I can't find any qat to buy. I don't know if I'm glad or sorry: it's hard to stay awake all night without it, but it makes me so thirsty afterwards, long into the next day.

The days pass slowly for me, hungry, fixed on the prospect of the evening, waiting for *maghreb* to eat. The nights drag, punctuated by meals at odd times, and I strain to stay awake, waiting for dawn when I can sleep. Everything is turned upside down. The days are quiet; people who can, sleep. There are women and children about, but few men. Around *'asr*, the time of the afternoon prayer, the streets begin to liven up. I live in a whirl of invitations; it seems everyone I run into invites me to break the fast with them at sunset.

On my way back from a *dowra* to the cistern, I meet the younger daughters of the gas cylinder merchant.

'Come and *efter* with us!'

We gather round a plastic cloth on the floor of the room behind the shop. We eat a little of everything first, and then again when their father comes back. The married daughter who was staying with them before has gone back to her husband now, but another daughter is there. She's married in a village round the mountain, but she in turn has come home to her father *haniq*, angry with her husband.

I visit Selma Yahya in the night. Her sewing machine is in a constant whirr. It is raised up on a hard elbow-cushion and she sits on the floor in front of it, circling the handle without rest. She sews all night, while we *semer*. She has a pile of made dresses, bright colours and sequins and glitter, and a great bale of material from the merchant she makes them for, and she's turning them out non stop. This is the peak time: everyone will want new clothes for 'Id at the end of the month.

'How many can you do in a night?'

'Four or five. But I only get six riyals a dress, the merchant gets four. I get four for dresses for children – but they're more trouble, not less.' She sighs. 'Life would be easy but for the sewing machine.'

'Couldn't you do less?'

'When he's away we eat from it.' She means when her husband is away.

'Doesn't he send you money?

'Not enough.'

'Don't you do dresses for individual customers?'

'Yes, for twenty, but that's not enough work.'

Her husband sits with us for a while. He complains to me, 'She won't sleep with me.'

'It's true, I have too much work; it's fine not in Ramadan, but now it's forbidden in the day, and there are always people around at night.

I'm tired, Ramadan is hard work, other times you can get the work done in the morning and then rest.'

After he goes out, I ask if he won't be angry.

'He knows I'm busy and tired.'

Later he comes back and helps her, using a second machine. I'm surprised. 'Does he know how to sew?'

'He taught me.'

I consult Selma on a point of behaviour: 'A man asked me if I was fasting and I said yes. But actually I've got a period. What should I say to a man then? Is it *'aib* to say?' Periods disqualify women from fasting because they cannot be ritually pure.

'Say you're fasting,' she advises.

A voice from the stairs startles me. I'm just getting up, at nearly 6pm.

'Neither Thuraya nor I baked bread today. Can you give me some lettuce?'

It's my neighbour Khadija, with some *lehuh* for me in her hand, instead of *khobz*.

I dress quickly and rush up to the roof to pick a lettuce from the containers there, and down to take it to the house across the alley.

'Where are you having *feter*?' Khadija asks me.

'I'm not sure, a boy from the neighbours asked me but I'm not sure who he was, and he said go to Fatima's but I've just seen Fatima on the roof and she said nothing.'

'I'll send Karima and you can eat with us if you haven't been called.'

She gives me some *helba hamudh*, sour *helba*, and a radish to be going on with, even if I come to them to eat; so I think she has a nibble and then prays, then eats more. I am developing a great liking for the sweet-and-sour *helba hamudh*. Later the same boy comes again to ask me, and later again to get me, and I sit and eat with the neighbours-across-the-roof. Afterwards I go to *semer* for a bit with my neighbours across the alley. Khadija is sitting in the upstairs *mafraj*, Thuraya's living room, where Thuraya is unceasingly turning the handle of her sewing machine. She too is frantically trying to keep up with Ramadan work. I've commissioned her to sew a dress for me, and she's already measured me up in handspans. Other neighbours are sitting there too, women from the tall house opposite ours with five brothers and their families.

'Do you pray?' one of the women asks me.

'*Min haqina*, our way.'

'*Min haq el jinn* – the way of the *jinn*!' she says: a no-good way. She doesn't expect me to understand, but I do, and everyone laughs.

A boy knocks at Thuraya's door and comes in.

'Can you do some work for my father?'

'I can't, I've got too much!'

Another boy comes in. This time it's to fetch Thuraya to collect post. She returns with two letters, in the form of audio cassettes, from Saudi Arabia. They are from one of her uncles. They're done up in sticky tape, and addressed to Khadija's small son, as the man of the house. She will listen to the letters on a cassette player, and record her reply.

In another house, another evening, I finally discover the identity of the mysterious Ramadan *shuraba*. It's a thin, savoury gruel, perhaps with onions in. Still puzzled, I ask, 'What is it?'

'From a tin.'

'Can I see the tin?' They produce it. To my astonishment, it's Quaker Oats.

The Thursday market is different now; it gets going by 5.30am and stops early. There are extra vegetables and fruit – green peppers, grapes, dates.

About the middle of Ramadan people start coming round the town begging, collecting Ramadan alms. They go from house to house, and come into our house and up to our rooms. Some are boys, some adults. We give the boys 5 riyals and the adults 5 or 10. Some give us elaborate blessings in return. Except for a few boys, all are from outside the town and come here specially, we are told, because it's seen as a rich place.

Three-quarters of the way through Ramadan, I'm just about to go to bed one dawn when I hear stones rattling on to my roof.

I climb up and out in a rush. It's Thuraya, standing on her roof opposite.

'I've finished your dress. I've been trying to get hold of you.'

I hurry down through our house, across the street, into her courtyard and up her stairs. Thuraya gives me two rounds of bread to take home, and the dress. I try it on. I think it's beautiful: thin blue nylon I bought in Sana'a with silver embroidery and sequins in a swirling paisley pattern, with a different blue showing through from the lining. It's very well made. I get out 20 riyals, the price we agreed for the sewing.

'No, no.'

'Yes, of course I must pay you, you've done the work!'

'No! We're *khwat*, sisters.'

I keep trying. I try to stuff it down the front of her dress, as I've seen people do. When the *muzayyina* refused payment for organising and making music at the wedding of a girl whose family lived in the same large house as her, because, she said, 'She's a daughter of the house,' the girl's mother tried to push the notes in at the neck of her dress.

Thuraya says, 'I've sworn, I've vowed to heaven not to accept the money.'

Rightly or wrongly, I give up at this. I have my new dress for 'Id, and I'm very pleased with it.

Late in the month. I see Thuraya on her roof, beckoning, and go over to her.

'Can you do some errands for me? Could you go to *beit* Salim, and ask the visitor they have staying from Mahwit for news of my uncle, and whether he's coming? And can you go to *beit* Fa'ini next to it, and ask for my *mada'a* hose, they have it.'

Tim and I set off together, with our own errand to do; we are half carrying, half rolling along our empty gas bottle. I am not very successful with my tasks from Thuraya. At *beit* Salim the visitor says he'll come and talk to her later, and her uncle isn't coming, and the household invite us to *feter* with them. As I go through the gate to *beit* Fa'ini, a woman comes out and pre-empts me by saying they've already returned the hose. At the meal in *beit* Salim next door, one of the girls says this is not true. We eat a very fine full meal. The young men of the house, who usually work away from the town, are back for Ramadan. Afterwards we sit with the men and watch a Ramadan competition on Saudi TV: a guessing game for viewers where girls do a sort of mime with a song, with prizes given by big companies. Then we go to the house of the man who trades in gas bottles, but it's the long Ramadan *'asha* prayer, and the man we need isn't there.

Well into the night, we climb with no moonlight down the rugged path to a house below the town, carrying our qat. The descent is tricky with loose stones and twists in the path and thorny plants. I stubbed my toe badly on this path once before. We pick our way slowly, peering in front of our feet by the weak light of our torches. Mine is the small one I keep in my bag all the time, for dark stairways and power cuts at night. A Yemeni country man, at least in daytime, would spring down a path like this, sure-footed, skipping and jumping, keeping balance against his own impetus – that's how they can get down to the wadi, by short cuts, as quickly as a car can inch down the rocky bends of the road.

We are glad to arrive, at a one-storey country house with smallish rooms and animal stabling next to it, and a kitchen at the side. We were invited earlier in the day when we saw the man of the house in town, and we have photos to bring, ones I took of the family when we spent an afternoon there a few weeks ago.

The men and women of the family are chewing together, comfortably settled against the walls of the room, with our host's brother and mother and a woman relative of his wife's. They are very pleased with my photos, which are shown round the room. This surprises me because they include some of the host's wife. But her husband seems quite happy and she likes the pictures. I also show around the photos I've taken of the area and of where we live in London, which are all looked at with great interest, but Safaqayn with more interest than London.

They press more qat on us. The house is in the midst of their qat terraces and there's a plentiful supply. 'Qat isn't *haram*,' our host declares, 'because it grows, it isn't prepared from ingredients like wine – so Allah would have said if it was wrong.' He tells us the legend we've heard many times, how qat was first discovered because a shepherd noticed his sheep enjoying it in the wild.

'In Saudia the penalty is two years in prison for chewing qat, fifteen years for selling it. This is so that the Yemenis can't make a lot of money exporting it to them. The Saudis have petrol, the Yemenis have qat; they sell their petrol here, but we can't sell them our qat.'

As the night wears on we watch a Yemeni soap opera. This is the first one I've seen that is made and set in Yemen. This one is appreciated for its Yemeni-ness, the recognisable language and customs and clothes and settings. A young man comes from the country to Sana'a and gets a job in a company, but is wrongly imprisoned for embezzling. In a previous episode he married a wife who'd been educated. She didn't know how to cook or make tea for him, and sat reading magazines all day.

'Everyone will have new clothes for 'Id,' our hosts say. I'm keeping back my new dress till the day.

'Did you sit up at night like this in Ramadan before there was electricity?' we ask. There's been electricity in the town, from generators, for only about six years.

'Yes, we did *semer*, we sat up with an *iteriq*' – a pump-up paraffin spirit lamp.

They press us to stay till morning, but we leave at 2am. Going back up is much easier. We stop off at our downstairs neighbours, still long before dawn, for sweet, spicy tea and a chat.

The next day, Thuraya invites me to *semer*.

'Come to me, I have guests coming.'

As I enter Thuraya's long *mafraj* and settle myself against the cushions, the women sitting round the walls are arguing.

''Id isn't till Thursday,' says one. It's Monday night now.

'No, no, tomorrow's already the slaughtering of the animals.'

One guest leaves at about 1am, saying: 'I'm going to bed, I don't *semer*, I can't sleep in the day.' Women with small children have a particularly hard time in Ramadan, if they can't make them sleep in the day. Tim's friend Yahya tells us about the *beni kelbi*, a creature which looks like a man, takes children, and at night changes into an animal and eats them. He says this bogeyman is used to frighten children, especially in Ramadan when parents want to keep children quiet so they can catch up on sleep in the daytime.

'When I was a child I went somewhere where there was a man with a long nose, I was sure he was a *beni kelbi*, I was very afraid of him,' Yahya says.

Early on Tuesday there's a small *suq* with animals being slaughtered. On Wednesday, Ramadan is over and it's 'Id.

Firecrackers pop all day. It's hard to adjust to being up in the day, and I sleep till late. Everyone has new clothes. Little boys are dressed in suits and Saudi-style long shirt robes, rather than new *futas*. Women get visits and money from their male relatives. I visit Thuraya, wearing my new dress, with Tim. We give some money to our downstairs neighbours, and receive an outpouring of ritualised pious thanks.

Women have fresh henna for the celebrations. Amina suggests we henna together, but when I take some henna powder down to her house she's already done hers, and I find her applying the ammoniac *shedher* to herself and her daughter, to turn the henna black. So I go home and do my own.

'Why didn't you ask me to henna you?' says Nuriya downstairs when she sees the results the next morning.

'I wanted to see if I could do it.'

'It's not right on your feet, the henna comes too far up your toes, it should be only halfway.' My feet are rather uneven, and there are unhennaed patches on the heels where I leaned on them. I think my hands are not bad, though.

'Why didn't you ask us?' everyone says.

Death of an old woman

'The old woman in our house has died.'

Small, energetic, ready to make himself useful, Ali seems to pop up everywhere running messages. He helped us carry our stuff when we moved; he runs errands for Thuraya across the alleyway. I know where his family live, in a couple of rooms in a big old house with many floors and multiple occupants. I go over to see what's happening.

Women stand crying in the street outside the house and people are swarming in. They encourage me to go in too, so I join the crowd climbing the stairs and looking into a room on the first floor, to see the body of an old woman lying on the bed in the room where she lived alone.

She wasn't the only old woman in the town living on her own, in a room like a bedsit, with pots and a charcoal brazier in a corner to cook on, and only herself to look after, released from the duty of cooking for others. When we buy water we give some to another old woman who lives alone.

'Who will give me water after you go?' she says near the end of our stay. I'm taken aback – we give her so little, a few litres every two weeks or so. I ask about her. A son left in the days of the Imam, a daughter is married in Sana'a, but she has another son who lives in the town.

'Doesn't her son give her anything? Or come to see her?' I ask other women.

'He comes to see her if she's ill. She lives off the town.'

'Isn't it *'aib* to treat his mother like that?'

'Yes, it is rather. People say he's undutiful to his parent. His wife is bad.'

'He's *da'if*,' weak, poor, someone else says in excuse.

Now, in the house where this other old woman has died alone, people are saying: 'She died in the house, with the door locked, they had to take it off the hinges to get in. She died cooking, just like that!'

Shortly before *maghreb* some men come and take the body away, wrapped in a blanket, to her son's house. She too has a son in the town.

Later that Ramadan night, about 9pm, we go out and find men in the graveyard, an expanse of dusty earth beyond the town. There are markings of small white-painted stones around the graves, but nothing to show who is buried there. The men are digging the grave. They come across bits of old bones, and carefully put them in a box to bury beside the new body. A group of about twenty women, carrying *dabba*s on their heads, cross the dusty open space and take down their loads at the grave. They have brought water. The diggers, the sons of the dead woman, mix it with earth to form balls of mud. A small generator has been brought to power a neon strip and strings of light bulbs. The grave is over a metre deep. As soon as it's ready men go off to get the body.

After about fifteen minutes they return, and this time they are accompanied by a procession that makes its way slowly from the mosque. There are a hundred or more men, a good part of the male adult population of the town. Boys lead the way, singing, or perhaps it's closer to chanting. They are organised by their teacher, a Yemeni, not an Egyptian now. The men sing in chorus, alternately with the boys, deep voices answered by higher ones. The effect of the many male voices all rising and falling in unison is powerfully moving. They never stop singing, a constant hum all the time, a background to the burial.

'Is it the same where you come from?' people ask me, as I watch as best I can, in the dark, from a discreet distance. The women who brought the water have left. Men are crowded round the grave. There are no women at the burial and I see only one little girl. The body, wrapped in a white cloth, is first carried on a wooden bier and then lowered into the grave, face towards Mecca, on a blanket with a red headcloth held above it. One man we know quite well is, it turns out, the grandson of the dead woman. He looks drawn and white. After the body is put in heavy stones are laid on top, 'because of the rain,' someone explains, and the balls of mud made earlier are passed along a line of men and pressed on to the stones. The men join in pushing the pile of earth over the mud.

Then the crowd disperses.

At the end of the funeral, money is given by the family of the dead woman, to go to the poor and to have chapters of the Quran read by one of the educated men of the town. The sheikh is standing by to record the amount, said to be 3,000 or 4,000 riyals.

'Who will benefit from this money?' Tim asks. He has had a vantage point in the crowd of men.

'The school director, the teacher, poor men...'

'For example our neighbour?' Tim asks – the poor man who lives downstairs, whose source of income is Quran reading.

'Oh yes,' says one man and shouts out to the sheikh to put him on the list.

When I'm sixty myself I reread my field notes with a sense of shock and revelation. How often I've mentioned an old woman: in the corner of a gathering, unwrapping a small bundle of goods, an item or two of clothing, a *sharshaf* or a shawl to sell to other women; joining me and other women on an outing; eating a snack or a meal in someone's house; spending days on the hillside outside the town looking after cows and sheep; waiting with the bride at the end of wedding festivities – always an old woman around, it seems, in every situation – and, in too many instances, I have not noted who she was or anything about her, or whether or when it was the same one.

Once, I ran a delicate errand for a young woman, taking a cassette she'd recorded to a man who was courting her, delivering it discreetly to his shop.

'Who was in the shop?' she quizzed me afterwards.

'Just one old woman.'

'Who was it?' She was anxious; I wished I'd recognised her but – inadequate, obviously, at the role of go-between – I couldn't remember.

In fact, even when reading the field notes I can distinguish several old women, attached to different houses by ties I sometimes failed to clarify, or else conspicuous by their solitude and independence.

'What do you think is a good age?' Hamda asked me once. 'A woman here is 120 – the one who walks in the market with a stick. She was married at twenty, she was twenty-five years married, she's been thirty-five years a widow.' That adds up to eighty, which seems a more plausible age.

Old women were often spoken of disparagingly. Did I absorb the disregard they were held in, the local assumption of their insignificance? Was it because I was (relatively) young myself?

Top: View of Safaqayn from the graveyard.

Below: Smoke from bread ovens.

Top left: The road down from the town.

Below: View to the next village, from our roof.

Top right: The house we lived in, beside its larger neighbours. Note the blocked doorway, behind which long-drop latrine solids accumulated.

Top: Rooftops, seen from a house at the top of the town.

Below: View over part of Meruwagha, towards the cistern, with the new clinic high on the right.

Top: Houses in the town.

Below: The town cistern.

Top left: An old door in the *suq*, with old and new locks.

Top right: Hand mill for grinding sorghum batter for *lehuh*.

Below: A kitchen.

Top: Coloured glass windows stacked in a workshop.

Below: Terraces below the town.

Top: Doorway to an old house in the town.

Below: Houses in the town.

View from further down the mountain.

A better reason, and a real one, was that they were the hardest people of any to understand, even harder than old men, though those were hard too. The women spoke in old, squawky dialect and were less likely than younger people to adapt their language and diction for me. What they said would surely have been interesting, but it was inaccessible.

'People here don't live to be old,' Khadija tells me. 'Except for that old woman in the market.'

'How old is she?'

'I don't know.'

Khadija herself looks ahead to a bleak old age. Her son will marry and bring to the house a girl from his father's extended family, a first or second cousin. Khadija doesn't expect to get on with her. When I ask about this, she says to me – perhaps a real question, but certainly also for rhetorical effect: 'Do women like their mothers-in-law where you come from?'

III
LIVING IN
THE TOWN

Hamda's cow

It's a lovely morning in November, fresh and clear and still, a welcome change from yesterday's damp and fog. Hamda's house is on a promontory outside the town on the edge of a great drop, a bowl of air formed by the mountains, with views to remote distances, ranks of mountains behind each other fading out. It's a good place to come on a fine day. From here you can see down and down through a gap in the faintest mountains to a wadi just visible in monochrome far away. The nearer view is striped with tiers of terraces running round the folds of hills, footpaths criss-crossing, little groups of houses perched on rocky outcrops to save the cultivable land. Immediately below, you look down on to the square, flat tops of a cluster of houses. The cries of sheep and chickens come up from below.

Hamda has a kind, open face and a good-natured, easy-going manner. She always makes me welcome and gives me *gahwa* when I pass her house outside the town. Once she said that she wished we were neighbours. Now, as we stand outside her house, she gives her cow a pat and it lumbers off to drink water from a small cistern a hundred metres away.

'She goes by herself, and she comes back for lunch. We give her all the spare bits of bread and leftovers.'

The cow is big, dun-coloured, rather gaunt with bony ridges. On each side she has a burnt-in mark a handspan wide, a square made of four lines.

'Is that a mark to show who she belongs to?'

'No, that's where we gave her a burn to cure her when she was ill. She gave thin milk, like water.' I am interested to learn that cows as well as people get curative burns.

'Do cows have names?'

'Yes, the one I had before was Khamisa and this one is called Rizga. She knows her own name, and she knows her owner, she could pick me out from among twenty women. She can follow me, she can track me by smell. I can say "go and drink from the pool" and she will go and come back. She's only unable to speak, otherwise she understands.'

When the cow comes back Hamda says, 'She's not herself today, she didn't want to go. She wants her friend.'

'Where is her friend?'

Hamda lowers her voice. 'They slaughtered her yesterday.'

The cow gives the family milk, butter to clarify for *samn*, and buttermilk – all delicious, real local produce. This milk and butter is much tastier than the substitutes in the shops: Nido or Nina tinned milk powder, tins of vegetable ghee or tinned slightly rancid butter from Denmark.

'How do you make the *samn*?'

'You shake the milk,' she demonstrates the jiggling action of her knee, 'in a gourd.' She shows me a container made of an hourglass-shaped gourd. 'I keep the fat for several days, then boil it up. I milk her in the morning, at noon, and at night – but not now, she's seven months pregnant and only gives a little in the morning. I'll stop milking her soon.'

'How many calves has she had?'

'Maybe twenty, one a year. She'll calve in two months.'

I sit and watch Hamda in her kitchen. The cow's shed is next door, and the cow stands munching, breathing out grassy breath. Hamda is clarifying butter to make *samn*. She heats it till it bubbles and puts in a pinch of something, and now it gives off a familiar smell of *samn*.

'What do you put in it?'

'A pinch of *helba*, fenugreek, burnt, to make it taste nice.'

She gives me some to eat, with bread dipped in. It's rich and spicy, a taste of the *baladi*, the locally produced. Yemenis prize *baladi* food above everything imported and shop-bought. I think they're right.

Hamda says she's feeling ill. But she still has to go down the mountain to get fodder from her land for the cow.

'Do you want to come?'

She knows Tim is away, and I suspect this is why she's inviting me. In recent days other women have already said, 'You haven't got any work to do, you haven't got to cook lunch for Abdullah, come and sit with me.' Everyone reckons I am free in the mornings because I haven't got to cook Tim's lunch.

'It's steep,' she adds, 'will it be tiring for you?'

'I'll be all right.'

Before we leave the house she says, 'My husband owes you fifty riyals.'

This is welcome news: it clears up a puzzle for me. One day in the Thursday market a man whom I knew I ought to recognise asked to borrow a small amount of money from me, saying he'd give it back to me at home. He looked like an absolutely typical Yemeni mountain man, like many others, with a long, bony, beak-nosed, tanned face, high cheekbones with hollow cheeks beneath, a rough-trimmed beard, a cloth wound round his head like a turban with one end hanging down behind, a jambiya dagger in his belt. I'm relieved to know who it was, and that I'll get it back. I had worried less about the money than that someone had pulled a fast one on me and knew they'd got away with it.

Hamda and I pick our way down a path which is steep, but not as bad as the path from another side of the town, where I've scrambled down to spend the afternoon several times and where we went in the dark in Ramadan. As we plunge down I lose sight of the grandeur of the landscape, the mountain peaks fading blue one behind the other to the far distance, the fertile terraced slopes that surround and face us, the near and distant hamlets of stone houses, and concentrate only on my footing on the path.

'Are you all right? It's *hiyud*.' Steep, difficult, precipitous. This is a word women in remote places, women who every day carry twenty-litre jerrycans of water on their heads up paths that would be hard unladen, use almost with pride: '*andinna hiyud*', it's steep, inaccessible, where we are.

'Yes, I'm fine.'

We get to the cluster of houses that you can see from Hamda's plateau, which belong to people from Hamda's husband's family. Hamda calls, a drawn-out, rising and falling screech women use to carry across mountain distances: 'We-e-eh *ya* Zohre-e-eh!'

Zohra appears in the doorway, in a black dress with a small flowered pattern, bright eyes, a worn, handsome, smiling face, and welcomes us in. The house is a fine, spacious, solid stone-built country house, with rooms for animals on the ground floor, and with its own tiny domed mosque and ablution pool. Hamda's husband still has a locked room in the house, she says, with nothing in it. We go in and greet a cluster of women: mother, daughters, sons' wives of the house. We sit down against cushions, glad to rest, and they give us *gahwa*.

'*Ya rukba!*' groans Hamda, O my knee!

The women of the house turn to me.

'We came to visit you the other day, but you were lying down. Abdullah gave us tea, and said not to wake you,' says one. It's true that when I'm ill or have a bad headache I prefer to be left alone; it feels too demanding to have a row of visitors chatting by my bed. People here expect to visit the sick, and find my seclusion hard to understand.

I say there seem to be a lot of families with the same name as her husband in and around the town.

'Yes, lots – their grandfather had three wives, ten daughters, fifteen sons' – Hamda names a few that I know.

We say goodbye and follow the path down to the terraces that step down the mountainside, narrow strips a few metres wide, each with a well-built retaining wall of stones. They are planted with qat, straggly bushes growing some waist high, some taller than a man, and with more compact coffee bushes. The terraces are are all intermingled – this one belongs to Hamda's husband, the next to someone else, then some of Hamda's. Even a single terrace, all on one level, has a part belonging to someone else. And then we reach her property. I can't see any marker, but she knows exactly where. It belongs jointly, undivided, to her and her son by her dead husband, who was a cousin of her present one. The son, working in Sana'a, gets produce from the land; labourers are employed when needed.

Hamda takes out her *sherim*, a small sickle, from where she was carrying it tucked into the close-fitting top of her dress, at the back of the neck. She starts to collect bundles of grass and plants from the terrace sides and the stone-faced edges of the next terrace up, cutting off handfuls with the curved blade. I pluck what I can get by hand.

'Don't trouble yourself, rest, *etneffesi*' – relax, enjoy the air and the view. She makes four or five bundles and ties them with dry banana leaves. Further on, when we're a long way from a banana tree, she ties one with a twist of grass. Then we pick some of her coffee.

'Only the black berries, the ones that'll drop off if we leave them; I'll come back early some morning for the rest.'

Hamda checks the qat trees to see if, after the recent rain, there are tender shoots fit for chewing. She is disappointed to find hardly any.

'But there's been lots of rain,' I say.

'It wants sun.'

I ask Hamda which is better, living with the extended family, brothers and their wives and children, in the big house we visited, as she did until recently, or up on the promontory in the new house with her husband and children.

'The new house is better, there's more *haya*, life, up there near the town. And when you all live together there are problems – it's better to have your own house.'

On the way back up we get covered in thorns and burrs stick to our clothes. Hamda worries again that it is *hiyud*, steep, and *ta'ab*, tiring, for me. We climb slowly, Hamda carrying a big bundle of fodder on her head.

'Let me take a little bit.'

'No, no, it's hard for you.'

I'm not a competent enough load-carrier to insist. I go slowly up after her, while she carries the whole lot. As we walk up the hill I ask Hamda about *jinn*. Other people tell me they lurk on remote hillsides. But she says firmly that there aren't any, they don't exist. We more often hear people say they must exist, as they're in the Quran.

'I'm hungry,' Hamda says, as we approach the house along the way. We stop off there and have fresh-baked, good-smelling bread, and *gahwa*.

When we get back to Hamda's house it's about two. Hamda's daughter, aged perhaps twelve, has cooked rice – not very well, Hamda says, there are burnt bits. We eat it with radish leaves from

Hamda's garden, then *lehuh* and homemade cottage cheese, *geyta*, which is delicious.

Hamda lies down, saying she's ill: 'O my back, O my knees...'

'Why do you have a cow, when it's so much hard work?'

'He wants milk and *samn*.'

I leave her to rest, refusing the qat she presses on me from the small amount she collected, and step out into the air and the view.

Having a cow is, together with fetching water, the hardest work left now. Women in the town no longer go out on day-long trips to gather firewood, which is mostly bought from trucks. They no longer grind wheat in a hand-turned mill for hours every day, but get it from the mechanical mill in the town. A cow is like having a *wadhifa*, a post, a job, women say. It ties them down: a cow can't be left, it lives in a shed and has to be brought fodder – livestock are not left to wander free on the steep terraces filled with precious crops. Girls don't want to marry into a household where they'll have to look after a cow.

'How many cows are there in the town?' I ask the man in the house where we buy buttermilk.

'Only a few left, and three in Meruwagha. Women don't want the work now.'

Ten weeks later, Hamda tells me her cow miscarried. 'She's ill, neither living nor dying.'

'Will you get another one?'

'No, it's *ta'ab*, hard work.'

Later, however, she says they probably will get one, to have nice food for Ramadan.

Near the end of our stay in the town another German, a vet this time, visits the area. He brings us our accumulated post from Sana'a. He too is working for the development agency, investigating what veterinary interventions might be useful; a phosphorus supplement, perhaps. I take him to talk to Hamda. She says her husband will buy a new cow from a bigger town and bring it back, and they will have three days in which they can return it and get all their money back.

The vet asks: 'What if you were cheated, and sold a cow which was said to be pregnant but wasn't?'

'I'd know. We'll buy one that's very pregnant, so you can see the calf moving around, or one with a small calf.'

'What happened to your old cow?'

'She was slaughtered by the butcher for the vultures; she wasn't fit to eat. I decided, and watched him; my husband went away, he didn't want to see. My daughter is still crying for her.'

When I visit the town four years later, I find Hamda doesn't have a cow.

'We did get one, but we sent her back after half a month because she wasn't good, she didn't give good milk, just went walking about.'

Two visits to the health centre

'I'm going to the wedding house in Meruwagha,' says Hamda, 'do you want to come? It's my cousin.'

'Who's the bride?'

'From outside, down the mountain.'

We head off from Hamda's house across the flat, open space, where the scouring wind, today, blows up the grit in our faces, towards the town. Hamda is wearing a headscarf and a *saramiya* cloth over it. She's carrying rounds of bread on her head, covered with the *saramiya*, and a tin full of *ra'ib*, buttermilk, in her hand, with one end of the headcloth over it. As we approach the town, halfway through the dusty expanse of graveyard, she says, 'I'm *fatish*!', unveiled. She tries to rearrange the *saramiya*, holding the free end of it in her mouth, 'for the *suq*,' as she explains: not the Thursday market, since it's a Friday, but the market town and its men.

On the way a car slows down and a woman leans out of the driving seat window to ask me if I want a hose. I was asking all round the market yesterday on behalf of Khadija, whose hose for bringing water from her roof is old and cracked. When she's gone on I ask Hamda, 'Who is that woman?'

'Mohammed Saleh's daughter.' She's from a local family.

'She's driving a car?'

Hamda shrugs. 'She drives.'

Other women don't; she does. When we try to get to the bottom of such differences in behaviour, people say, '*Kull wahed 'ala mizajuh*,' everyone according to his disposition.

In the wedding house everyone is busy in a hurly-burly of cooking *gheda* for the bride and her family, who will arrive today from their village down the mountain. I'm bundled up to a sitting room out of the way, from where I can't see anything interesting, so after a bit I take my leave. A man asks me if Abdullah will come in the afternoon, and the women tell me to come. I spend the afternoon with a small roomful of women chewing qat, hardly anyone I know, some women and girls from villages nearby, some neighbours coming in briefly. I dance with a girl from the nearest village, and learn a slightly different, back-and-forth step. She invites me to come to her village to *rabakh* the next day. I walk back with a woman I know, and see another girl driving.

'Who is she?'

'*Bint* 'Ali Ma'arif, she's from Bani Ayub – here, only *bint* Mohammed Saleh drives.' These are the only two women I ever see driving.

Hamda doesn't stay to *rabakh* because she feels ill. I go to see her soon after.

'My knee is still bad.'

'You should go to a doctor.'

'*Ma ejzim*, I don't dare, don't feel I can, alone.'

'I'll go with you. I can check first if there's anyone there.'

'Tomorrow,' she ends up saying. 'Then I'll have the money,' she says to the neighbour sitting with us.

'I can lend it to you,' I say.

'Tomorrow.'

The next day I check that the clinic is open and there is a doctor there – Sudanese, one of a succession of Sudanese or Egyptian doctors and health workers stationed in the town, who mostly don't stay long. At Hamda's we sit around for a bit. A neighbour visits. At 11am I say, 'We should go. I'll lend you the money.'

It's only 2 riyals for an entrance ticket to the health centre. This is still the old one up in the town, in an old house; a new polyclinic has been built just outside the town but it isn't in use yet. The doctor says rheumatism, and gives her ampoules of dextrose solution to drink, vitamin B complex, something to take when it hurts, and something else I don't identify, all from the pharmacy store attached to the clinic, and a prescription for something to get from one of the town pharmacists.

They are not exactly pharmacists, rather they are untrained entrepreneurs who keep a stock of drugs and do some prescribing. At least one is referred to as '*doktur*' by the people of the town. Subsequent years will see a state crackdown on these enterprises.

After we've got the medicines, we stop in the tunnel where the alley goes under part of a house, for Hamda to ask me again which medicine to take when.

'From the government?' she asks about the bundle of medicines, surprised, I think, that it didn't all cost more.

None of the pharmacists has the prescribed Aroma ointment. We give her our tube of Tanderil. (We had some Aroma, but we gave it to a friend of Tim's for a bruised hand. Tim goes to the friend's house to try to get it, but he's not there, so Tim doesn't go in, though invited by his mother. He assumes it wouldn't be proper, but later the friend says, 'Why didn't you go in and drink tea?')

Hamda gives me bread and *samn*. I wonder if the rather strange collection of products will do her any good. I feel sorry that her accessing of modern medicine, with so much effort and persuasion, was not for a problem it could more conclusively cure or help.

White sheets curtain off the back room of the clinic. I have come to see the Sudanese doctor. Another sheet covers the entrance to the room he sits in. Something is going on.

'Go in,' says the attendant. 'It's a woman in childbirth.'

Two boys, the patient's children, are sitting in the outer room. Some women, people from the town, emerge from behind the sheet curtain with harrowed faces. A couple more peer out from behind the curtain. They beckon me to peep in.

On the bench built into the wall, a woman is lying, with a man, her husband, sitting behind her, his legs stretched out on either side, supporting her and holding her head. I don't recognise either of them; they come from a village. She is dribbling, and I'm not sure if she is conscious. A blanket covers the bottom half of her body, leaving only the lower part of her legs showing. She is otherwise fully clothed.

The doctor is working by feel alone. He has bloodstained surgical gloves on.

The doctor goes out for a break, and one of the women pulls down the blanket to cover more of the sick woman's legs. I go and sit outside. After a little all the women in the room come out, intensely upset, at least two of them in tears. They tell me: 'She's been in labour for three days!'

They shake their heads to each other and say, from out of a fellow feeling, a female solidarity, that excludes me, 'You haven't had children, you haven't given birth.' I'm moved by their empathy with a woman they don't know.

The next day, the Sudanese doctor tells me about her. It was her eleventh birth, and she had uterine inertia, obstruction, placenta praevia – she needed a caesarean on at least three separate grounds. He was only carrying out resuscitation before sending her to Hodeida, the big city down on the coast. He doesn't hold out much hope: it had been going on too long. This is a common pattern. He has a boy in the room upstairs with bronchopneumonia who was ill for ten days before his family brought him in.

'They kept thinking he'd get better. He needs to be sent to Hodeida, but his family won't agree, they say he'll die on the way. So I'm refusing to treat him.'

Afternoon gatherings of women where I'm *rabakh*ing discuss the woman in childbirth at the clinic.

'That Sudanese doctor doesn't have any *khibra*, expert knowledge, in childbirth cases.'

'He looked at her and put his hand up inside her,' says another woman.

'There were people coming and going.'

'Men could look.'

'Her legs were *kashif*, exposed.'

Finally they turn to me.

'Would you let a doctor, a man, put his hand inside you?'

'A female doctor would be better, but yes, I would, if otherwise I or my baby would die.'

'Death is preferable!' says Selma Yahya, and no one disagrees.

For me, it's a moment of alienation. I feel upset, homesick for my own culture. I can't get my point of view across, and no one listens much to what I want to say.

I never find out whether the woman survived.

Gardens

'What shall I give you?' Hamda asks, herself more than me.

She looks round her garden as I leave. Unlike the women in the pressed-together town houses, she has a walled-in plot all around her new one-storey house on the promontory outside the town. She has well-tended plants in the ground here: onions; the Yemeni flat-leaved onion greens, like something between leeks and chives, called *bay'ah*; big white radishes with edible leaves; chilli peppers, mint, fennel, dill, coriander, tomatoes – all the ingredients for *zahaweq* relish and the salad accompaniments to a meal. And for medicinal uses: fennel for pregnant women if their legs itch, or in *gahwa* for stomach pains; dill for urinary problems.

'You don't have to give me anything,' I protest. I've already enjoyed her hospitality, relaxing in her sitting room, sipping *gahwa*.

'We're friends,' she says. She picks a handful of mint and presses it on me despite my refusals. 'I haven't baked today,' she says, as if not giving me bread needs an explanation.

'*Ya* Mariam, *ya* Mariam, your *mishqor* are thirsty!' The neighbour girls from across-the-roof are out on their roof, a step above ours, and calling down our stairwell, scolding me.

I struggle up the steep, irregular stairs with a small plastic *dabba* of water, hunch through the doorway and emerge into the sun.

'They get thirsty just like people, it's *haram* to neglect them.'

Wicked, a sin. I hadn't meant to neglect my plants; I'm very pleased with them. Lush green growth spills out from the top of my collection of old containers. My cracked *barmil*, the one I failed to carry water in, has Swiss chard from English seeds. A broken blue plastic ten-litre *dabba*, with one side cut out, holds four small crunchy lettuces. The cutting of purple-bracted basil that Thuraya gave me is growing bushy in its tin. Old, round yellow Nido and square blue Girl Ghee tins hold bright nasturtiums, also a useful addition to our diet. I have the green kind of basil too, mint, and morning glory with blue flowers trailing from another tin.

I wrote to my mother, 'Please could you send me lettuce seeds, a small kind, and nasturtiums?' and waited for the unreliable post to bring them. Now the plants flourish, colourful and pleasing against the dusty white-painted roof.

'*Ya* Mariam, can you give me seeds for your green flowers?' I'm asked one day.

Green flowers? I'm puzzled. Then I realise she means blue morning glory, and it's one step on the way to my understanding that they don't use the Arabic word *azraq* to mean blue (though I do hear it used for an olive green) and that *akhdar*, green, covers what we would call blue as well as green.

'Wear your green dress,' someone instructed me, planning an afternoon's *rabkha*.

'I don't have a green dress.'

'The one Thuraya made you.'

'That's blue!'

But only schoolchildren use *azraq* for blue. Similarly, *ahmar*, 'red', extends to my brown hair, browning a chicken ('cook it till it's red'), the yolk of an egg, the orange yellow of a Bic biro, bright yellow berries on a solanum plant, and the purple side of a matchbox.

Later I have to write again for another batch of nasturtium seeds to give as presents. I'm always on the lookout for acceptable things to give, and these have proved popular; people have been very pleased to get them. A tiny garden at the bottom of the town has the orange and yellow flowers cascading down a miniature terrace. Women who've seen them growing in other women's pots ask me if I can give them some. I've been gratified to see flowers from my seeds decorating women's headscarves, and even a bride wearing them for her wedding.

Outing with Amina

It's a sunny morning in late April. There's a knock on our door and Fuad, Amina's son, comes in. His head has been shaved; three or four scars from *misam*s are visible on the top near the front.

'My mother says, will you come to her this afternoon?'

'Yes, I'll come down after lunch.'

'Come early, come at two your time, she wants to go out of town.'

I ask him about the scars on his head.

'My mother did them, for illness, one every month.'

'Didn't it hurt?'

'Yes, it hurt.' I don't manage to find out what the illness was.

After lunch, and before the *'asr* call to prayer, I hurry down through the town. Amina is ready in a clean dress for the afternoon, dark brown with a small flower pattern. She picks up her fifteen-month-old baby and settles her on her hip, where the child grips with her legs, as Yemeni babies do (later, when I have my own babies, I am surprised to find they don't), and Amina holds her with an arm around her. She arranges her *saramiya* over her head and shoulders. Her elder daughter Hasiba, a sober, responsible eight-year-old, comes too. We skirt the edge of the town and take a steep path going down. I watch my feet, looking out for good footholds and the easiest route past stony outcrops, wary of loose gravelly patches where one can slide downhill out of control, making use of safer tufts of grass. I can feel the path through my flip-flops and get an extra grip and balance with my toes.

Amina says, 'This is the first time I've taken Fatin out.'

She must have been a bit less hidden away already, though, I think, because she has a healthy colour now; last time I saw her she was very pale.

'Why do you keep babies inside? Are you afraid of the sun on them? Or people's eyes?' I'm remembering what Amina told me about her children who died as babies.

'People,' she says shortly.

'And the sun, is it good or bad for babies?' I ask this because I've read that in another part of Yemen mothers keep babies in because the sun is considered bad for them.

'Good.'

I wonder if, in those other areas, the sun was the real reason or, just possibly, a proxy for fears people didn't want to talk about. Or if it all comes to the same thing, a fear of exposing babies to the wider, dangerous world.

As we leave the town behind, Amina stoops to pick up a handful of pebbles from the path, and circles the handful round Fatin's head, muttering under her breath – counting the circles? – then throws the pebbles ahead in front of the baby. A little further along the path she does the same thing again.

'Why are you doing that?'

'Because I haven't taken her out before.'

'But why...?'

'This place is bad.'

'What's bad about it?' I press her.

'There are no people.' I wonder if that means there are *jinn*, but I don't like to ask, because I've been told that talking about *jinn* encourages them to gather.

A little later the conversation takes a turn I don't like: Amina starts to urge me, 'You should convert to Islam!' I try to deflect the topic, but she's not going to let it go.

'You and Abdullah would get a salary, you could have any job you want, a house and everything, from the government.'

Again, I try and fail to change the subject. 'But why not?' she persists. The default position is I should convert; not to needs a reason.

'Hearts don't change. It's better for people to stay in their own religion.'

As we walk, I take the opportunity to ask Amina about something I've heard of, an illness of children called *redda*. She's happy to explain.

'Children get ill. If a woman washes, for purification, after her period or anything like that,' (sex, childbirth, I suppose) 'she should wait most of a day before she goes near a child.'

'Even the child's mother?'

'No, it doesn't matter if her hair's still wet from the wash, she's the baby's mother. The mother, father, brother, uncles, aunts, grandmother... those who are from your kin do no harm.'

A little further along the path she shows me a tree. 'That tree, *talaga*, is a house for *jinn*.' And now I ask, and she tells me, more about *jinn*.

'There used be some near my house, and I saw one in my village, in a remote place. It looked like a woman.'

'How did you know it was a *jinniya*?'

'It was there one minute, then gone. *Jinn* change into a cat, a dog, an old woman.'

'Some people where I come from say dead people come back at night, a bit like that, suddenly there and then not.'

'Someone who's dead is dead – they can't come back. These would be *jinn*.'

'What do they do to people?'

'They're dangerous, if you go alone, at night.'

'What do you do if you see one?'

'Recite.' She recites a long passage. 'The holy Quran is good for many things.'

'Are *jinn* afraid of the Quran?'

'Yes.'

Next she tells me about the past, before the road came to the town, the long walks into the countryside to get firewood.

'Before there were cars here we would go all day till 10 at night, our time' – that's 4am! 'It was *ta'ab*, hard. But our relaxation was better then too, and people would *semer*, sit up chatting at night, more than now, and they were strong from working so much, and never ill. We're weaker now.'

We're heading for a cluster of houses below the town, which belong to members of Amina's husband's family; the same house I've been to with Hamda, who is Amina's husband's brother's wife, though living on opposite sides of the town they don't have the intense relationship of brothers' wives who live in the same household.

On the way we meet one of the women of the house we're going to, Zohra, bright-eyed with high cheekbones, neither young nor old, going up to the town.

'I'm going to *rabakh* at Marawi's, I haven't been yet.' I wonder what's happening at Marawi's – wedding, sickness, birth, death? – that means she ought to go, that I haven't heard about, but I fail to find out.

We arrive at the solid old country house with storage and stabling on the bottom floor. We climb the stairs to a sitting room on the first floor, and spend a pleasant afternoon relaxing there, chewing and chatting with the women of the house. One of the girls is soon to be married. Her sister cries, perhaps talking about her departure and how she will miss her.

We talk about veiling. I say we don't wear veils where I come from.

'That would be *'aib* for us.'

'Did your grandmothers wear a veil?'

'No, nor our mothers. Just a headscarf.'

'Why not?'

'There weren't any *lithma*s and *sharshaf*s in the shops or the market before the *jumhuriya*.' That's the republic, after the deposition of the Imam in 1962. 'Before, people only had one dress, made out of plain cloth. There was no bedding or furnishings – people slept on cattle fodder. There was no electricity.'

Veils, it seems, are part of all these relatively recent improvements, consumer goods and amenities.

'So do you like veils?' I ask the woman next to me.

'They're good, they're cover, protection. If men come, you can just pull your *lithma* up.'

'And before, what would women do?'

'They would run away.'

'So it's better to be able to sit, and just pull up a veil?'

'Yes.'

'Have you got a *sharshaf*?'

'Yes, four. They cover you from people.'

I wonder what anyone can possibly do with four. They all look the same. She adds: 'You should get one. A *lithma* is good because it keeps you warm.'

'What about in hot weather?' I think of the clammy nylon covering the face.

'There's no hot weather here in the mountains.'

'And in Hodeida?' Down on the coastal plain the heat is extreme.

'Yes, it's very hot, but the women there are used to it.' She asks me: 'Why don't you go uncovered here?'

'But you just said I should get a *lithma* and a *sharshaf*!'

'To learn how to use them.'

What I wear is neither one thing nor the other, neither their custom nor mine, but a compromise. I wear a scarf on my head, always, but don't put on the other coverings adult women use. I wouldn't feel comfortable now with my head bare. What I wear is actually, I realise later, the degree of cover of girl children well below puberty. I'm like a child in my movements as well, going around the town freely, going to the market. This freedom, which I take for myself as an outsider, and which nobody seems to object to, means I can run errands for women, who don't go to the market or the shops.

Earlier the woman sitting next to me mentioned contraceptive pills, and now she shows me part of her collection. She has two packets. I read the labels: one says Microgynon 30 and one Anovlar. The packets are quite different in design.

'Those are different,' I point out. 'That's not good.'

'I have two more different again,' she says. 'I only take them on nights when I have sex with my husband.'

I start trying to explain that she needs to take them every night even if she doesn't have sex, and that they should be taken for three weeks, with a week's gap. I hear my 'week' and 'seven days' being repeated to the other women there as '*thaman*', eight days, which – like *huit jours* in French – is used to mean a week; I don't know whether this means they would take eight days off. I begin to realise the enormous difficulty of getting all this across: the taking of pills even when you don't have sex, the stopping for a week, when there'll be bleeding and so no sexual relations, but not exactly coinciding with the time not taking the pills. And that you are protected for the days when you don't take the pill but the bleeding hasn't started, and that you need to start taking them again after seven days even if the period is still going on. There are three separate sets of events going on, three cycles – when you have sex, when you have a period, and when you should take the pills – which don't quite mesh.

I ask if they use condoms. They've heard about them.

'A woman in Sana'a had one come off inside her, she had to have an operation to get it out.' I have heard this before, more than once; it's the most usual response to any mention of condoms.

On the way back we meet Zohra again, coming down as we climb up, returning from her afternoon's *rabkha*.

We pause to chat. Talking about her daughter's impending marriage, she starts crying.

'I'll have no one left.' She has a small daughter and son, but she'll miss her elder daughter's help and company.

As we climb back up again Amina searches out plants to add to the ones she's told me about before. She tells me the names and what they are useful for, and I pick samples for later identification. I'm getting a long list.

There's a kind of sorrel, used to wrap qat, and for sore eyes, and good for babies. A leaf you rub on spider bites. *Humadha*, oxalis, sour leaves eaten raw by pregnant women: nausea makes them want to eat sour things. *Gushab*, with roots good for internal pains and leaves for *sufre*, malaria or hepatitis. Different fleshy aloes – *ksherrabah, seber* – are split open and the sticky translucent gel used to dress wounds. *Sib'eya* is burnt and the smoke used to purify the gourds that women shake milk in to get butter, so it doesn't taste bad. *'Aden*, the strange-looking plant like a miniature baobab with improbable bright-pink flowers, is, I'm told, 'like penicillin' for wounds and burns. White sticky sap from *dherah* twigs is a depilatory for pubic hair. There are dozens of plants with medicinal and domestic uses.

Amina remembers one we saw last time we went out. 'That plant I couldn't remember the name of the other day, for curing skins – it's *'athek.'*

Her daughter Hasiba says, 'Let Mariam stop and write them down!'

I'm grateful for her understanding. We stop on a convenient rock just before it gets too dark.

'Is there anything for these on my foot?' I show her the verrucas on my sole. 'I don't know,' she says, adding without much conviction, 'maybe menstrual blood.'

I think Amina is glad to have a companion so she can go further afield to visit; women don't leave the town alone. Whenever I go on outings with her she finds plants for me and tells me about them. I suppose she knows so many because she comes from a village. But she's also, in general, particularly interested in health and health-promoting activities, new information as well as old. She tells me that vitamin C is good for health and is found most of all in limes and green peppers.

Men who come from villages, as well as women, know plant names and their uses and tell me more. I learn of plants that treat worms, pains, fever, kidneys, burns, sore eyes, cuts, nausea and swollen legs in pregnancy, problems of menstruation, headaches, diarrhoea in cows. Duckweed, on the surface of the cistern water, is recommended to me for urinary problems. ('Put it below your navel,' a man advises me. After the advice to ask my neighbours Khadija and Thuraya for more exact instructions, I realise that this is a euphemism.)

There are plants to use as twine for tying things, berries whose juice can be used as ink, berries you can eat, a round-headed thistle with an edible centre inside its prickles, something like tobacco growing wild that people used to smoke, and a plant you can tie an animal to, because the roots won't pull out.

Later, out on a *dowra* with some townswomen, I find I know more plant names than they do.

An afternoon with men and women

'Did Abdullah give you the *'uzzab* for your ear drops?' the women ask me.

I'm sitting in the house of Tim's friend Yahya in his village, twenty minutes' hard scramble down below the town. He's an intelligent young man with a full moustache and a mass of wiry hair parted over to one side, pushed down flat but springing up again. I am with him and his wife Zeinab, his father and some boys and some neighbour women, relaxing against grubby unmatched cushions in a small comfortable room with a television in the corner and the ubiquitous set of metal shelves with cologne sprays and pots of plastic flowers. The sickly smell from the cologne lingers in the air and on the front of our clothes, and as we start to stroke our leaves for chewing the sharp qat smell joins the smell of tobacco from the *mada'a*.

I haven't brought any qat, but our host presses some on me.

'I don't want any, I chewed so much yesterday.'

'Then you should have a bit, otherwise when you do chew it will keep you awake. That's what happens if you only chew some days.'

Last week Tim came here to *rabakh* on his own and explained I couldn't come because I was ill in bed with a fever. So they gave him *'uzzab*, a herb like marjoram, and careful, repeated instructions about how to apply it, dropped into my ears in hot sesame oil, four drops only.

I thank them, then ask them about cows. 'Who has a cow in the village?'

Several of the women say they don't. '*Ta'ab!*' they explain: too tiring, too much work.

'It's like the town here now,' says Yahya's father, 'the women want to have rest like the women in town.'

Then Tim and Yahya's friend and some more men come in through the door, and the nature of the gathering changes. At the arrival of the men the neighbour women scuttle out fast, but Yahya's wife stays, and takes part in the conversation with us and the men.

One of them tells us about his mother. 'She was educated, she was employed in the Ministry of Health. But my father made her come to the country and look after cattle. You can't find an educated husband with a job for an educated, employed woman, who will let her work – he'll tell her to stay in the house.'

The room becomes more and more smoky. Cigarette smoke is added to the smoke from the *mada'a*. The conversation turns to bride prices.

'It's forbidden to pay more than 25,000 riyals.' Everyone, wherever we go, is discussing the new limit, imposed by the government, either central or local (accounts vary) on the bride price paid by the groom's family.

'Twenty-five thousand for a virgin,' (a little over £3,000). 'Out of that twenty thousand goes to the bride's father, her father's brothers, her mother – she would get one thousand. Five thousand is *mahr* for the bride, she buys gold with it.' There are still the other expenses of the wedding: 'Sheep, qat, meat – three to four thousand. For a divorced woman or a widow the bride price is fifteen thousand, divided into ten for the bride's family, two and half for the bride, and two and a half for clothes and so on.'

'Do you think people are keeping to the limits?' we ask.

On this question opinion is split. Some people say yes, strictly. Others say they're exceeded in secret. Both sides seem equally certain.

'Some people do pay more, secretly.'

'No, they have to swear an oath that they haven't paid any extra.'

'In Mahwit the limit isn't observed, there was a man from there wanting to get a wife here because they're cheap – here the officials are enforcing it, in Mahwit they aren't.'

One man remembers, 'Saleh Mohammed Marawi's daughter was married for 100,000 riyals, just before the limit.'

'Ah, how lovely she was!' says Yahya's wife. 'It used to be one thousand *haq el bab* to the bride, "for the door", when the bridegroom enters the room, and another thousand *haq el fetsh*, for her to remove her veil – that's what I had. And a thousand, or gold, *haq el fersha*, to lie down together. Is there still *haq el bab*?'

'No, these payments don't exist now,' the men tell her.

'It's much better now, with the new limits,' one man says. Others agree: 'Rich and poor are alike.'

'And girls aren't married against their wishes to the man offering their father the most.'

'Before, unwilling girls were given to the highest bidder, by fathers who didn't care about them.'

A man sitting in the corner, with a cloth wound round his head as a turban, adds, 'Girls used to kill themselves – not here, but in Sana‘a – when they were married against their will, and their fathers wouldn't agree to a divorce.'

I note the crux, the point that really counts: not marriage to a man you don't want, but being unable to get divorced if you find you really can't stand him. It's *min Allah*, from God, just one of those things, if you don't love your husband, women say. But they also say it's possible to stay and get to love him *habba habba*, bit by bit.

'In our country that's not allowed,' I say. 'The girl has to choose for herself, it's not up to the parents.'

'That's much better,' says the man in the corner.

Yahya disagrees. 'A father knows his daughter, he knows what's best for her.'

I think of the women I know who have told me they were married young because their fathers didn't care about them, were thinking only of their own interests. The man in the corner modifies his position: 'Before, girls had no education, they couldn't meet boys, their fathers knew what was best for them.'

They talk about a woman married to a prominent local figure, who now has a young second wife.

'She's not divorced, he still wants her, but she doesn't want him. She never wanted to marry him but her father beat her so she went to marry him, still protesting. She ran away back to her village after a month, even though everyone knew her father had said he would kill her. She said she'd shoot her husband if she was forced to go back to him.'

'Why does she hate him?'

'It's from Allah that she just can't bear him.'

'So who is wrong, the father or the girl?' I ask.

'The father for forcing her,' says one man. Another, a young man, concurs: 'She should have the right to choose, you can't force a girl against her will like in the past.'

Zeinab says, 'The father is wrong. But if someone runs away from her husband like that, women will laugh at her and say she is afraid of men in general.'

'What will people say if a girl doesn't want to marry the man her father chooses?'

'If she wants to choose the man herself,' Zeinab says, 'people will say she's a *gahba*, a whore.'

'And if the man wants a second wife, can the first wife leave?' we ask.

'Her father will say to her, he's your fate, your lot in life, he provides for you – he pays for your food and clothes,' Yahya says.

His wife disagrees passionately. 'If the house was full – stuffed with food and goods – I still wouldn't accept another wife!' She adds: 'Some women would stay. If she loves him a lot, or if there are children. Some would leave *because* they love him – they can't bear it, they want to die.'

Sitting with us in our house one day, another young man, 'Ali, tells us how he wanted to take a second wife, but his wife threatened to poison him. He comes to see Tim to learn English; he has had little chance of education and this is an opportunity to improve himself. He complains about his wife, saying she's rough, uneducated, a village girl.

One day he pulls a piece of paper from his jacket pocket and reads us a poem he's written, a poem addressed to a beloved, not his wife.

'How can you meet women?' we ask.

'It's easy in the countryside, girls go out getting fodder for cows, or getting water, and you can sit and *rabakh* together, with people not knowing you love each other, thinking it's just normal.'

'How would she read the poem?'

'I'd go and read it to her, or record a cassette. The poem doesn't mention her name, it has references to where I saw her, things only she would know, so only she would know it was about her.'

'Have you written love poems to your wife too?'

'No, I've written insult poems to her.'

One evening I get my grammar confused, and use, when speaking to 'Ali, a feminine possessive suffix with a noun, *-ish* instead of *-ak*, as I'm used to doing because I mostly talk to women. The result is that I'm speaking to him as if he were a woman rather than a man.

'If you said that to the *mudir*, the prefect, he'd be angry.'

'And if I said *-ak* to a woman, what then?'

'No, that doesn't matter.'

I ask why.

'A man is *ahsan*, better, than a woman.'

'Why?'

'A woman can't go out, go to the town on her own, for example.'

Women say the same thing: women are poor things, pitiable, because they can't move around freely.

Behind the scenes at a wedding
Voices rise and fall in the dark, voices singing in unison and then many more joining in a chorus of 'Allah, Allah'. The neighbour

girls and I crane from the rooftop, women's vantage point, to see the lights of lanterns and the dim outlines of figures as the men's wedding procession twists round a corner and pushes, crowding, into a narrow alley.

Men hold aloft pump-up lanterns and lamps on gas canisters. A woman, half veiled, a torch in each hand, carries a round basketwork tray on her head, filled with biscuits and popcorn, and in the centre a small dish of flaming wicks. The lantern light catches on heavy silver ornaments hanging by her ear, on the metal strap of her watch and her silver rings.

Here is the groom, solemn, set-faced, eyes down, wearing dark glasses despite the night, carrying a silver sword glinting in the torchlight, a red shawl draped over his head and hanging down, a long spray of *heynan* tucked into his headcloth. He's closely surrounded by men singing, making good cheer, and beyond them a press of young boys. The town musician, the *muzayyin*, blows a *mizmar*, a double reed pipe. His cheeks are puffed out huge, like two qat bulges, or as if he has two half tennis balls stuffed inside them.

Gunfire at weddings is currently banned – in the whole province, on the orders of the governor, we are told, after people were accidentally killed – and it's not till a later wedding that I see the ban flouted, with pistols and rifles let off, green fire streaming up into the night sky. And that time, we hear, the groom's family had to pay a fine of 1,000 riyals for the impetuous actions of their guests from outside the town.

Earlier that day, I went to the noisy wedding party in the usual place, the big room like a barn. The bride is easily the youngest I've seen, but also one of the most cheerful. Many women tell me they were married long before puberty, in the past, but no bride I see is that young.

'Isn't she young? Is she older than you?' I ask one of the neighbour girls.

'Oh yes, she has *ku'ub*.' Fatima gestures how her breasts hang down. She seems to me completely flat. I hear women assuring others that she's reached puberty, maturity, *gdih kumelan, gdih balugh*. There seems to be a feeling that her post-pubertal status needs confirming, emphasising; that it wouldn't be normal or permissible, now, to marry off younger girls. Legally, at this date, there is a minimum age of fifteen for the marriage of girls, even if it's not enforced. Few people know their exact age anyway, but when they do try to estimate it, it is assumed that fifteen is a standard age at which girls start menstruating.

I leave the crowded hall with Thuraya, and as we go out people are giving money to the bride.

'Give her twenty,' says Thuraya, so I do. It's only the next day, when Thuraya hands me a 20-riyal note, that I realise the present to the bride was from her, not from me, and I've given the bride nothing. Thuraya says it doesn't matter.

The afternoon procession of men comes very slowly from the mosque. One man leads the singing with a portable microphone, and the others chorus responses. In the light of day, the groom looks young. As before, he carries a sword, and a spray of dangling, trembling *heynan* projects over his face. He is closely flanked by two men, also with set, sober faces. One holds a Kalashnikov in his left hand, while his right covers the groom's hand, over its grip on the sword. His jambiya is wound about with a silver chain. The companion on the other side, who is wearing dark glasses, has his fingers interlinked with the bridegroom's. An older man behind them rests his hand on the bridegroom's shoulder. Like the bride in her procession the bridegroom with his withdrawn look seems closely supported, almost guarded by friends.

The men in the procession all link hands and make a passage for the groom to go through. Then they stop to dance. They form a ring round two dancers in the middle who circle and turn, with a sort of sprightly hopping, holding their bare jambiyas aloft and brandishing them in the air, turning them this way and that. I see Tim, a head taller than the others, taking a turn. The jambiyas wave at his eye height. He tells me later it was quite dangerous for him, not understanding the dance well enough to know which way people were going to move or when. Then the groom dances in the middle of the circle of men, with his ceremonial sword and the long coloured scarf across his body, opposite another man with a Kalashnikov on his shoulder.

The bride sits in a room, veiled in a black *sharshaf*, and receives money. The *muzayyina* flourishes each note and announces loudly who it's from. This time, men are crowding in to give money, and the bride is getting a good amount, plenty of 100-riyal notes. She puts it all in a scarf, a fat bundle. Tim comes in and gives 10 riyals; he wanted to give 20 but didn't have the right notes. I don't give any because I'm under the misapprehension that I have already given her some. When most people leave I get up to go from where I've been sitting.

'*Aib!*' says the *muzayyina* firmly. 'You have to stay for supper.'

So I stay and eat *lehuh* and *zahaweq* and *mareg* meat stock, and meat, of which I'm given a generous amount, and then some more. The bride has taken off her *sharshaf* and sits looking relaxed, laughing and talking.

'How did you learn to play the drum?' I ask the *muzayyina*. 'Did your mother teach you?'

'No, but I learnt when I was small,' she says, showing a child's height with her hand.

When I finally leave, quite late, I'm told the bride will now go to the bridegroom's house, and wait there, while he chews qat in his uncle's house.

'Is it necessary for the bride to bleed the first time she lies with her husband?' I ask the woman I'm sitting with one afternoon.

'Yes, even just a little.' she shows me with three drops of spittle, licking a finger and dabbing it on the palm of her other hand. 'Otherwise she's not a virgin. The bride's family look the next day to see the blood.'

'What happens if she doesn't?'

'Her husband won't want her, she'll go back to her father, he will beat her. Later she'll remarry as a *raj'a*, a woman who's been married before.'

'Is it important that the marriage is consummated on the wedding night?' we ask Tim's friend Yahya, sitting in our room one evening.

'No, it could be the next night, people won't talk right away.'

We talk about customs in other Arab countries we've read about where a man is expected to perform on his wedding night.

'This is very wrong. A man is not iron, it's from Allah – some days he's weak, some days he's strong.'

Other men say that a public display of the bride's blood from the consummation would be barbarous. 'We're not *bedu*,' they say. *Bedu* is used to denote darker-skinned Yemenis who live at lower altitudes, dwellers in the wadis, but also implies savage or uncivilised.

'*Itfaddalu 'andinna*, come to us! There's a *gheda* for the wedding.'
Standing on our landing is a man I photographed, because he asked me to, in the market the day before yesterday – a broad smile in a wrinkled face showing stained, gappy teeth, stubble, tanned brown skin. I don't know his name. He's inviting me and Tim and our friend the Sudanese teacher, who happens to be in our house.

It's 12.45 on a Friday now. Earlier today, when I went to get water, I could see tray after tray of *bint* sweet pastry being carried into the groom's house. My neighbour Thuraya was busy baking bread in the *tannur* and trays of *bint* in her gas oven. Some of the *bint* got burnt, and she gave one to us, in its dish. Underneath the burnt top it was delicious.

The messenger leads us out of the town to one of the newer houses on the outskirts, the house of a man we know. 'It's the house of the bridegroom's uncle,' he explains, his mother's brother. Although the meal is in honour of yesterday's wedding, I can't see the bridegroom or the bride actually there.

'Do you want to go with the men or with the women?'

It's interesting to be asked. Up to now, when we've been invited to celebratory meals with lots of guests, I've always eaten as an honorary man, the only woman among the men. When my sister visited, we were asked to a big *gheda*, and we were both honorary men.

'With the women.'

With the women is like being behind the scenes while a performance is put on. In the kitchen five or six adults, and some young girls, are frantically busy, bustling in all directions, running to and fro, chopping, stirring, beating, pouring, putting dishes together, washing the used trays and bowls. There's a smell of fresh bread and hot fenugreek and boiled meat. Men of the family keep rushing in, taking dishes out, bringing them back, and coming back shouting for the next.

'*Helba!*'

They shout for, and take away, a large, flat dish of spicy-fragrant meat and vegetable stew with fenugreek foam on top. The juice from below is still boiling in the earthenware dish, breaking through the green topping, as they carry it away.

I look round for anything useful I can do, but the best thing seems to be to stay out of the way, so I just watch. It seems like chaos, but a meal is getting sent out there, and I know from the times I've sat with the men how the dishes appear from nowhere, how everybody concentrates on eating without talk, how quickly the men sitting round the dishes on the plastic cloth dip in their right hands and eat up the food, and each at their own pace finish, praise God, *elhamdulillah*, for being full, and rise and leave the room. And how before that the men will call loudly for the *helba*, and a man or a boy will bring it in bubbling, or take it from a female hand stretched round the door, and the host will stir in spicy *zahaweq* relish as his own final touch, and then distribute lumps of meat. And how the back-scene bustle doesn't show or obtrude on the dignity of the male host enacting his hospitality, summoning food as if from nowhere for his guests.

The women in the kitchen are busy washing the serving dishes in between sittings. At least there aren't individual plates to wash, since everyone reaches to dip into the central one. The dishes go out, first *bint*, then *shfut*; *susi*, bread cooked with stirred-up eggs and butter; rice with raw tomatoes and onions and *zahaweq*; *helba*; chunks of boiled meat; meat stock to be served in little glasses; *muhallabia*; quartered oranges and apples. From the order the dishes go out I reckon there are three sittings of the meal in succession; the first two take about half an hour together, so the men are eating fast. I'm invited to eat with the third sitting of men, and accept gratefully – there's no sign that the women in the kitchen are ever going to sit down and eat, and the sight and smell of all the food have made me hungry. The dishes of *shfut* and bread with eggs that I saw in the kitchen don't appear at this sitting, but there is a plentiful delicious dinner.

We leave after lunch. After a rest at home, I set off for the afternoon, still pondering who I'll visit today, when a little girl comes running behind me and pulls at my hand.

'Come to the *hariye*, the bride's party!'

So I follow her, and find a place in a smallish, very crowded room. I know a couple of faces. The women I don't already know ask me the usual questions.

'Haven't you got any children?'

'No, I don't want them now.'

'What do you do not to have them?'

'I take pills.'

Fatima, who I've met before, with a wide, tired face, leans towards me and says earnestly,

'Give me some of them! I've had four children, they all died, my husband doesn't want any more, he has children from his first wife.' (The first wife is dead.)

'I can't give them to you, it has to be from a doctor, they have to check you.'

'It's *haram* to take pills like that,' says another woman.

'They give you haemorrhage,' says another.

I say they've never given me haemorrhage, but it is important to see a doctor. Then we talk about marriage. They all agree more than one wife is good for the man but bad for the woman, and they would be unhappy if their husband took another wife 'on top of' them.

They say: 'Women marry again here after divorce. Do they where you come from?'

'Yes. Can a woman divorce her husband here?' I ask.

'Only if he doesn't pay her keep for a year, or two or three, then she could go to the government.'

'To the hakim, or the town prefect?'

'Any government. Otherwise a woman can't divorce.'

'What if her husband beats her?'

'She will go home for a bit.'

The words of the evening call to prayer break out in the distance, rise, reach a crescendo.

'*Maghreb*! *Gduh maghreb*!'

The women adjust and retie the *lithma*s over their mouths and foreheads, reach for their outer coverings, arrange shawls and skirts, compose themelves to leave, and say their good evenings.

Outings with Khadija

I find Khadija in her yard busy with a sack of grain. She's cleaning *dhura*, sorghum. First she measures it, in a flat-bottomed wooden container which counts as a half-measure. The grain fills it eight times, so she ties four kernels into the corner of her *saramiya* headcloth as a record of the amount. Then she pours some of the grain into a wide, round metal tray and stands up and shakes it in the wind for the chaff to fly off. She sits down again and shakes it in the tray. Blackish bits come to the surface, and she scoops this top layer off into a plastic bag.

'This is for the chickens,' she explains to me. Then she sorts it handful by handful into another tray. The last bit she shakes till small stones fall to the bottom, then picks up handfuls, shakes the grains from them, and throws away the stones.

'It comes from the family lands down the mountain. It's not good, from the rain.' She finishes and leans back. 'My back aches. It would be nice to be dead and rest, life is *ta'ab*. Do you want to come for a *dowra* to warm up?'

We go into the house for Khadija to put on her *sharshaf*, black overskirt, cape, gauze veil over her face. When we set off, as always she doesn't take the direct route through the town and past the mosque, where men gather, nor the more exposed path round the outside of the town, but weaves discreetly through between the houses.

It's a fine, clear day. The sun feels good after the recent days of mist that crept in round the mountain and up to the foot of the town. Then mist penetrated the whole town till we were effectively living inside a cloud. Everything was cold and slimy to the touch. Green mould the colour of verdigris appeared on our wooden kitchen door and furred Tim's spare jambiya belt where it hung on the wall. I got up out of bed one morning and slipped and fell over on the wet lino. People huddled indoors over charcoal braziers and complained of the cold.

'Is it cold like this where you come from?' Khadija asked me.

'Much colder sometimes, and snow. But we have heating in the houses.'

'The Imam is there, poor man.' Khadija doesn't remember Yemen's former ruler with any great affection: 'The days of the Imam were hard, there were no doctors, no medicine, people died of hunger, but the Imam refused wheat from Canada, threw it in the sea... He took his money out, put it in Switzerland before he left.' Still, she feels sorry for him exiled in the snows of London.

This morning when we saw sun again Tim and I washed clothes and shook out blankets on the roof. Now it's good to feel the warmth of the sun, breathe in the clear air and see the blue sky with just a few small white puffs of cloud, and the road curving out of sight in the distance before it twists down to the wadi, peaks rising up, distant villages, and further still the side of Milhan to the west.

We walk out beyond the town to an outcrop of rocks, Khadija's favourite spot, a promontory jutting out over a drop to a valley, a fold between mountains. We find flattish places among the rocks and make ourselves comfortable on the smooth stone, slightly warm to the touch where it's been in the sun, still clammy in the shadow. Birds are singing around us, larks perhaps. Khadija puts her veil back over her head, takes out binoculars from under the folds of her *sharshaf* and scans the land below. The terraces look like contour lines sprung to life, faithfully following every curve and projection of the mountain slopes, each a mere few metres wide, some narrower than the height of their retaining walls. The strips of land they hold are coloured solid green or bare ploughed-earth brown, or filled with a pattern of regular dots, sparse and small or larger and fuller, depending on how old the bushes are. From up here the land looks flat below us, like a frenetic abstract pattern on paper with loops and swirls and spots in greens and browns, something vaguely 1970s. The bushes are mostly qat, the newer plantings perhaps replacing coffee bushes, since qat is more profitable now. More Yemenis, rich – at that time but never again – with remittances from Saudi Arabia or the Gulf, can afford more qat, as indulgence or conspicuous consumption.

Here and there a single white-painted house sits on a rock among the fields, or a little group forms a hamlet. Behind the brown-and-green foreground, the next mountain peak is a little paler and greyer. The next behind that is almost monochrome grey-blue, the jutting angularities of the rock defined by darker shadow. Behind that, the same, but faded. Then peaks in silhouette, one, two, three, four behind each other, of ever paler blue, till the last one just shows faint against the sky. At least seven successive rows of peaks, seven distinguishable shades of blue fading backwards.

Khadija points out the terraces below and tells me who they belong to, and which are the lands of her dead husband's family, worked by sharecroppers, where she goes to pick qat and coffee. A kestrel sails past below us, over the great drop, on unmoving wings. I can see the orange-brown colour of its back.

'*Etneffesi*! Breathe in, relax, enjoy the view.'

The connection the word holds between breathing and relaxation and enjoyment seems particularly apposite here, where the expanse of the view and the keen pure air lift up the heart.

'When my husband was alive I couldn't come out for walks. He didn't allow his wives and daughters to go out except at '*asha*, not in the daytime, so no one saw them.'

'Not even to *rabakh*?' I ask, shocked, for the afternoons relaxing in company seem a vital, inalienable part of women's lives.

'No.'

Even now, Khadija doesn't go visiting among the townswomen, except to the hakim's house and the houses of the sheikh's family, and for special obligations like mourning visits.

An old woman with a brown wrinkled face, Shu'iya, comes out from a nearby house to join us, and we sit and chat.

'Look at the tractor down there, whose is that?'

'It's new, it belongs to *beit* Ismail.'

It's the first to be seen in the whole mountain, bought by the family we stayed with in our early days. Some say it's a crazy waste of money, there's not enough flat land it can be used on. Others say it's a wonderful idea and will pay for itself in four months.

Shu'iya and Khadija point and discuss and argue about the lands spread out below and whom each bit belongs to.

As we talk the mist comes rolling up, like an advancing tide, through a gap to our right between the spur where we're sitting and the mountain beyond.

On another sunny day Khadija takes me on a *dowra* to get qat from the family lands below the town, the land we could see from above. We skirt the town and take an easy path down. On the terraces, down among the qat bushes, she examines them judiciously and picks carefully selected shoots.

'Not the ones from low down, those will grow.' She puts the qat straight into a sheet of plastic. She also collects and carries firewood, mostly twigs, and she puts the qat underneath.

'Let me carry something for you.'

'No, it'll get sun on it.' I think she doesn't quite trust me with the precious qat.

There are also fruit trees on the land, and Khadija keeps giving me fruit to eat – an apple, a peach, a pomegranate. They are very small, all unripe, crunchy and revoltingly astringent. I try not to pucker up my mouth at the taste.

As we climb back up the hill, Khadija with her load, she sends me on ahead to fetch her daughter to help her. After I've delivered the message I go on some errands of my own, chasing up the post, and then go to look for Khadija, but don't find her. There's a *sharshaf*ed woman coming through the *suq*, but I'm not sure if it's her; I give her a look but she says nothing, doesn't respond at all. Only later she says yes, it was her.

Khadija says 'yes' with a lift of her head, sometimes a click of her tongue too – a gesture that in other parts of the Middle East, certainly in Turkey, would mean 'no'.

Exchanges with the neighbours

Khadija beckons me from her window. I'm on my way back to our house; I've just been to the houses of two women who have asked me for photos of their children, but they were both out. So I go in to her house instead, and she gives me *gahwa*, and we sit in her living room with the view on to the street, and sip together.

'I've been *ghathi*, depressed, this morning,' she tells me. 'I didn't get up till 2,' (8am) 'and I cried three times, on the roof, in the kitchen...'

'Why?'

'I don't know – maybe thinking of my father.'

'Is he dead?'

'No, he's still alive. I'm often like this, I have been ever since leaving my *bilad*, my own part of the country. It's a mountain like here, as green as Ta'izz [a fertile area further south in Yemen]; you could see the sea and Saudi Arabia from it. I haven't been back there for twelve years.'

'How far away is it?'

'Four, five hours driving.'

'What about your mother, is she alive?'

'No, she was already dead when I left to get married.'

'Did you want to?'

'*Nasib min Allah.*' Fate is from God.

She was one of four wives, settled in different towns where her husband had land. Her husband had twelve wives in his life. Sixteen of his sons died when they were small.

'I had a boy die before he could walk, from whooping cough, and a girl. My husband would stay with me only a little, then maybe not come back until three months after the birth of the child.'

She asks me, 'Do you want to see the party on the *sullabe*?' This is the flat, open stretch of wasteland just beyond the town. We go up to her roof and sit on the smooth whitewashed surface to watch what's going on. The sun warms our skin and the sounds of conversation, speeches and drumming come floating up. The occasion is a reception party for a TV crew from Sana'a who visit different areas of Yemen in turn. The resulting TV programmes never show any qat, and Tim and I have been wondering how they will manage here, where no picture of the surrounding land could really avoid it. The women I was looking for were probably up on good vantage roofs, watching the gathering and the visiting drummer. Later we see the drummer leaving the town at the end of the reception, in the back of a pick-up truck, still drumming.

I pick up the conversation again. 'Were you sad to leave your *bilad*?'

'Yes, I'm sad to this day.'

By the time her children come from school and she gives them *subuh*, a morning snack, Khadija has recovered her equanimity. She seems cheerful and jolly.

I'm lying in bed, ill with a fever. But now there's a rattling on the roof door, pebbles falling against it again. I drag myself out of bed and up the stairs to see what it is. Thuraya is standing on her roof.

'What are you doing?' she asks me.

'I'm ill, I was lying down.'

'Who will help me?' exclaims Thuraya, with a dramatic gesture of helplessness, a shrug of her shoulders, hands spread out.

'What do you want?'

'Guests arrived suddenly, I want two chickens for supper.'

I am becoming established, now, as her errand-runner. I'm happy to be able to do something in return for her kindness to me and her patience at explaining. Dizzy and weak, I force myself to the shop that sells frozen chickens from France. I struggle over to my neighbours' house with the two chickens. There's a great bustling, frantic preparations. Thuraya is tying her things up in bundles to clear her smaller room for the guests, men from her family, to sleep in.

I collapse back into bed.

The guests who descend on our neighbours across the way always cause a great to-do. Another day, I'm just going into our house when Nuriya my downstairs neighbour comes out of her room to say, 'The *naqib*'s wife was calling for you.'

I go across the alleyway to Khadija and find her very busy. 'We've got guests, from my husband's family – can you cook my chicken on your gas burner?' The chicken is cut up and ready in a pan, with *samn*, plenty of *filfil* ground chilli pepper mixture, salt crystals and water. I carry it carefully back and put it on our gas ring.

After a while Khadija comes over to see if it's cooking as it should be. After some more time Karima comes to tell me to bring it. Later she comes again, to the bottom of my stairs, with *helba* and bread for me. 'I couldn't shout from the roof,' she says, 'because of the men.'

'How many guests have you got?'

'A lot! I don't know how many, I haven't seen them.'

I'm struck by the image of the women working away below, running around and coping with the sudden demands, while their unseen and uncounted guests sit at ease up in the *mafraj*.

Market day, and I climb Thuraya's stairs to ask if she has errands.

'No, I don't want anything. Ask Khadija if she does.'

I go down a level to Khadija.

'I wanted okra, but Karima's already been, she said there wasn't any.'

I manage to find some okra. I wander around the market a bit, enjoying the bustle, then take it back. Khadija is up on her roof washing clothes.

'Wait till I come down, I'll give you some *lehuh*.'

Khadija asked me for garlic two days ago. 'I put a whole head in when I cook beef, to make it nice.'

I forgot to take it. Now I remember and go across the alleyway with it.

'It doesn't matter, because they didn't come yesterday.' She was expecting guests, once again men of her dead husband's family. They went off down the mountain to see their lands further down and to deal with a dispute between their agent and a sharecropper.

'Do you want *gahwa*?' Khadija asks.

'Aren't you busy?' It's noon, the run-up to lunch.

'Yes, I am.' I feel pleased that I know better, now, than to accept the offer of *gahwa* at this time of day.

In the early afternoon I hear pebbles rattling on my roof. When I put my head out at the top of the stairs, Khadija calls from her roof to me to come and get bread. Once I'm in her kitchen she gives me a large piece of sweet *bint* and some slices of melon.

'Where's Abdullah?'

'He's at home.'

'If he wasn't here you could have had *gheda* with us. I got a whole meal ready for the guests, and they haven't turned up.'

'Won't it keep till tomorrow?'

'They want it fresh.'

'Will you do this every day till they come back?' I ask, amazed she has gone to all the work of cooking a full-scale formal lunch for nothing.

'Yes.'

I am sorry about the *gheda*, certainly nicer than what we'll be eating, and the convention that means she can't invite Tim into this female household, and the assumption that I couldn't eat with them and leave him to look after himself. I take back her bowl a couple of days later, feeling guilty that I forgot it yesterday, when she probably needed it for the guests.

'They went today.' She takes me up the stairs and shows me the top *mafraj*, not yet cleaned, littered with qat residue, the bits of the bundles that weren't tender enough to chew. The acrid, mouth-puckering smell hits you as you go in. The discarded twigs and leaves lie heaped, drying and curling. She gives me a bunch of leftover qat, still fresh from being kept carefully covered and cool.

Khadija calls me early in the afternoon.

'Here's some *jehin* and *khobz* for you,' she says when I go over, handing me the rounds, two different kinds of flat bread. 'There's a *ma'shara* ceremony this evening, I'll ask where it is. Can you bring your blender over? I want to use it for *filfil* pepper.'

I bring her the electric blender, and she tells me where the tray ceremony is being held, the beginning of another wedding. After I get back from the *ma'shara* we grind the dried red chillies to powder in the blender.

'My sister has a blender like this, but it's got no top, so the pepper makes you sneeze.'

The television's on, and she asks me, 'Is that fat man real?' He's only moderately fat, but really fat people are not seen around here. '*Filfil* keeps Yemenis thin,' says Khadija.

'It needs thyme to go with the pepper,' she says.

'I have some, I'll bring it tomorrow.'

The next day I go round with the thyme and my camera. I'm hoping to photograph Karima's hand, which she showed me yesterday, decorated with black *khadhab* in swirling patterns that go all up the arm.

'The girls are at Hasib getting water, they went there three hours ago.'

We sit down and drink *gahwa*. I mention that Tim is ill and lying down.

'Then can I borrow a bowl of sugar? I was going to ask Abdullah to carry a sackful for me back to the house, I'm getting it on credit from the shopkeeper.' It's hard to manage, she says, on the meagre allowance the family give her; she has to borrow and get things on credit. 'They have lots of money, trunks full,' she says. I picture Indian painted tin trunks, full, perhaps, of silver Maria Theresa dollars.

'The government is weak,' she goes on, 'the officials are corrupt. Eight women are registered as employed at the school as cleaners and so on, they draw salaries and never set foot in it.'

'The same is true for the clinic,' I say.

'The school management take levies from the students for things like a water tank for the teachers, but then they keep the money. And the municipal government – far more street cleaners are salaried than ever do any work.'

'There's a lot of dirt in the streets, and sometimes human shit in plastic bags and on pieces of cardboard.'

'People with no bathroom throw it out. I have to empty the room underneath our bathroom myself, no one will empty it now, they refuse.' Like our house, hers has a long-drop latrine where the solids fall into a closed chamber beneath.

'How do you do it?'

'I take it outside the town in cardboard boxes. There used to be a day labourer who did it for fifty or one hundred riyals a day.'

'Can it be used for fertiliser?'

'No one wants it. Our other bathroom, which was the men's, has a drop the height of the house and has never been filled up. Also rats eat it.'

She turns to look critically at a loose hair on my jumper.

'Your hair's all falling out, do you use hair oil?' We are interrupted by the noise of drumming outside. 'Go out and see. I'm going up on the roof to listen.'

I follow the sound and it leads me to the wedding house. Outside it is a boy I recognise, a butcher on market days. He is sharpening a knife. I hear drumming from inside, then a sheep is brought out, then a group of unrecognisable, completely veiled women emerge as the sheep is slaughtered. The bride treads on the freshly killed sheep, I'm told afterwards, though I don't see her do it because the women are in the way. The group goes to the *diwan*, the big room where the wedding party is being held, leaving behind them the slaughtered, still twitching sheep, which the butcher then skins, cleans and cuts up on the spot. A woman brings him out a bowl of water from the house.

The gathering in the *diwan* for this first day is pleasanter, a bit less crowded and noisy than the second day. I give a woman from the sheikh's house a copy of a cassette I recorded from an earlier part of the wedding, and she gets me to dance with her. She is very short and I find the bending movements hurt my knees, and feel I'm doing it less well than before.

'Have you got money to give the *muzayyina*?' she asks. 'You have to give her some, for playing as we danced.'

I feel embarrassed, because I've danced before and not known to give her anything. I go to get money from my bag, but when I try to give it to the *muzayyina* she won't take it from me, she absolutely refuses to accept it.

'We-eh, *ya* Mariam!'

It's Thuraya, calling to me as I make my way home through the alley. 'Can you bring a spanner for my gas?'

Tim and I go over together, with a spanner, some Tang orange juice powder we bought in Sana'a, a photo album Thuraya asked me to get her there, and a headscarf as a present. We change her gas bottle.

We are glad to be able to do things for our neighbours. We have fallen into a patron/client relationship with them, and unlike many anthropologists in the field, especially in postcolonial settings, we are the clients, the weaker party. We are drawn into the web of small exchanges that enable them to get by. They often give us bread, and sometimes food. More importantly, they are kind and patient with my slowly improving speech and understanding. We are learning from them what it means here to be neighbours.

Earthquake

The house is shaking and trembling all around me. It goes on shaking for long seconds.

I am used to the floors of our shabby little house vibrating as we walk on them. But this is much more, all over. My first thought is that our house is falling down. I rush to go out on the roof. This is perhaps unwise, but it's my immediate instinct, the way I'm used to seeing what's happening. But the door is locked and Tim – maddeningly, *jinni bizzuh*, a *jinni* take him! – has gone out with the key. Before I really have time to panic, after perhaps twenty seconds, the shaking stops. Tim comes back almost at once. It was an earth tremor, he says. Our house, with the rest of the town, seems undamaged.

We only find out how serious it was when we listen to the evening news on the radio: it's the first item on the BBC World Service, a large earthquake in Dhamar to the southeast of us. I need to contact my parents in England to tell them we are all right. The next day I knock on the door of the *muwasalat*, the communications office. The office is one small bare room off the street near our house where the town telephone is operated by the communications representative. This is the only telephone I know of in the town apart from the town prefect's, and possibly one privately owned by the sheikh. The communications representative keeps the numbers of frequently contacted relatives in Saudi Arabia and Sana'a and dials for the townspeople on request. I spend money, and a 20-riyal connection fee on top, trying to reach my parents in England. I am frustrated and the money is wasted: it's impossible to get through.

I try again later in the afternoon and succeed this time, though I'm overcharged by the communications representative. Men are sitting around in the office, passing the afternoon and discussing events. 'The earthquake went all round the earth,' they inform me. Meanwhile, at his afternoon qat chew, Tim is told that the Day of Judgement is at hand. A few days later, he hears that an eighth of the *zakat* Islamic tax money from each area is to be given as aid for victims of the earthquake. Tim pays 300 riyals for the benefit of earthquake victims to an official in the government buildings and gets an official receipt.

The Yemeni television news always begins with an account of the activities of the president, making visits, receiving dignitaries, showing him incongruous, short, somehow amateur and informal in his bearing beside the stiff, dignified leaders of other countries. This is only four years into his presidency, before anyone could have predicted it would last another thirty years. Now the news shows him visiting the stricken area. The earthquake, it says, was six on the Richter scale; at least eight hundred people were killed, 150 in a school which collapsed, and a thousand injured, and eighty villages destroyed. The programme shows pictures of Yemenis giving blood to help the victims. There are also trained dogs, from Germany, sniffing for people under the rubble. This is a source of amazement to people we hear talking about it. Feral dogs roam the town, picking over rubbish, feared and despised. Skilled, helpful dogs are a revelation.

The prime minister talks about tectonic plates on the television, but Tim hears a group of men discussing how the quake was caused by men sleeping with their sisters and drinking alcohol, and by Bilqis, the Queen of Sheba, rising from the grave to set a licentious nation to rights.

In the evening, before *maghreb*, the mosque broadcasts prayers for the dead.

I go over to take Thuraya some shopping from the market, a sweet that she asked for, *mushebbek*, batter deep-fried in spirals and soaked in sugar syrup. She told me to pay 20 riyals for it. Women know the price of everything in the market even though they don't go there.

'The man said twenty-five, but you said twenty so I knew.'

'He was trying to overcharge you,' Khadija says. 'People overcharge you and Abdullah.'

Men from the family are there, a brother and an uncle of Khadija's dead husband. They have come over from Mahwit, three hours' drive away, because the phone lines there aren't working after the earthquake, and they need to contact their senior relative in Saudi Arabia. A house with three families in, women, full of stuff and Maria Theresa dollars, is cracked and likely to fall down, and they want to know what to do.

'Did you get through to your mother?' Khadija asks me.

'Yes, but she wasn't very worried. She said she looked at a map and saw the earthquake was quite a long way away from Safaqayn.'

Khadija sighs, wistful. 'Reading is wonderful.'

'Can your mother read?' Karima asks me.

Khadija says bitterly, 'We're *guresh*.' Cattle, domestic animals, kept in dark stables. It's not the only time I hear women say this. 'We are *guresh*, *baha'im*' – cattle, female donkeys – is a stock way they describe themselves: their lack of knowledge of the world, their situation, uneducated and confined.

Khadija was determined that her daughters should go to school, insisted to her dead husband's family and got her way. '*Bi samil*,' she says, shaking a clenched fist; by force.

A visit to a village

'Are you pregnant?' I ask. Lively, bright Warda who explains things to me, and who said she hoped to get pregnant when her husband returned for last Ramadan, has just complained that her stomach hurts.

'No.'

Her *salifa*s, the wives of her two brothers, say, 'Oh yes she is! She's just shy about it, *tistaha*.'

'And *she's* pregnant,' says the elder brother's wife, indicating the younger, 'and so am I.'

'You're not shy, then?'

'No, I'm used to it.' It's her sixth pregnancy. She already has three children, and two that died.

It's mid-afternoon, but they've only just finished lunch. I'm in their small living room, barely big enough for Warda's brothers and their wives and the children, sitting against cushions drinking tea, because Warda has invited me to go back with her to her husband's house. His village is an hour and a half's walk away. A girl came to me earlier with the message that she was going today.

Warda's husband is working in Saudi Arabia, but her mother-in-law needs her labour. Warda's mother went to stay there for a while to help with the cow, giving her daughter a chance to enjoy life in the town. It's obvious that she prefers to be here. She manages to get back quite often, is at every wedding, a vivacious presence at gatherings, teasing and joking. I guess she's reluctant to resume the life of hard work in the countryside, under her mother-in-law, that her marriage entails.

'My mother warned me,' she tells me twenty-six years later, when her mother-in-law is dead and she's had nine children and has left the village and is living in Sana'a. 'She said, it'll be hard work in the country, looking after a cow. But I wanted to marry him. He had two cars!' She shrugs, laughing at her own youthful folly.

I'm looking forward to the walk. It's a fine day with a high, clear sky. You can see the village we're going to, huddled on its own flat spur of the mountainside, away below the town, and I itch to set off down through the landscape towards this often-glimpsed target. Even more, I'm looking forward to the chance to talk with Warda along the way and get to know her better.

But one of her brothers takes us in his car out of the town along the motor track, and then she finds a man who's going that way soon, and persuades him to take us now. 'My luck's good, isn't it!' says Warda as we scramble into the cab. I feel that mine isn't. The ride is neither quicker nor easier than walking. It's jolting and bumping as we are thrown now to one side, now to the other, inching along an appalling track.

The house we arrive at, in the late afternoon, has a village-house layout like others I've seen. Downstairs is space for animals and a *safil*, a storeroom, with sacks of flour in it, and the kitchen. The best room or *mafraj* is on the first floor looking over the flat roof of the main building below. There is a small room beside it on the first floor as well. Downstairs, the sister and daughter of Warda's mother-in-law, currently staying in the house, sleep. The sister is visiting from the mountain to the east 'to warm up', she says. The daughter's husband is also in Saudi Arabia.

All over the mountain, young men are away working in Saudi Arabia. Many are saving up to get married. If they are already married, their wives stay in their marital household with the husband's parents, or go back to their natal household and return when their husband visits. They are still, always, under the protection of and answerable to a man somewhere. Where many men are absent, decisions don't get made: girls go unmarried for want of fathers to arrange it, children miss vaccination because there isn't a man to take them.

Warda's mother-in-law has white hair coloured orange-red with henna, and wears a Saudi robe. The older neighbour women who come in, all very chatty and friendly, wear smocks, *qamis*, with wide sleeves, an older local fashion which you don't see in the town. Of course, they also wear trousers underneath. They give me some qat. They all leave at *maghreb*, then come back again at 8 or 9pm to *semer*.

In the meantime we have supper, *lehuh* and tinned peas and cooked fresh ones. The neighbour women are splendid coarse old ladies who make jokes about peas and farting all evening with lots of laughter. I sit hard on the heel of the leg tucked underneath me. The electricity generator tries to struggle into life, then gives up, so we can't watch television. We sit up talking instead till 11 or 12, a very enjoyable evening.

We talk about marriage. I ask: is it usual for girls to cry before their marriage?

'They stop after the first night,' says Warda.

'*You* didn't,' one of the women says, laughing, teasingly, 'you cried next day.'

'From happiness,' says Warda unconvincingly.

They tell me plant names to add to my growing list.

Warda shows me where I can relieve myself, and where they also go with bowls of cold water to do their ablutions, at the back of the side of the house, quite secluded behind stones and tall cacti. 'It's much better in the country,' one woman says, 'you can go outside. Poor things, town people are close together and have no room outside, they have to have smelly bathrooms in their houses.'

'Which do you think is better,' I ask Warda when we're on our own, 'a bathroom, or outside?'

'A bathroom.'

Warda and her mother-in-law and I go to sleep in the little room next door to the reception room, Warda on a high bed and the mother-in-law and I on foam mattresses. In the morning when I get up the mother-in-law's bed is already empty, but Warda stays in bed till 9, complaining of backache and feeling ill. Her mother-in-law comes and tells her to get up: '*Gumi! Gumi!*'

When Warda does get up, she washes her face and hands and arms in a bowl of cold water, without soap, scratching at her arms to get the dirt out. Then she and I go to get water, from a spring that runs into a pool. Back at the house, women drop in all morning and we sit first out on the roof, then in the *mafraj*.

Warda's father-in-law must be dead; it's an all-female household. They have another house, in the middle of the village, where their two cows have a room each and there are sleeping rooms upstairs which the family use if men come.

Warda's husband's sister goes off to look for qat. There's very little at the moment, it seems, and there's discussion and speculation about where to get it, whether a man over there is bringing some. But the women who come to *rabakh* for the afternoon bring a supply. There are a lot of black dresses, less colour than in the town. Except for

Warda, women wear almost no gold, but silver instead, lovely old beautifully worked necklaces with big, round silver beads. Everybody thinks Warda knows some of my language, because I understand her better than I do them. But she is just one of those people who are good at making themselves clear, and at grasping my meaning.

I half mean to leave, but I stay to *rabakh*, then get given lots of qat by the women, who keep hardly any for themselves, despite my protests; and then it gets obviously too late.

'Stay till Thursday, there'll be cars going to the *suq* in the *merkez* then.'

'I must get back to Abdullah.'

'Will he be worried about you?'

'No, he knows I'm with Warda.'

The English news comes on, and they ask if I understand every word.

'Well, yes, it's my language!'

'I've been to London,' Warda's mother-in-law says. 'With a relative, we went from Saudi Arabia.' This seems to me staggeringly unlikely, but when she says how cold and rainy it was, and that the cats were big and fat and walked slowly, unafraid, in the streets, not running away like Yemeni cats, I begin to think it's true.

'I didn't go in an English house, just a hotel. And I went to another country and stayed a month there – but I don't know its name.'

The evening is much less fun this time because the electricity is working and we watch videos. First there's a costume drama about the Arab hero Antar, with escapes, fights and dungeons; then an Iraqi film of women dancing. In the end I nod off.

'Go to bed, you're sleepy!'

Next morning Warda again lies in bed while her mother-in-law shouts, '*Gumi*! *Gumi*!'

'I feel ill,' she says, 'my head, and everything.'

A local man whom her mother-in-law calls *doktur* visits, sitting in the *mafraj*, giving the mother-in-law Novalgin pills for a bad knee. His diagnosis is that Warda's body and her foetus are missing her husband.

'That's the reason she's ill. If she's not better soon, I'll give her an injection.'

I say goodbye to Warda, who is still in bed, and leave. Her mother-in-law comes out to see if there are any cars, then comes out along the road with me, to shout at some men going on foot to show me the path. The route turns out to be hard to find, but not very hard walking. I'm glad to be out in the clear air, feeling the small stones and tufts of grass beneath my flip-flops. One man very chivalrously and courteously insists on taking my hand where the path goes over smooth rock without footholds. I keep up quite well, at least until we reach an uphill bit; I feel pleased to hear the man say to another, '*ma lha she*,' she's OK. The other, a man from the town, replies, 'Mariam's a man and a half.'

On the way towards the town I hear a shout from Yahya's village. It's Tim shouting for me. So I alter my direction to go round that way, and find Tim helping haul stones with a wheelbarrow. He spent the night there. We are very pressingly urged to stay, but after drinking tea we succeed in leaving to climb up home. I am desperate for a good wash in warm water, and my head is overloaded, buzzing from talking.

I go out later to take messages to Warda's brother's house, and to her neighbour, my friend Amina: her mother, I am to tell her, is coming from the village tomorrow.

'The women in that village are not nice,' Warda's older brother's wife says. I can't get an exact reason out of her. I enjoyed their company.

Taking photos

'Katiba! We-eh, *ya* Katib-*eh*!' I call as I turn through an arched stone doorway and enter the dark and cool of a big old house.

A girl comes out. 'There's no Katiba here!'

'I'm looking for Katiba, she wanted a picture of her children,' I explain. I thought she said this was where she lived.

It's a morning in March, sunny and bright and good to be out in: my second March in Safaqayn. I'm out on my rounds with my camera. This is before the days of cameras that slip in a pocket. My SLR weighs seven hundred grams, so I don't usually take it out with me.

When I do, I take innumerable pictures of people's children. I photograph grubby children in torn clothes that are too big or too small for them, and children who have been carefully got ready, dressed up in new best clothes, some bought in Sana'a or Saudi Arabia. When I find Katiba, her daughter, a child of five or six, wears a dress with endless elaborations: lacy additions, a waistcoat, bows, ruffles and frills. I also photograph her kitchen, newly recoated in smooth earth. 'It has cracks, we want to pull it down. The room upstairs is hardly used – I sit downstairs with the children and my husband doesn't *rabakh* in the house.'

Next to the kitchen is a storage space with sacks of flour and sugar and a carton of milk tins. She has six children, and three dead, and is pregnant. She didn't want to be, she explains; she got pregnant two months after the birth of the previous child, while she was still breastfeeding. 'Before, I breastfed for two years and didn't get pregnant. I'm worn out, there's no one to help me. My eldest girl is not very big, and now she can't go to school because there's no one else to help me in the house.'

Her brother's daughter is there, lending a hand, but she's just leaving to go home. Katiba's baby is in a swinging cradle. The cradle swings too far and the baby falls out, on its head, and cries for a bit, but quietens down.

'I've been examined in Sana'a, Hodeida, several times – they say my blood is weak. Life is hard, too much work, I'm too tired.' I offer what sympathy I can.

At another house I take a photo of a swaddled baby, neatly tied up like a parcel from head to foot with a ribbon wound round and round a black-and-white headcloth. The bundled-up baby seems serene, as if to bear out what women say, that swaddling keeps their babies calm. Then the mother unwraps it and I take another picture, of a wriggly, kicking baby with a mobile face and wiggling toes, in new, slightly-too-big clothes and a pointed *gargush* hood.

In the next house I go to, a small girl carefully holds another baby, jolly and plump in a green bought dress and a matching *gargush*, and tickles it under the chin to make it chuckle for the photo.

Someone hails me from a window. 'Mohammed 'Atanah's wife wants her pictures!'

First I go to the wrong house, and photograph *their* baby. Then I find the house of Mohammed 'Atanah's wife, Nuriya – who hennaed me in my first few days in the town – and give her some prints of her baby that I took a few weeks ago. She wants more pictures of him now he can sit up, and also some of her little girl. She knows I gave Abdul Mughni's wife seventeen pictures of her children.

'Do you want money for the pictures?'

'No, no.'

She gives me some raisins.

Then I move on to the house of a recent bride. On my way up the stairs I hear my name called. It's another woman who lives in the same house, inviting me in. She lives in one room, a recent widow who will soon remarry, once her waiting period is up. I've often sat next to her, *rabakh*ing with her neighbours. Now she gives me a snack of watermelon. Then I climb the stairs to the rooms I was aiming for.

I photographed the bride with her new husband, standing side by side as a couple, and now I have the prints. She's pleased with the pictures, but not with her marriage.

'How are you?' I ask, and get a frank reply.

'He's no good. He's dirty, just a day labourer. He knows nothing of love, he comes back tired out and goes to sleep.'

She doesn't like her mother-in-law either. 'She expects me to go out getting fodder for the cow. I'm not used to this kind of work – I don't know how to use a *sherim*.' That's the small sickle that women tuck into the backs of their dresses and use for weeding or gathering fodder.

Her mother-in-law is from outside the town. This is the clash of expectation between a girl brought up in relative urban leisure, and a married-in country woman of an older generation who worked hard on the hillsides.

In Selma Abdullah's house, I find her lying on a high bed, its legs raised up on the usual old baby-milk powder tins. It always seems to me symbolic or ironic that the beds of new mothers are propped on tins from this ubiquitous product that – given instead of breast milk, mixed in wrong quantities by women with no access to clean water – has been responsible for so much damage to the health of Yemeni babies. Selma gave birth recently. Her mother is there and her schoolgirl daughter Semira, a serious student who has completed elementary and is now in the first intermediate class, is at home to help. Her younger sister doesn't study at all. On a previous occasion I asked Semira why. 'My father won't let her, she has to stay at home and help my mother.'

I also found out then that Semira knows her exact age, fourteen. This is so unusual that I asked her how she knew. 'My father can read, he writes down all the births. If my mother gives birth in the night, he writes it down in the morning. In an exercise book, kept in the trunk.'

I hand Selma two tins of fruit, the standard offering to women lying in. (It seems standard to me, since that's what I always see people giving, perhaps a tin of apple slices and one of pineapple; but women have complained to me that 'the big people want more', two tins of fruit isn't enough to be an acceptable gift for the elite of the town. A woman from the sheikh's family will have earned 5,000–6,000 riyals by the end of her lying-in, they claimed.) The room smells of rue and feverfew. Semira tries to give me a bunch of rue but I refuse it. 'Thanks, I don't like the smell.'

We hear voices and laughter outside the door and a group of women and girls, Fatima Abdu, her two little sisters, and her cousin with her baby come in. Selma unwraps the baby from his tight swaddles. His eyes are smeared with blue-black *kohl* and his small face is yellow with turmeric.

'What's his name?'

'Sultan... Faris...' she suggests tentatively.

'Ramzi,' Fatima Abdu suggests. 'There isn't a Ramzi here.'

Selma has had five children still alive and four dead. I photograph the baby, the father of the family with a small boy, and the daughter holding a younger boy on her hip.

'Come with us and see my brother,' says Fatima Abdu, turning to me. I leave with the little group. First they decide to go and visit their cousin Fatima, whose wedding I went to a year ago. She has a baby girl, another *kohl*- and turmeric-smeared baby, wrapped up in clothes and a towel. I photograph the baby in the arms of her father, a young mechanic in an oil-stained shirt who holds her tenderly in large, competent hands. Fatima's two boys and a girl from her first marriage are there. 'Are they living with you?' I ask.

'The boys go back in the evening to their father.'

I photograph one more child in Meruwagha, the son of a woman whose other children I photographed yesterday. I'm not sure who she is. Fatima Abdu and her little sisters and I climb the hill together to Safaqayn, and take the short cut up the rocks to the site of the old town gate overlooking Meruwagha. Just through the gate is Fatima's parents' house, a tall many-storeyed town house which abuts its neighbours so that they make a wall to the outside of the top part of the town. We duck through the doorway, feel our way up the stairs, and emerge into the room where Fatima's mother is lying on a high bed with a swaddled baby beside her.

Fatima herself is pregnant, now, with her first baby. Her mother has had six children that I know of, including one that died. After exchanging greetings, I excuse myself to go to a house nearby, where another Fatima, with a wide-boned face, asked me recently to come and photograph her daughter. I've known her since the early days when I went out visiting with Katiba, when she asked me if I could give her contraceptive pills.

'*En el fa'ida*,' she said then, where's the use, what's the point, in having more babies. 'I've had four, they all died.' Now she has a healthy baby girl. She takes her out from where she's lying – invisible, under the high bed in a sling suspended like a hammock – for me to take the picture.

'*Ya* Mariam! Come in to us!'

Voices call me in to next door.

Zohra is lying on a high bed; she too has recently given birth. She looks drained, exhausted, even more than all the other women I know that are depleted by frequent childbearing. I regularly assume women are ten or fifteen years older than, it turns out, they possibly can be. I take it for granted a woman is well over fifty, then am startled when she mentions her periods – feeling unwell, or performing the necessary washing after one.

'I gave birth in Hodeida, in the Chinese hospital there, after I was in labour here for four days.' So she was taken three or four hours by car, at that point, to reach the big city on the coast.

'Which is better, giving birth in hospital or at home?'

'Hospital. They gave me an injection and it came out after five minutes. There were only women in the hospital, and a woman doctor and nurse.'

The baby lying with her is tiny and red-faced.

'A child every year, every year. I've had eight, four living and four dead.'

When I leave, another woman calls me from her house, leaning out of the window, 'I've got a small baby, come and take a picture.'

I go to her, a little further along the line of houses. But my film is used up.

Religion

It's well after '*asr*, mid-afternoon, when I go round to Khadija's to *rabakh*, but she's busy praying, dressed in a loose white robe, performing her prostrations on a mat. She waves at me to go and sit down.

After a few minutes she joins me in her sitting room, still in white, and still reciting prayers when there are gaps in the conversation. She sits in her prayer clothes, smoking her *mada'a*, drinking coffee, and going over her beads muttering, all at the same time.

'Are you praying for *'asr*?'

'*Dhohr* and *'asr*.' Noon and mid-afternoon.

'Isn't it late?'

'Men have to pray at the right time, but if women are busy it's no sin for them to pray late, and two together.' She goes back into the other room to finish her prayers.

When she comes back she asks me with interest, 'How do you pray?'

Of all the women I know, Khadija is perhaps the most preoccupied with religious practice. She fasts extra days – three days in the month before Ramadan, as many other women do, and for the month of Rajab.

'The whole month?' I ask.

'Yes, for *ajr*.' Reward in heaven. '*Ajr* **kathir**!' she says with great emphasis, *lots* of *ajr*. It seems very concrete, rather as she might have said, 'Lots of money!' as if she can see it piling up for her.

But despite her own piety, Khadija never goes on at me to convert to Islam. In general, Tim has a harder time than I do. During the long afternoons chewing qat, in their dignified male emptiness, as it comes to seem to me, with the immediate, real-life concerns of children and family life that fill women's afternoon talk filtered out, men pass the time by competing to urge him, even threaten him with hellfire. It goes on for whole afternoons.

'If you convert your children would be beautiful, everything would be good for you, your salary would be increased, food would taste better...' Men who, in groups with others, are particularly pressing, who keep on the topic for hours together, are the same who at other times approach Tim in secret to ask if he has any whisky.

Of course everybody would like us to convert.

'Will your government stop your grants if you convert? You could convert and not tell anyone at home.'

In answer to the pressure we point out that, as monotheists and *ahl el kitab*, People of the Book, of the Scriptures, we are not necessarily damned as heathens are.

Now I show Khadija how Christians kneel to pray, and then I do my best, phrase by phrase, to translate the Lord's Prayer for her. She is delighted.

'*Qarib! Qarib!*' she exclaims with excitement. 'It's close! It's close!' Close to Islam: she quotes parallels and equivalents.

'We wished you would convert, and not go to the fire.'

It's the year 2000, and I'm sitting with Selma Yahya, reminiscing about how we used to sit together thirteen years ago. She's much more *murtah*, relaxed and happy, now. She's not sewing much. Her children are grown-up except for one young girl, Ashwaq, and a small boy.

Pretty, bright Ashwaq jumps to my defence. 'They're close to us, we learnt about it at school.'

'We're People of the Book,' I add.

'Yes, they're People of the Book, it's all the same God.'

I feel ridiculously grateful to her, and to education.

The town is populated by a mix of Shafi'i and Zaidi, the two main denominations of Islam in Yemen. The Zaidis historically ruled North Yemen. The villages around, we are told, are Shafi'i, so presumably the mix in the town reflects the migration of people from the Zaidi areas to the north and east to this outpost of central government. Shafi'is are Sunni, while Zaidis are Shia, although a branch that is close to Sunni Islam. It's not obvious to me who is which, and everybody says that it's not important.

One man refuses to tell us which he is. 'I don't know, these differences are only spoken about by crazy people.'

To us, at least – perhaps as outsiders – people consistently make little of the differences, of this fault line that could be seen as dividing much of the Muslim world, and certainly Yemen. The difference has been important in the country's past and will be so in the future; but here and now, it is made as little of as possible.

Once, I'm at Hamda's house with her daughter, who is sitting hennaing her hands, and the wife of a government official, who declares, 'I'm a Shafi'i.' But this is because she's been asked about the way she speaks – 'ich' instead of 'ish' – and she's talking about where she comes from, the mountains to the southwest, to explain it. So she's talking about regional identity more than religious affiliation. 'Which are people here, Zaidi or Shafi'i?' I ask her. She doesn't know.

I ask Hamda's daughter, but she seems not to understand what I'm talking about. Hamda comes back into the room and I ask her.

'I'm Shafi'i. It's mixed here. My husband is Zaidi, and my first husband was, and my son. The only difference is in how you pray, with your arms crossed in front or by your sides. My husband does sometimes one, sometimes the other.'

'And what do you do?' I ask the daughter.

'I pray with my arms by my sides.'

'Which people here are Shafi'i?'

'People from the villages. In the town it's mixed.'

'Can they marry each other?'

'Yes, but *qaba'il*, tribespeople, can't marry *jazzar*, butchers, people who slaughter animals.'

Hamda's daughter asks me: 'Are you Shafi'i or Zaidi?'

Another woman I ask says much the same.

'There are both here,' she explains. 'Shafi'is pray with their arms crossed, and Zaidis with their hands by their sides.'

'Which do you do?' I ask her.

'Sometimes one and sometimes the other.'

'Can Shafi'i and Zaidi marry each other?' I ask.

'Yes, but we can't marry butchers.'

'Why can't you?'

She simply shrugs.

I ask a group of women in Meruwagha as we sit and chew qat one afternoon; they have been asking me about my religion and how we pray. They all say they are Shafi'i. One quotes something about the Prophet saying that if you hold your arms crossed a *sheitan*, a devil, sits in the elbow crook; but that is how they say they pray. And they all emphasise that there's no difference really. There are some variations in the repetitions of the call to prayer, and whether '*amin*', amen, is said aloud or mumbled. These are the only distinctions between the denominations that I ever hear mentioned.

They say the mosque in Meruwagha is Shafi'i, but when I ask about the one in Safaqayn there is some argument; they don't seem sure.

I ask another woman, when I'm sitting with her family in her father's house, and she turns to ask her father which denomination she is. He seems put out by her ignorance and tells her sternly: 'You are from Zaid, son of Ali, son of Husain, son of Ali.'

We ask Tim's friend Yahya, one evening when he has come to sit in our room to chat and learn English.

'I wouldn't necessarily know which someone was,' he says, 'unless I stood next to him in the mosque and happened to notice how he was praying.' He says the Safaqayn mosque is Shafi'i.

One man, much given to talking at length about religion, informs Tim that the Prophet was half Zaidi and half Shafi'i, and prayed sometimes one way, sometimes the other.

'They're all the same really,' everyone says. One man declares, 'It's all one *madhhab*,' one denomination.

This is the way, again and again, that people talk to us about the two denominations. They repeatedly minimise any difference, and they focus on the position of the arms when praying, on externals rather than doctrine. It's a marker of regional identity rather than belief or politics. And in practical terms, it doesn't make much difference. Certainly, as the women show in their replies about who can intermarry, it doesn't make as much difference as the gulf between tribespeople and 'butchers'.

'Butchers'

I ask a group of women, 'Can Zaidis and Shafi'is marry each other?' and as often happens, get the reply, 'Yes, but butchers and *qaba'il*, tribespeople, can't.' These women then say they are all *qaba'il*.

'What's the difference?'

'The butchers are *naqis*, deficient. They used to serve us.'

This is a distinction where everybody knows who is which. Yet it's months before I do. I came primed, from my reading, to find this sort of division between different social strata, with *qaba'il*, 'tribespeople', distinguished from a lower-status group or groups including butchers (*jazzar*), musicians and wedding attendants. In former times, before the revolution of 1962, the men of this low-status group did not wear jambiya daggers. But at first I'm not sure who everyone is, and anyway I will learn with time that it's more complicated than that. The lower-status group are often referred to as 'butchers' in general, though they don't all actually work as butchers. 'Butchers' and 'tribespeople' all look the same. 'Butcher' men wear jambiyas now, as an indication of theoretical post-revolution equality. 'Butchers' and 'tribespeople' live cheek by jowl and whichever group they are from, women have the typically intense relationship of women who are neighbours. The women I spend afternoons with include both, often in the same room. (Women's visiting seems to me at the time more free and less structured than perhaps it really is, because of the access I have and the welcome I'm given everywhere. Even so, as time goes on, it's an effort to keep my wide range of different contacts on the go; I'm pressed to return to the same people for the afternoons, and aware that some of my associates disapprove of others.)

Tim's descriptions of male gatherings have a different feel. Sometimes low-status men are publicly mocked and teased. Sometimes they act in a serving capacity, look after the guests and tend the *mada'a* and the qat spittoons. One afternoon a group of young 'tribesmen' spend several minutes mocking a 'butcher', and they get Tim to write down all the words they use to humiliate him: *naqis*, 'deficient'; *dowshan*, a public crier or praise-singer. (There are no *dowshan*s living in the town now.)

The young 'butcher' is actually a practising butcher; we see him in the market, confident and vocal with his customers, shouting and haggling. The despised butcher, after all, sells meat, the most valued food; he potentially controls the quality of every man's dinner. In this gathering, Tim says, he sat almost silent for two hours. When I hear about these afternoons with men, I think how much less emphasised hierarchies are in the afternoons I've spent with women.

As I get to know who people are and the relationships between them, it gradually becomes clear. There is no intermarriage between the 'butcher' group, nearly a quarter of the town, and the others, the *qaba'il* or 'tribespeople'. The occupations that mark someone as a 'butcher' and are considered shameful, or would be shameful for a 'tribesman' or 'tribeswoman', include selling bread, running a restaurant, being a barber, playing music at weddings. It's not clear what is shameful about them, and the 'tribespeople' never say anything to explain it. It strikes me that many involve taking money for the basics of hospitality that are honourably offered for free. Near the end of our stay, a restaurant is started up in the town by a 'butcher' and a 'tribesman' in partnership; when we ask about this people explain the 'tribesman' is 'only helping'. The 'butchers' are not all involved in slaughtering animals or other 'shameful' occupations, but some of them are, and the whole group is densely interrelated. They have to be, since they can't marry out of the group.

The 'tribesmen' make their view of 'butchers' quite clear. 'They are *bani khums*, children of the fifth; of the fringe, wedding attendants,' a 'tribesman' tells us. The literature I've read mentions this expression, 'children of the fifth', but I haven't seen a satisfactory explanation.

'The butchers serve the tribesmen all over the world,' declares another.

'They are different from us,' another explains. More than once men tell us, 'They have a different number of teeth from us.'

I don't as often hear women talk like this. Perhaps this is partly because of the overriding importance of relations with immediate neighbours, which will often cross this divide.

I wonder how the 'butchers' see it. The dominant voice, of the 'tribespeople', seems to define the situation. Nothing I've read has given the point of view of the 'butchers'. It is only many years later that I will hear it expressed.

One morning, I'm out with my camera trying to track down people who've asked me to take pictures. I'm invited into a house by a little girl, into a small room crowded with women and children: an old woman, a younger one, Zeinab, plump and relaxed, and Seyida, sallow and harassed, with her own children plus her younger brother and sister to take care of.

'Their mother is dead, and their father remarried,' she explains.

'Seyida is my sister,' Zeinab says. I start to try to piece together the relationships and fit them with other people I know.

They give me *lehuh* with cold meat and *filfil* chilli pepper powder, an unexpectedly delicious, sour-meaty-chilli combination. They urge me to eat a piece of cold, hard liver.

'We slaughter,' Zeinab says, I think in explanation of the abundance of meat as a morning snack, offered at a time when men are out of the house, by women to women. Here is a positive side, the possibility, perhaps, of pride in this identity.

They joke about whether I should photograph the women.

'My husband wouldn't mind really,' Zeinab says, but decides against it anyway.

'Come and *rabakh* at my house!' says Seyida.

'I don't know where it is.'

'My daughter will show you.'

Another day I go to Seyida's with the pictures I've taken of her children. We sit and chat. Her two rooms aren't enough for the family, she complains.

'My husband's father had a house in the town, but they pulled it down and sold the stones. Now we're building a house outside the town, but there isn't enough money. My husband's shop doesn't give much money, it all goes on qat and coffee.'

She comes from a village down the mountain. 'Which do you prefer, town or country?' I ask her.

'They're different. Here is better, the country is more work, cows and all.'

I ask her if girls or boys are better.

'Boys are better,' she says. 'Girls are grief, they wear you out with worry.'

'Why?'

'You don't have to fear for boys when they go out.'

'Will your daughter get married soon?' I ask her. She's already told me that the daughter has *kumelan*, reached puberty.

'No, I need her help in the house.'

Then she tells me she has two sisters in Meruwagha, Hamda and Selma. I piece together the puzzle in my mind. I need to get this clear. 'So the other day, Zeinab said you were sisters, but you're not really, are you?'

'No, she's a butcher and I'm a tribeswoman.' Across this divide, unbridgeable by marriage, they are figurative sisters, women friends who help and support each other.

Another time I ask someone, 'Are you related to Ahmed Fulan?' and get the reply, distancing the other family: 'No, they slaughter.'

A 'tribesman' friend tells us how he fell in love with a pretty 'butcher' girl after he saw her at a wedding. 'I wanted to marry her, but my family and friends were angry and didn't let me.' Now, he seems to think they were right:

'My children's *khal*s, maternal uncles, would have been butchers!'

'Can *qaba'il* and butchers ever marry?' I ask some women – 'tribeswomen' – one afternoon.

'*Aib* – it's shameful, not done.'

'What about Ahmed Mohammed, I heard that he married a butcher woman?'

'He *wanted* to marry Fatima Saleh, who's now the wife of Hamadi, but all his family beat him, he gave up, he didn't actually marry her.'

'*Why* can't *qaba'il* marry butchers?'

'Because they slaughter.' The woman who's speaking makes a cutting gesture, a slice with her hand.

These marriages that didn't happen, and the very occasional ones that did – possibly one in the town, since people say our landlady's husband is a tribesman, and one in a nearby village – are all between 'tribesmen' and 'butcher' women. The other way round, a 'tribal' family giving their daughter to 'butchers', is unheard of.

At last, in 2009, I hear more of the point of view of the 'butchers'. I am visiting Safaqayn with my daughter and her friend, who are doing an Arabic course in Sana'a in their gap year. We are sitting talking with a woman who was born while Tim and I were staying in the town, twenty-seven years ago. Now she's an educated married woman with a post in the girls' school. Her children are asleep and we're sitting *semer*ing, chatting at night, in her new clean sitting room in her family's comfortable villa outside the old town.

She asks my daughter and her friend about *unsuriyya*, racism, in our country. Then she talks about the racism, in her own country, of the tribespeople's prejudice against the 'butcher' group. It's the first time I've ever heard anyone talk like this.

'They still don't respect us. We marry anybody. But they won't marry us. If we arrange an engagement with another family, in Sana'a perhaps, and they find out our origins, they break it off. Look at our girls who are sitting at home, unmarried, there's no husband for them because of this.'

'What should happen? What should the government do?' I ask.

'Raise awareness, talk about the problem in schools and on television. At the moment it's simply not talked about.'

'Do you *rabakh* together?' my daughter's friend wants to know.

'Yes.'

That's what makes the issue so confusing, so hidden. There are women in the town from elite families – Khadija, the sheikh's womenfolk, the hakim's – who don't often go to houses besides each others'. But women whose families can't intermarry often sit and *rabakh* together. The ordinary *qabili* and 'butcher' women socialise together, may live in different parts of the same house, and can't be told apart except by knowing about their family, who they are related to and married to.

In contrast to Tim's afternoons with men, I don't regularly hear women make negative comments about 'butchers'. I did once from Amina. She disliked her neighbour, our landlady, with whom she had a neighbour's quarrels and disagreements and an ongoing dispute about a piece of land. One day I was present at a bawdy conversation among a group of neighbours that included her and Amina, with rude words, for female genitals, spoken with glee and relish. Later Amina said to me: 'It was *'aib*, the women saying those words at Nuriya's the other day. It's all right for Fatima Yahya, she bakes and cooks for people, she's a butcher.'

Most 'butcher' families, however, seem to guard their reputations as much as *qaba'il*. Perhaps they even work harder to compensate, to maintain their respectability. They have also been quick to seize on new sources of wealth and power, like the family who own the generator and receive payment from every other family for electricity, and who are building the most conspicuously expensive new house in the town.

To look for an objective reason for the status of slaughterers is probably beside the point. The way 'tribespeople' speak of the 'butchers' and look down on them, as my friend said 'don't respect' them, is reminiscent of how any dominant group attributes bad character to the members of a despised category while exploiting them: like racism, or as men do with women.

An afternoon with Na'ma and Fatima

'*Ya* Mariam, *ya* Mariam, *itfaddali*, come in!'

Na'ma had sent her little daughter to fetch me that afternoon.

I kick off my flip-flops and duck through the door and am welcomed in out of the grey, chilly day to the *makan*, small sitting room. Na'ma (five children and five dead) and her daughter-in-law Fatima, a toothy, raw-boned young woman pregnant with her first baby, install me in a comfortable corner position by the window, arrange cushions for me, and unfold blankets to put round me.

'*Etki*, lean, like this,' says Na'ma, pushing me into position and propping my elbow on a firm cube of cushion. She has a face that is still beautiful despite showing the wear of her life: sculpted bones, high cheeks, shining eyes.

I settle, cosy under the blankets, and I think how extraordinary it is to be here, to be taken into a world that isn't mine. The room smells of tobacco smoke from the already lit *mada'a*, and soon there is also the bitter smell of snapped qat shoots and chewed leaves. I've brought a little qat, and they have a little.

Na'ma has been telling me the words to wedding songs while I write them down as best I can in a notebook. She is a gifted explainer, clear and patient, miming and acting out meanings, but she slightly impedes the process by tapping, with encouraging writing movements, on my right hand while I'm trying to write. I reflect that anyone who knew how to write herself wouldn't do this. Now she explains and tells me about the sequence of celebrations in a wedding: 'First is the day of the trays, and the henna; second, with a small party, the day of the *shedher*' (the stuff that turns the henna black). 'Third, day of the *zaffe*, the procession, with a big party and the bride going to the groom's house. Then *yum es sabah*, the day of the morning, with a big dinner in the groom's house; all the bride's family come, a sheep is slaughtered. The bride stays in the house for fifteen days, she mustn't go out at all; her mother will *rabakh* with her every day. Then *wafe' el khamstash*, the completion of the fortnight, with a women's party in the afternoon. The next day the bride goes out, to the cistern if they need water, or on a *dowra*, an outing, in a car with the groom.'

I note the gradual, supported transition, and the involvement of both the families. I ask about the little girls I saw on my way in, playing in the alleyway at holding a wedding, one of them drumming on a tin and others dancing and ululating.

'The little Rafani girl wants to be a *muzayyina*, she's practising.'

'Is it good work?'

Fatima says with emphasis, '*Fulus!*' – money, lots of money. It's also an occupation only open to 'butcher' women; it would bring shame upon tribespeople.

'The *muzayyina* gets one thousand riyals for the three days, or two thousand if she goes to a village outside the town, and stays there three or four days. Also she will have sugar, honey, *samn* sent to her.'

I have brought my little cassette player, and we listen to a tape recording of Na'ma. She is singing with the *muzayyina* at the wedding of her cousin.

'I didn't have a *muzayyina* at mine,' says Fatima. 'The local girls sang and drummed for me. They sang well, I've got the tape at home.'

'It's not *'aib*, for tribeswomen?'

'Not if they don't take money.'

Then we hear a recording of Na'ma singing a song on her own, in a clear, sweet voice.

'It's a wedding song. I was singing for my children, so they could hear me if I died – I was pregnant and ill.'

I would like to record Na'ma singing, but she says there are women sitting next door who will hear and come and comment. And when, another day, I eventually do get a recording she doesn't sing as fully, there is some shyness coming out in her voice.

I ask them about *jinn*.

'Once my son Ahmed came back late at night from Bajil, 7 o'clock' – 1am – 'and walked to the house with someone he thought was Saleh Fulan, talking on the way. But Saleh was asleep in his house all the time: it was a *jinni*.' Tim heard the same incident described by her husband.

'They live in the house. They see you but you don't see them. They live in the *safil*, the storage room at the bottom of the house. This house has seven *safil*s from one door.' She adds: 'If you don't wash after sex, *jinn* can take you – but you can wait till the morning, some people do, some don't.'

'In Sana'a,' says Fatima, 'they don't wait, they wash straight away.'

I am struck by how complicated it is, the fears of pollution and its consequences, the individual decisions women take about how to mitigate the dangers, the importance attached to washing and the difficulty with no running water or bathroom.

'If my husband is away,' the young woman says, 'I don't sleep alone, one of the children sleeps with me.'

'Why? What are you afraid of?' I'm wondering if it's *jinn*.

'Men. There are men who prowl the town after dark, trying the doors of houses where women are alone. Some women let them in, the men pay them money.'

'What would a woman's husband do if he knew?'

'Beat her, send her back to her father, divorce. He would remarry and she would remarry.'

'What do women do if they know their husband goes to other women?'

'They call him names when they quarrel – O visitor of whores, adulterer, you bring shame on your father – and he is ashamed.'

'Would she leave in anger, *haniq*, run away?'

'Not because of this. If she goes to her father he'll say, *nasibish*, he's your fate, your lot in life; he provides for you, your food and house and clothes. It's not enough reason to leave in anger.'

They add, 'Men are like this.'

Na'ma moves conspiratorially to sit next to me. 'One night when Fatima was a new bride, and our husbands were both away, Fatima and I were alone except for the children, and this man came knocking at our door. We poured a *matfal*, a qat spittoon, on his head.'

I think of the thick green gloopy spittle in a *matfal*, and its nauseating smell. Na'ma goes on gleefully, 'He still didn't go away, he lurked around the house. We took a tin and all peed in it in turn, and then stole up to the roof with it' – Na'ma mimes these actions vividly, the passing round of the tin, the tiptoeing up the stairs – 'and poured it on him. He had a *shal*, a cloth wrapped round his head, it all dripped down, he ran away and never came back. I told the old man when he came home.'

It's a good story and Na'ma makes the most of it. We all laugh a lot, and Na'ma provides exuberant repeats and clarifications and elaborations and more miming. 'We sat up all night after that, keeping watch and laughing.'

I wonder if always having a small girl to sleep with you, as women do when their husbands are away and they would otherwise be alone, is a way of protecting your reputation, so people can't talk. I have never felt worried when Tim was away, even though I don't have a neighbour girl to sleep with me. Actually, even with all doors locked, access to our rooms is extremely easy, as I found out when I locked myself out and climbed in through the window.

I shift position.

'What's the matter?' Na'ma asks.

'My knee hurts,' I admit.

'Stretch your legs out, be comfortable.'

I gratefully obey. To sit with my legs stretched out is a measure of ease and informality. It's normal and polite to sit with them folded, one up and one down.

Na'ma and Fatima tell me another tale.

'There was a man in Howd, the village near here, who had a good friend and they quarrelled. So he decided to go to the man's wife and make her pregnant while he was away, so he'd divorce her. He tried to get in by the door and couldn't, so he decided to climb through the hole in her kitchen roof, where the smoke comes out. Just his legs got through, then he got stuck. The woman asleep below woke up, got up, took matches and – "*Bss! Bss!*",' says Na'ma, imitating the sound of the matches, 'put a match to his arsehole and his legs and everything.'

Fatima elaborates, adds more places where the woman put the match.

'He tried to get out' – Na'ma acts out his struggles – 'but he was stuck, he couldn't go either up or down. A small girl from the family fetched a neighbour.'

'Is this really true?'

'Yes! He went to prison.'

'Do some women get pregnant while their husbands are away? What do they do?'

Na'ma mimes very hard pushing and massage to the stomach. 'To make it come out, when it's still small. The woman would say she was ill, and bury it. A woman down the mountain, a long time ago, got pregnant when she was still unmarried. She told her parents she had an '*ulla*.'

'What's that?'

'With eyes, in your stomach, it eats your stomach from inside. Then it was born and it wasn't an '*ulla* but a baby. The parents took a cloth, smothered the baby, and buried it secretly.'

'How do you know about it, then?'

'Women talking...'

I know for myself how local talk can spread stories and rumours. When we had a car accident near Sana'a, in which, thankfully, we were not very badly hurt, we heard how people were saying we had been killed or variously maimed.

I ask again about the *'ulla*.

'It's filth, something horrible in the stomach. It stays in the woman's stomach, makes her ill, hurts' – Na'ma makes clawing gestures – 'it's like a *gishwe*, a wild beast, it has two eyes.'

She keeps emphasising the eyes.

'Some are like a snake. After the baby's born it may come out, bite the woman as it goes, go back in, kill her. And it may kill the women who are with her when she gives birth. They had one in that house over there, they were ashamed of it, they buried it secretly at night.'

'How does a woman know if she has one?'

'She goes to Sana'a, a doctor examines her, says she has an *'augari*. The woman bleeds when she's pregnant, from her mouth and from below.'

'Augari is a word I recognise, used for a similar creature, from literature about other areas of Yemen. It seems to me that this horrific entity embodies the fear and uncertainty and danger of women's childbearing lives, something terrifying growing, seeing but unseen, and attacking women, in their vulnerability, from the inside.

Maghreb sounds, and the afternoon breaks up. I get up, take my leave, and go out into the chilly mist.

No periods

'I've never had a period,' says Safeya. She has had seven children, four living and three dead.

'What, not one?' I ask.

'One, when I reached puberty. I'd already been married seven years. Since then I've always been pregnant or breastfeeding.'

I've brought my qat to the house of Madani, a friendly oldish man with a jutting white beard, and we're sitting, a mixed group: Madani, another man whom I don't know, Safeya, who is Madani's much younger second wife, with an ill-looking baby small for its age, and Adiba, his daughter by an earlier marriage. We sit comfortable against cushions, in a room with windows looking over the small open area in the town, *ras es suq*, where the road round to the top meets the market alleyways, the point where cars arrive and leave.

Safeya has traces of prettiness, but like so many women I know she looks worn out, hollowed, her face thin. She leant out of her window earlier in the afternoon to call me to come and *rabakh*. As she settled me in and gave me *gahwa* she said, 'I saw you from the window the other day, but I couldn't call out because there were men outside, soldiers.'

I try to ask Madani if they slept together when she was so young, but he misunderstands my question, and evidently thinks I mean now. Unfazed by what he thinks I've asked, he asserts firmly: 'Every night!'

'Don't believe him!' says his daughter. 'He's had an operation.'

I don't get an answer about young brides this time. Other times, the answers vary. Some, asked what husbands would do with a girl so young, say, 'Everything.' Some say a patient husband would wait. Some explain that the marriage contract can include a formal undertaking on the part of the groom's family to 'bring up' the girl, without consummation of the marriage, till she's older. One man who says he and his wife were both seven years old when they married, when we ask 'What did you do?' says, 'Nothing, we played together in the street.'

'I have ten children,' the old man tells me, 'and ten in the graveyard.'

'Why haven't you got any children?' Madani's friend asks me.

'Pills like that are *haram*,' says Madani after my explanation. 'They harm women, that's why you're so thin.'

'How old are you, do you think?' I ask Safeya. I'm assuming she's about forty; certainly much older than me.

'Maybe twenty-five,' she guesses. Fifteen years younger than I thought. 'How old are you?'

'Thirty,' I say.

They ask, checking, 'How old were you at the revolution?' I do a quick calculation: the deposition of the Imam and the beginning of the republic was in 1962. 'Ten.'

They calculate in turn. 'Yes, then you are thirty now.'

'I must be twenty-one or twenty-two,' says Adiba, the daughter – young, pretty, with a light-hearted manner. She has three children and one dead, and is pregnant again.

'Different women take a different amount of time to get pregnant again,' says Adiba. 'I get pregnant two months after the *wafe*.' That is, after the completion of the forty days' confinement after a birth, when women wash to become ritually pure again, henna themselves, celebrate and have a party, and when relations with their husbands can resume.

She runs through her children, and how soon she got pregnant again after each.

'I don't get pregnant again so fast, with breastfeeding,' says her stepmother Safeya.

I have brought prints of pictures I took a while ago of Adiba's children. I get them out of my bag. She looks at them critically. 'They're looking to one side.'

'I'll take some more.'

'Will you send us a picture of your baby, if you have one?' Adiba says.

I promise I will.

'Who will you address it to?'

'To you: Adiba, daughter of Madani.'

They look at each other. 'They do this where she comes from.'

Adiba turns to me. 'For us that's *'aib*, it must be addressed to my son. Address it to Kamal, or Fuad' – her own little boy, or the son of her older co-wife.

'If *inshallah* the new baby is a boy,' says Safeya, 'he'll be called Murad, you could address it to him.'

'Which is better, a boy or a girl?' I ask.

'A girl would help, I'd prefer a girl.'

'And your husband?'

'He'd prefer a boy. But it's all from Allah.'

As I make my way home past *ras es suq* I see a knot of women, busy over something. It turns out to be a carload of firewood, a heap of awkward lopped branches. My neighbour's daughters are taking it into their yard, piecemeal as best they can, from where it's piled in the street. Other women, neighbours and passers-by, have joined in to help them. It cost 600 or 700 riyals, Karima says, and should last them four to five months. I stop to help too, take a manageable light load of the knobbly wood to dump just inside the door of their courtyard, and come back for another. The helpers keep working till it's all done.

Long pregnancy

'How long does a pregnancy last?' I ask a group of women as we sit *rabakh*ing one afternoon. I have read that Yemeni law recognises durations of up to two years. But everyone sitting around the room this afternoon says, 'Nine months.'

'Can it be more?'

'No.'

We ask Tim's friend Yahya when he comes to sit with us in the evening.

'A pregnancy can't go on longer than nine months unless it stops and starts again. This is very possible. Then it picks up again from where it stopped. There's a woman in the village of Ma'arif, over there, who's been pregnant for twenty-five years or more, she's old now. My wife's sister was six or seven months pregnant when her husband went to Saudi Arabia, then the pregnancy stopped. The baby was *raqid*, sleeping. When he came back and slept with her it started up again and she gave birth two or three months after his return.'

'Could a long pregnancy be a cover for a woman who gets pregnant while her husband is away?'

'No, it couldn't, because she would have to be already pregnant when he left, with her periods stopped and so on, and people would know.'

Everybody knows of cases of long pregnancies. Another friend says, 'Ali Mahwiti's mother carried a baby for seven years. She felt it moving in the first year, then thought it had died. She had strange flows of blood on several occasions in the next years, then after seven years she gave birth.' He adds: 'My own brother was a year in the womb.'

The hakim, who issues judgement on marriages and divorces, and the Egyptian doctor (a real doctor this time, not a nurse, though he doesn't last very long in his post) have a public argument on this question. From our roof we overhear the dispute coming up from the alleyway below. The hakim is asserting that pregnancy can last three years. When the doctor insists this is not possible, the hakim goes away muttering, 'You are wrong, *ya doktur*, O doctor, you are wrong.'

Sitting with my downstairs neighbour in her dark little room one evening, I ask her, 'How long is a pregnancy?'

'Nine months.'

'But can it go to sleep and wake up?'

'Yes, it goes quiet, if the woman gets a shock; it can stay a year, then wake up again and finish. When it goes quiet there will be blood, *nazif*. Hamud's wife was pregnant for seven years – he kept beating her, it would go quiet, her stomach would go flat, then she would get big again.'

'Is it *'aib* for a man to beat his wife?'

'Yes, it is *'aib*.' Poor Nuriya is trying to watch the serial on TV, and I am pestering her with questions.

'Doesn't she run away?' Other women have made it clear to me that they wouldn't stand for being hit.

'She's got nowhere to go.'

Leaving in protest

It's a clear, bright day, but there's a constant, wearing wind which spoils my pleasure in being out, and dust gritty in my mouth, swirling up as I cross the flat area outside the town. I'm heading towards the cluster of new houses beyond it.

'*Ya* Mariam! Where are you going?' a little girl calls to me.

'*Dowra*,' I say. For a walk.

'Are you going to see Selma Yahya?'

'Yes,' I admit.

'*Haraban*, she's run away, she's gone to her father's house.'

I change direction, back towards the town. Selma, small, bright-eyed, never still, is sitting in her father's house. She is busy all the same, turning the handle of her sewing machine. Her neighbour, Zeinab, whose smooth, plump face makes me think she's much younger than she is, is sitting with her, keeping her company.

'Why are you staying here?' I ask Selma.

'I left *haniq*, angry, a week ago.'

I ask her why.

'He said bad things to me, he insulted me and my mother and father.'

I remember how, early on, people explained to us: 'This is how we swear at people here: *Ya gahba bint gahba, ya nasrani ibn nasrani*' – O whore daughter of a whore, O Christian son of a Christian. Perhaps he said things like that. We often hear such cursing. People curse each other as Christians in our presence without any apparent awareness that it might apply to us.

'I won't let him in here. And he can't talk to my father, because he's away at his house in Sana'a. I telephoned my father to inform him, from the communications office, and he said to stay in his house.'

'So what will happen?'

'He'll have to pay,' says Selma, angry and emphatic. Compensation for the insult.

'Who to? You or your father?'

'To me.'

'How much?'

'Three hundred, four hundred, five hundred, to teach him to be better mannered in future.' About £40–60.

'Where are your children?' She has four.

'With their father. There's only me in the house here. I cook myself tinned ful beans, or I eat with the neighbours. My son brought the sewing machine, but I can't get the dresses I'm working on, they're in my tin trunk and he has the key. I gave it to him to get his money out.' She means her husband.

At my string of questions, Zeinab asks, 'Don't women *harab* where you come from?'

'No, not much. When you choose your husband yourself, you're the one who's responsible.' I add, 'Anyway, I couldn't run away to my father now, it's too far.'

'You could always come to us if you need to,' the women assure me. I'm touched that they don't want to see me denied this vital recourse. I ask Selma, 'Have you run away angry before?'

'Lots of times.' She adds, 'Come and see me, while I'm here.'

I wonder how Selma's husband is managing. Another man whose wife was away angry complained to Tim that he had to eat in the restaurant run by our landlady, who, he said, was taking all his money. The wife's withdrawal of labour has an impact like workers going on strike.

Over the next few weeks, I do go and see Selma at her father's house. It's much easier to talk to her here, where she hasn't got lots of work in the kitchen. The next time I go, there's another neighbour sitting with her. They are eating *ksu'*, a morning snack, of *lehuh* spread out on a piece of material from the dress Selma is sewing. Neighbour women come and go while I chat to Selma. She explains to me what she was saying to the other women: the recent earthquake happened because in Dhamar men slept with their mothers and sisters. Zeinab, the plumpish woman I met there before, is one of the neighbours who comes in.

'I'm tired,' she says, 'the mother of the dead boy was with me yesterday, and I'm worn out from crying with her. I knew her before, I saw her in the street and brought her in – she wanted to throw herself out of the window.'

I remember the incident, some time before. A crowd gathered outside the prefect's office. A small boy had been brought there, dead. He had been playing with his father's gun and shot himself through the head. There are always so many guns around that I'm only surprised this doesn't happen more often. The family came from an outlying village, and had brought the dead boy to the government offices to make sure, people said, that there were no problems – accusations or gossip about the death, I suppose.

A couple of weeks pass and Selma has still not gone back. She seems to be enjoying the break from her life of endless work. This time I find her in the house next door to her father's, sitting with the neighbours: sleek Zeinab and older Na'ma, with high cheekbones and bright eyes, who I often visit to *rabakh*. A *mada'a* bubbles in the middle of the room, and they pass the mouthpiece between them.

Zeinab has no children. 'I've been married for fifteen years, since I was young. We went to a doctor in Sana'a, he said there's nothing wrong with me, it's a weakness in my husband. They said he should go to Cairo or Saudi Arabia to get something to strengthen him. Maybe we'll go and do the Hajj.'

She seems quite content. She looks noticeably smoother, more youthful, than the other long-married women I know, who have been giving birth every year for many years.

Selma's husband comes shambling in, looking sheepish. He sits for a bit, joined by another man, Zeinab's father. Selma's husband tries to approach her, but she pushes him away. After he's gone she says, 'I've had enough, I don't want to go back'.

'She's joking,' Zeinab says, 'she's got children.' She passes the *mada'a* hose to Selma. Selma refuses it.

'And she's pregnant, look, she's *'awif*,' Zeinab adds: nauseous from pregnancy. She turns her head to make the spitting gesture that indicates the nausea of a pregnant woman.

I remember Selma saying last year, 'When he comes back, I get pregnant.' Her husband came back from working in Saudi Arabia during Ramadan.

'Do you want a boy or a girl?' I ask Selma.

'It's from Allah. But girls are better – boys marry and leave, girls love their mother more.'

Zeinab agrees. (I find out much later that Selma had her wish: the baby turned out to be a girl.)

'I wish I could give it to you,' Selma jokes to her friend.

I ask, 'Have you ever run away angry, Zeinab?'

'Never, I've had no reason to. I've never had a problem with my husband.'

Next time I visit, Selma is still relishing her holiday. 'I don't know when my father is coming back. I telephoned him in Sana'a, and he told me to stay as long as I like.'

A week or two later, I'm visiting Hamda, out beyond Selma's house. A neighbour is sitting there, who I've seen at Selma's house. She asks me, 'Is Selma still in her father's house?' She doesn't know because she doesn't visit her there. It's about ten minutes further away, she's no longer a close neighbour.

Five days later I go to Selma's father's house but this time she isn't there. I am welcomed in by her father's wife, a calm, youngish, pleasant woman; not Selma's mother, who is long dead. She welcomes me in and gives me a handful of nuts and raisins, *gahwa* and bread. We sit against cushions and sip and snack. Her daughter, a girl of perhaps fifteen, brings in a bowl of bread dough for her approval.

She criticises the dough to her daughter, but once the girl has taken it away again, she says: 'Adiba's good, she does all the work. She's engaged to a man in Sana'a, she'll be married soon. Then I'll have to work again.'

I ask her about life in the past. 'It's much better now.' But then she gives me a long, enthusiastic description of the food they had in the old days.

'When women ground local wheat, you could smell it two houses away – it smelt as good as meat! The wheat now has no taste. We had *ra'ib*, buttermilk; lots of grain, *dukhn*, millet – this much!' She makes wide gestures with her hands.

'Weren't people hungry?' I ask, remembering what others have said about times of hunger under the Imam.

'No, everyone got lots from their land.'

'Wasn't it hard work?' I'm thinking of the grinding.

'Yes, but we were strong then.'

'Did women *rabakh*, chew qat?'

'No – there was too much work to *rabakh*, and no qat.'

'Why don't you have a cow now?'

'I do, shared – it's with an old woman in *beit* Hamali.' I ask if she gets *ra'ib* from it.

'I did, but then I refused it; the woman is dirty, her pots and everything are dirty, I don't want it.'

I ask after Selma.

'She's gone to her husband's.'

'For money?' I ask, remembering Selma's determination that her husband should pay.

'Not for money, because he's poor.'

I go on to Selma's house, but today she hasn't got time to chat. She's in a flurry of activity, cleaning out rooms that have been left dirty all the month she was away.

'Congratulations! You're a bride!' the women joke to Selma the next day, when she arrives at an afternoon party for a real bride.

The next time I drop in to see Selma she's not there – she's out visiting Zeinab, the neighbour she made friends with when she was staying at her father's.

I hear more about leaving in anger, in protest, one afternoon with Naʿma and her daughter-in-law Fatima. They welcome me in, smooth a comfortable place for me in the corner of the little room furthest from the door, put down extra cushions, snuggle me in with blankets, give me *gahwa* and pass me the *madaʿa*. I've brought some qat for us all.

Yesterday Naʿma said her daughter-in-law, married a few months ago, was sitting crying for her husband, who was on a trip away down the mountain. Today she's looking a bit brighter; she's had a message that he's coming back tomorrow. Naʿma sings a little for me, in a high, clear, silvery voice, a fodder-gathering song.

She tells me about her first marriage, to a cousin. 'I was very young, like my son now' – a boy I guess to be eight or nine – 'and he was much older, and he didn't wait for me to grow up like some men do. I was very afraid of him, after the first night he waited two days then it was every night, he hurt me and I was afraid.' She mimes sitting huddled and trembling.

'My father was dead, it was my brother who arranged my marriage. After a year – my husband was away a lot of it – I went to the *hakuma*, the local government, with my brother and got divorced. Then he married three or four more women who all left or were divorced – he was bad.' She flicks her cheek with her fingers.

'A match should be with a girl's agreement,' she says. 'Both the girl and the boy should be in agreement with their marriage. If a woman doesn't like her husband, she will run away. But once she's pregnant she will stay for the sake of the child. She's *hanib*.'

'*Hanib?*'

'Like when you get your foot between two rocks,' Na'ma explains. Stuck, trapped. 'My husband now is much better.'

'Have you ever run away *haniq*, angry?'

'Yes. I didn't get *mahr*' (the woman's portion of the bride price). 'I was sorry for him because he had no money, till I got angry with him and ran away to my brother, and my brother told my husband I wouldn't come back till I got *mahr*, and he gave me four *nuss mishkhas*.'

She shows them to me, pulling them out from round her neck: four old coins with metal loops added, threaded on a string.

'Then when our son got married, the old man wanted to give them to the new bride. He said I was old, I didn't need them. So I ran away to my brother, and now I've got a paper to say they're mine. It's with my brother, he keeps it safe.'

'Have you run away other times?'

'Yes, twice – once I went and stayed in a room which belongs to my brother, in the house over there. I stayed there alone for ten days. Women gave me bread and sugar, my children came to see me. He had to pay two hundred for one time and five hundred for the other, to me and my brother. But the old man has it all back, borrowed off me.'

The daughter-in-law, Fatima, eager and helpful, a country girl from a village an hour or two's walk down the mountain, says: 'I've never left, when we've quarrelled we've always made it up. Perhaps if my father was alive... But if I needed to, I could go to my mother's brother.'

It's interesting that she mentions her maternal uncle as a refuge, but not her mother. She has remarried, and, I learn later, the new husband is no friend to the children of her first marriage, even though he's their dead father's brother. He is taking their property for his own children. On another afternoon at Na'ma's I meet one of these oppressed children, a young lad. He is being encouraged and urged by Na'ma and Fatima to be a man, to stand up for himself and his siblings and their rights. A widow with no children can remarry, Na'ma and Fatima tell me, but a widow with young children shouldn't, for their sake, lest she give them an oppressor. Fatima's mother was still attractive, Fatima says, and wanted to remarry.

Tim *rabakh*s with Na'ma's son, Fatima's husband, sitting chewing qat in his shop in the market on long, slow afternoons when only a few children trickle in to buy sweets, a riyal's worth at a time. They have got the riyals by pestering their parents as they sit trying to relax and chew qat. He says how good his wife is.

'She hasn't run away once. Other men's wives are always running away. A wife from the countryside is much better, used to hard work, going out getting fodder and wood; she'll be pleased with life in town and stay, not run away. And there are fewer problems with her family because they're further away, she's not always going there.'

Indeed, in one tall town house I visited, the wife, living with her husband on one floor, had only had to go upstairs to 'run away' to her father on the floor above.

Another friend of Tim's says, 'My wife must have run away twenty-five or thirty times! When we were first married she was not *mu'addab*, well behaved. She would stay two weeks then run away.'

A few weeks later, when I go again to *rabakh* at Na'ma's, I find a small group of neighbour women there. There's a widow who lives in the same house, a woman from next door. They are an interested audience for Na'ma's tale of woe. She is furious.

'Fatima ran away yesterday! My son went to Sana'a to get medical treatment, we don't know where he is, but he'll be back soon. Fatima kept sitting around miserable, locked herself up in their room with the cassette player, only wanting her husband, wanting his *dendeli*.'

Here Na'ma shakes a dangling hand to convey what the young woman wanted.

'I'm ill, there's no one to get water, Fatima wouldn't do anything, wouldn't get up, said they weren't her children, why should she get up for mine, we could drink our piss for all she cared.'

I remember how I've seen the conflict between mothers and daughters-in-law played out like this, the older woman urging, '*Gumi*! *Gumi*!', get up, get up, while the younger one sulks or pleads illness, lying on her mattress instead of working for the household.

'I told her to get up at half past four yesterday' – about 10.30 in the morning – 'and then we had an argument and she left, walking. She won't come back till my son comes back.'

The next day, the same group of neighbours are listening while Na'ma, half-crying, describes her trouble. The neighbour women make sympathetic noises.

'I treated her well, I never so much as called her *jinniya* before.' A *jinniya*, a female *jinni*, is something women often call each other, in joke or anger. 'I'm ill, the old man doesn't ask how I am, he takes the money the boy gets from selling Vimto and gives me to keep safe, I haven't got a *saramiya*, I have to use Fatima's, nobody buys *me* a new one, only the young one, Fatima. And she took the key to their room downstairs, which I need to get things out of, and the key to my trunk.'

In the long term, the daughter-in-law often wins this conflict. By the time of my second return visit thirteen years later, Ahmed and Fatima are a separate household, living in their own new building on the outskirts of town, with six children and another on the way, besides two that died. Na'ma is still hurt and angry that they left to set up house on their own.

One morning, I'm at Adiba's in the old town. I've brought her a few nasturtium seeds, all I have left from the packet my mother posted, and we're sitting in her small, dirty room eating *kak* and onion greens and drinking tea: cheerful Adiba; Fatima, her much older co-wife, slackened by childbearing – she is the one with the extreme number of six children who lived and nine who died; and another woman whom I don't know, no longer young, sitting quietly.

'She comes from down the mountain,' Adiba explains, 'she's run away to my father, he's her uncle: her mother and father are dead. She's divorced now.'

'Did she want to be divorced, or was it her husband?'

'The divorce is from both her wish and her husband's. She'll stay with my father till she marries again,' Adiba says. 'She's left three children with her ex-husband's mother.'

'Don't you miss them?' I ask the quiet woman.

'No, my heart has stopped feeling,' she says. 'My husband can keep them. What would I do with them?' When she marries again, her new husband won't want to take on the children of her previous marriage.

'The usual thing with us here,' Adiba says, 'is for the husband to keep the boys, if they're not very small, and the wife keeps the girls till they marry. This is the law.'

Adiba and Fatima are sitting together and seem friendly. I'm surprised; everyone says co-wives don't get on. Even men admit that having two wives makes problems. Women always speak of co-wives in the same breath as anger, upsets, quarrels, hate, jealousy. I'm not sure I've ever seen any other pair of co-wives even in the same room together.

'Don't you have problems if you live together?' I ask.

'Not if it's only for a few days. My house is being repaired,' Fatima says.

Adiba asks, 'Has Selma Yahya gone back? I haven't seen her.' Adiba's house is in the old part of town; with her return to her husband's house a little beyond, Selma's everyday social world has shifted.

'Yes, she's gone back. And you, have you ever run away angry?'

'Yes, three or four times! Once some men were working on my husband's lands down the mountain, and Fatima took their lunch down' (labourers always get *gheda*, and of course the women have to cook it) 'and didn't take any *gahwa*, and she was sent back and told we were both to come with a thermos each. I refused, and went to my father. Another time I took my *saramiya* and my baby son and went to my father. I stayed a night, and my husband had to pay my father eighty riyals, because he'd insulted me.'

'Doesn't the wife get any of the money?'

'Some families would give her some. Another time I stayed five nights, and another, six. Once my husband paid four or five hundred riyals. Another time he was let off. Another time we quarrelled at eight at night' – 2am – 'I was very pregnant, I was two weeks off giving birth, he was being unreasonable. I went out, I got as far as that house on the edge of town, he came after me and we made it up and I went back.'

'And Fatima, what about you?'

'I've run away a hundred times.'

Adiba says: 'It was only words, he didn't hit me. I don't run away now, my husband is better now.'

'He hit *me*,' says Fatima.

Adiba isn't happy to be pregnant again, with her fifth. 'I wish I'd miscarry. I was taking pills, but I had *nazif*, haemorrhaging. There are injections to make you miscarry, but I'm afraid of haemorrhage.'

'Is it *haram* to have an injection like that?'

'Yes.'

'Are there any plants or anything, that people used before?'

'No, only massaging or poking your stomach, and falling. I miscarried once at four months, by falling.'

I'm surprised that she is pregnant, because a year ago she told me she wouldn't have another baby: 'My husband has lots of children from his other wife, and from three wives he divorced; he doesn't want more. I went to Sana'a and had an injection after my last birth, when my baby was two months old. It lasts a year, then I'll go again.'

(On my next visit four years later, she has three more children. She says she tried contraception but has given up: children are from Allah, just what happens. I wonder if it is especially younger women who are interested in trying to control their fertility, and later they resign themselves to constant childbearing. Anyway, by the time I visit again after another thirteen years, Adiba has had nine children, and been sterilised.)

Adiba gives me a handful of fresh mint leaves as I go. 'Where are you going to *rabakh*?'

I say I'm planning to go down to a house below the town. It's the one down a steep path that we went to in Ramadan.

'I'll come with you,' says Adiba. I'm glad; despite going there before, I'm not entirely sure of the way. That afternoon Adiba, her mother, the divorced woman and I all go down together to *rabakh*.

Next time I go to visit Selma her *salifa*, her husband's brother's wife, isn't there.

'Lutfiya's *haniq*,' Selma tells me, 'she went and took her children.'

'Why?'

'We had a row. Her children are bad-mannered, sometimes I hit them.'

'Where's she gone?'

'To her father. She wants to eat separately from us, but my father-in-law won't agree.' She has four or five children, but her father lives in the town so she didn't have far to take them.

Running away angry, leaving in protest, is an important option for women, a safety valve, and a lever to improve their position, even if only slightly. It's one way they manoeuvre within the constraints of their hard lives. It's also a source of stories which women tell almost with pride, with a sense of having asserted their rights, having taken a step to make their husband behave better, in a spirit of 'that'll teach him'.

'I never loved him...'

'I never loved my husband, but I got pregnant right away.'

Selma is young and smooth-faced. We're in her kitchen, surrounded by her small children, and she's busy grinding, pushing a heavy rounded stone to and fro over a smooth, slightly hollowed stone base. She's making powder out of a piece of 'helba stick', *'ud el helba*. It has hardly any smell, it's just an undistinguished-looking brownish twig or root. The powder goes in, just a pinch, when you beat up *helba*, to make it froth up nicely.

'This will be enough to last a month or two. I have a blender, but it's not working.'

I came to bring her prints of photos I took of her children; she's handed them over to the kids and now they're passing them around, already torn.

She has five children after six years of marriage.

'I don't want more, I get an injection every three months. Five children is more than enough, my husband gets fed up and shouts at them. We used to live with my husband's family, but we moved out because there were too many children, all fighting.'

A little girl, eight or ten years old, comes in bearing a pumpkin, and announces: 'From Abdul Mughni's wife, she says can you give her some *lehuh*?'

I see this girl in many places. She comes to my house to fetch me to her mother Na'ma's to *rabakh*. She seems to run messages for everybody, and helps some women – hard-pressed women of important families, like Abdul Mughni's wife – in their houses. Whatever the benefits for her, it's an informal arrangement; when I ask why she does it, she says, 'because my heart tells me to', and denies that it's for money.

When she's gone Selma looks at the padded envelope that the photos came in, with a label in Arabic photocopied by my mother, who got the pictures developed for me in England. To my surprise, she reads out the address. I have hardly ever seen an adult woman read, just the once with the schoolgirls who came in to chant Quran verses in the house where people were mourning. Most of the women I know certainly can't. She explains: 'I went to Quran school and up to the fourth class of elementary school. They didn't teach writing or arithmetic then, I can only read. I was taken out of the fourth class to be married.'

'How old were you?'

'About fifteen.'

She was married to the younger brother of her older sister's husband, a not uncommon pattern. Often families are linked by repeated alliances, or a successful marriage is duplicated with younger family members.

'I didn't want to. My mother beat me, I was married against my will, and then I had a baby within a year. I miss my studies. The teacher was sad to see me go. I was very good at studying, I helped teach the others.'

'I never loved him, but I got pregnant right away,' is the cry of the unhappily married woman. She is trapped. If the marriage ends, she stands to lose her children.

Perhaps this explains something that has puzzled me: that even recently married women ask me for contraception. Maybe they are looking for a breathing space to see if their marriage will be tolerable.

After divorce

This is a restless, noisy afternoon's *rabkha*. I'm at the house of Fatima, the ex-wife of Ahmed in the house we lived in at first, whose second wedding I went to. Katiba is there too. Several mothers of small children are sitting against the cushions along the side of the room, busy talking to each other, or trying to, while the bored children fidget and cry and whine. I often see children sitting in on adult gatherings with a stillness that seems to me remarkable, but not this afternoon. The mother of one child who's being tiresome turns to me for help with her threats: 'Mariam, have you got a needle in your bag? We'll give him an injection!'

I say firmly that I haven't. Fatima is saying to the other women: 'I want to keep my little girl.'

Katiba says: 'My father will take her.' The little girl's brothers, aged perhaps two and four, already live with Katiba's family.

Another afternoon, when Fatima is talking about her three children and her wish to keep her daughter, her brother asks her: 'Have you got a *waraqa* from the *hakuma*?' – a document from the government, the local authorities.

'No,' says Fatima. 'My *wakil* – agent, representative – spoke to the sheikh.'

A young lad sitting in the room, who comes from the family of the hakim, warns her: 'This isn't enough. You should go to the hakim and get a document.'

And another afternoon, the women I'm sitting with tell me: 'A boy stays with his mother till he goes to school, and a girl till she marries, that's what we do here. Look at Zohra Ali and Selma Hamud, they kept their daughters till the daughters married.' But perhaps these were women who didn't remarry? They go on to say, 'But if a woman remarries, her husband won't want the children.'

Different Islamic schools of law give different ages for sons and daughters to go to their father after divorce, or in some cases to choose which parent to live with. But women talk about local norms and about individual negotiation. Their love for their children and the threat of losing them hang over their attempts to push for better treatment and to call their husbands to account.

Red-eyed from weeping, our downstairs neighbour Nuriya starts crying again as she goes out on the roof to tell our neighbours her terrible news.

'My daughter's dead, killed in an accident, they buried her yesterday.' The news came with a visitor from Mahwit, the mother of a woman who's married here. This was Nuriya's daughter from an earlier marriage before she married the Qadi. She seldom saw her; she lived three hours' drive away. It's not long since Nuriya told me that her daughter was getting married.

'I haven't seen her since Sabah was a few months old,' she said then. So about four years. 'My first husband took her, when she was three or four years old.'

'Were you sad?'

'Yes, I was. My son from my next marriage is in 'Are, so it's not so bad, I can see him.' 'Are is a village just up the road. 'Now he's at school here he comes to me daily. He gets on fine with the Qadi, and so did my daughter when she visited us, no problem. Some fathers leave both girls and boys with their mother till they're big, then take them. Selma Hamud, for example – she has a daughter by her former husband who went to Sana'a when she was older, now she telephones her a lot.'

At the time, I asked her, 'Are you going to your daughter's wedding?'

'No. They sent my brother one thousand riyals as the bride's *khal*, maternal uncle, and I get five hundred of it. He sent his back for clothes for her.'

Now I go down with Nuriya into her small sitting room on the ground floor of our house. Nuriya, between sobs, recounts the story to the women who come to condole. 'They sent word she was getting married, but they didn't invite me.'

The other women murmur, '*Aib*! That's not right.'

'Then she was going in her wedding procession, in the wadi, and the car was swept away by floodwater, and she was drowned.'

A dry, tranquil wadi can be suddenly filled without warning by a turbulent spate of water, running off from heavy rain on a mountain upstream. The neighbours exclaim at the tragedy, and ask God's mercy on the dead bride, and on Nuriya.

The next afternoon I go downstairs to *rabakh* with Nuriya, bringing her our qat spittoon because she asked me to. It's not often that she has women come to her small room. The first to arrive are

274

Khadija and her daughters from across the alley, then the hakim's wife from the next house, a very old woman from the tall house opposite, Amina with her daughter up from Meruwagha, and several other women I know, the majority from nearby, more or less neighbours, and a few from further away. There's a squash in the little sitting room. The women condole with Nuriya.

'*Allah ye'adhem ajrek.*' God increase your reward.

'*Ajrenna we ajrek il Allah,*' she gives the reply.

Khadija nudges me. 'Get us some drinking water,' and I run upstairs for some of our filtered water. When I come back Amina is saying, 'She drowned, so she's gone to heaven.' I've heard this before, that people drowned, burnt, or struck by lightning go straight to heaven.

The next day women visit Nuriya in the morning. These are women without any obvious strong connection to her; it's more as if, a few at a time, the whole town is visiting. I sit for a glass of tea.

'Women will sit with her for seven days,' they tell me in the house where I *rabakh* the next afternoon. I spend another afternoon at Nuriya's four days later, with an assortment of visitors from the town and up from Meruwagha. It seems like a fairly normal afternoon, not especially sad or low-key. I overhear Nuriya saying what good neighbours we are, she doesn't know whom they'll get when we leave. At the end, when nearly all the women have left, Nuriya retells the whole story of her daughter to the one or two remaining. I get up to go with the last guest, but Nuriya urges me to stay: '*Inti min el beit,*' you are of the house, from the same house. So I sit a few minutes more.

Walking around

It's a lovely morning, the sun warm on my skin through the cold, sharp air. Little puffs of cloud dot the skyline over the long ridge of the next mountain. Tim is away, working on surveys of water projects for the German aid company, and I set out to walk around, enjoy the air, and see who I meet. It's still early, smoke is curling up all over the town from women's baking ovens, and the early-morning woodsmoke smell pervades the alleyways.

In the street I run into a group of women in black *sharshafs*, veils and capes and full, swishing skirts. I manage to recognise them: the women from the tall house opposite ours, where five brothers and their wives and children live on five floors.

'*Sabah el kher*, *ya* Mariam!' Good morning!

'*Sabah en nur*!' I give the reply.

'Come with us, come for a *dowra*! We're going to see the new clinic.'

Someone has alerted my neighbour Khadija and she comes out of her gate to join us, also covered in black, from veiled face to skirts brushing the ground. The women are in an excited mood. We make our way down through the town, over loose stones and dusty earth, chatting, lively, a party of women on an outing. At the bottom of the town, beyond the stepped cistern with its covering of green duckweed, is the newly built polyclinic: about ten rooms, still bare and unfurnished. The women swarm into the new building as if taking possession of it, commenting loudly, black capes and skirts flapping as they move swiftly from room to room. Their cries and exclamations echo in the empty space. They go into all the rooms, try every door, rattle the handles of the locked ones. They marvel at the tiled white bathrooms. They talk about the rooms, what will be where, the accommodation for the doctors. They seem pleased with it all, proud of the new facility. I saw Khadija and another woman doing much the same with the new school buildings a while ago. 'Is it better than schools in London?' they asked me.

We sit down for a while, on stones just outside, to take a rest, then head back to the town. On the way we're invited into a house by the road. We all troop in and the woman of the house, whom I don't know at all, gives us all tea and bread and *lehuh* and buttermilk.

The women start back up the hill to go home. I stay down in Meruwagha and try Amina's house, but she's out. Her daughter Hasiba, who must be about eight years old, is in charge of the house. She welcomes me in and shows me the baby lying in her cradle, and the guinea pigs they keep. I don't see how she could be spared to go to school. The guinea pigs are for food and for medicine – 'Good for children's coughs,' Amina said.

I go past Warda's to see if she's there. She isn't, but her sister-in-law Nuriya says, 'Sit and have some tea.'

Her baby is lying in the middle of the room and she and her sister are in the middle of doing something strange to him. 'They don't do this in Sana'a or Hodeida, only here,' they tell me. I watch with interest. She has a cloth compressed into a smooth wad which she heats over coals in a clay incense burner. Then she presses it on the baby, on the palms of his hands, the soles of his feet, and up under his testicles, reheating it each time. The baby isn't crying or, mostly, looking uncomfortable.

'Why do you do this?'

'To make him strong.'

He has six small scars from *misam*, curative burns, on his stomach. They look like little cigarette burns, in three neat rows above the navel.

'My father's mother did those, with a *nugum* stick.' I know the plant; it has little yellow fruit like tiny tomatoes.

'Why?'

'Because he had green veins on his stomach. He would be unhealthy, crying, if we didn't.'

Next, women call me in to another house in Meruwagha. 'Come in, come in and drink *gahwa*.'

I go into a small ground-floor room, sit down against the cushions, and receive *gahwa* in a *sini*, a little handleless Chinese cup. The woman of the house has six children and none dead. Her husband has been away in Saudi Arabia for four years, and is expected back in Ramadan.

'My mother should have four more children,' the eldest boy says, 'so there are lots to fight if there's trouble.'

Another, half-familiar woman is there too. 'I've run away from my husband,' she says. 'I've been here three days. My father is dead, so I've run away to my sister.' She doesn't give any particular reason for having left.

'Have you left before?'

'Yes, the last time was a year or two ago.'

'Will you go back?'

'Yes, when we make it up.'

'How many children have you got?'

'Six – three boys and three girls – and three dead. And you, how many children have you got?'

'None, maybe I'll have one later, *inshallah*.'

'A child traps you, *yehnib*.' This, I suppose, is what has happened to her. She knows she has to go back for her children.

I head out of the tangle of small streets and go up and round the other side of the town to look at the view and see if Hamda is in.

'She's not here,' her neighbour says, 'look, she's over there.'

Hamda and another woman are sitting a couple of hundred metres away, on an outcrop of rocks. Pockets of water have collected in the rocks from the recent rain, and seizing this opportunity, the women have been doing their washing. The washing is finished now and spread out on the rocks to dry, and when I approach the two women are sitting on convenient flat stones, drinking *gahwa* they've brought in a thermos and eating a snack: *kak* and some dried roasted peas.

'Sit down!' They show me a good place on a rock, and pour me out some *gahwa*. I sit on the hard stone and feel the warm sun and sip the sweet spiced liquid from a small glass.

Hamda straightens up and calls '*we-e-eh*,' a drawn-out rising and falling cry, to a house up a small hill a few hundred metres away. It's the kind of call women use on mountainsides to carry over distances, hailing each other from one rocky outcrop to another across gulfs of empty space, a distinctive practice of the women who inhabit this landscape. Women I know demonstrate and exaggerate this creaky, screechy voice, a projected version of the way the older women talk. They get me to imitate it, and find this very funny.

'We-eh, *ya marat el katib*!' Wife of the scribe. She's calling the woman of the house up the hill by the name of her husband's post; he's a government official, clerk to the *mudir*. The woman from up the hill comes over to us with a pair of very good field glasses, and we take turns looking at the view, sharp and clear after the rain, neat rows of terraces descending into a valley at our feet, mountain peaks rising up beyond. We sit and chat.

'Do you have arguments with your husband?' the *katib*'s wife asks me.

'Well, sometimes. Do you?'

They all laugh and say they do.

'What do you argue about the most, with your husbands?' I ask.

They chorus unanimously: '*Gheda*!' The midday meal. '*Gheda we 'asha*!' And supper. Not having the meal ready when the husbands come home. If I'm out in the late morning, women always ask me, 'Where's Abdullah's lunch?' unless they know he's away. Then I'm free to have more interesting and productive late mornings.

I stand up to continue my walk. As always, the women tell me what to do. 'Go the other way, by the school, different from the way you came.'

I take their advice and wander in the direction of the school. It must be break time, the schoolgirls are out sitting on rocks. One calls me as I pass – my neighbour's daughter Nabila.

'Come in and see!' The girls lead me in through the door of the long, low, new school building. They show me three classrooms, one of which is theirs.

'We sit here, all together, four of us in fifth elementary, and the boys sit behind and on the other side. The teacher hits the boys but not us.'

One writes her name on the blackboard, Sabah, in English letters. She recites the alphabet and numbers in English for me. Nabila shows me her desk with books in, and gives me tea from a thermos she keeps underneath her desk. An older girl pupil is serving the Egyptian teacher milk tea. They tell me how many girls are in each of the higher classes – four in fifth elementary, one in sixth elementary, two in first intermediate, four in second intermediate. The school goes as far as third intermediate. To complete their secondary education, pupils must go to Sana'a. Some boys, who have family connections there, do this, but the girls' education is cut short sooner. Three girls have recently left to be married.

I say goodbye to the schoolgirls and veer away from the town. On the hillside a woman is hard at work rolling large stones downhill. As I get closer I see that it's Amina. She is moving stones for building. The stones have been blasted out of the mountain by dynamite, and she's getting them down to the track where cars can pick them up and take them to her husband's brother's house. I stop to help a little. We are joined by Khadija and Shu'iya, the old woman from a neighbouring house, on a *dowra*.

We all look together at a house in the process of being built. It's a shell of dressed stone walls, going only as far up as the top of the empty arches where the windows will be. The women talk about whose it is, how much it cost, how long it's taking to build, the family who will live there. 'It will cost them 200,000 riyals to build; they're paying rent of five thousand a month now.'

I walk back with Khadija towards home. As we get to her house she says, 'You must have *gheda* with us.' She knows Tim is away.

Lunch, when the children come in from school, is rice with potatoes and *zahaweq*, then fish and *filfil* pepper mixture and *lehuh*. Khadija got the fish from Bajil, she says. She must have either ordered them specially from someone who was going there, or snapped them up from the market (by means of her son or a messenger boy) and then salted them; there are some more hanging over a beam in the kitchen. They taste delicious, like anchovies.

As we sit around the plastic tablecloth on the floor, dipping our hands into the dishes, Khadija corrects my table manners. 'Don't lean forward, sit back upright.' This makes it slightly more of a challenge to get the food in my hand safely into my mouth, but I do my best. I wonder how many times I've been uncouth, hunched towards the food.

Shu'iya also eats lunch with us. Afterwards Khadija asks her, 'Have you got bread?'

'Yes,' the old woman says.

'Who gave it you?' Khadija asks, quite sharply, as if to check she really has some. Shu'iya gives a name, and Khadija seems satisfied with the reply.

'Come to us when you want lunch,' Khadija tells her. 'Don't go anywhere else, nowhere but here.'

Then we drink *gahwa* and the two girls go off to Hasib for water.

'If their father was alive now they couldn't go to school. He didn't approve of education for girls,' Khadija says. 'We moved here after he died because there's a school.'

Nabila and Karima both assert that they want to study, not to be married young. But then girls always say they don't want to get married. They say it vehemently, seem to mean it, but it's also a matter of form.

Khadija asks me, 'Where are you *rabakh*ing today? I've got no qat, the girls wouldn't agree to go down the mountain to our land to get it. I'm going to lie down for the afternoon.' So I cross the alleyway back to our house. Nuriya downstairs catches me on my way in.

'Where have you been? I wanted to give you some bread.'

Later in the day Nuriya and I go together to fill our *dabba*s from the water tank that Tim and I bought and keep by Thuraya's storehouse off the street. As we pick our way with the empty containers down the narrow street past the communications office, the men sitting there call out to me, '*Ya* Mariam!'

'Pay no attention!' Nuriya insists, and hurries me on though I want to stop. I would have liked to check it wasn't letters for us.

I struggle back with my load of water, feeling for my footing on the uneven stones, dodging the rubbish that litters the street.

An evening in Meruwagha

'I don't *semer* in my sons' house, because it's *ta'ab* with the children – I come here, to my neighbours, for peace.'

Tim and I are in Meruwagha *semer*ing, sitting chatting in the evening, with a small group of family and neighbours – Tim's friend Yahya, his sister whose house it is, and her older neighbour Sa'adia, my friend Warda's mother, energetic and bustling with a hawk nose and dignified bearing. We're relaxed and comfortable, leaning against cushions. The TV is on while we talk.

'In my sons' house they're all angry with each other, quarrelling,' Sa'adia says. Two brothers, their wives, and often also Warda, escaping her marriage or her mother-in-law while her husband is away in Saudi Arabia.

I reach for my vocabulary notebook to get down the word for 'quarrelling'. But Sa'adia, with a better memory than mine, says, 'You wrote it down last time!'

Yahya's sister, pretty, dimpled and lively, has had one child, who died. 'How old were you when you married?' I ask.

'Three or four years before I reached puberty. I've been married seven years now.'

'Do people still marry very young girls?'

'Not now, it's forbidden.'

We are chatting with one eye on the TV, which is showing a health programme. A picture of a baby with a bottle comes up. I ask about it.

'Breast milk is better,' Sa'adia says, 'better nourishment.' She adds: 'Some babies refuse the breast, because of the eye. The baby is *ma'yun*, "eyed". If a woman with the eye sees a baby feeding at the breast, this can happen, the baby's vulnerable to the eye when it's feeding.'

Yahya interjects: '*Khurafat*! Superstitions! What are you telling them this rubbish for?'

Sa'adia is not at all abashed. I tell Yahya that I very much want to know, since powdered milk in Yemen does a lot of damage and it is important to understand reasons women don't breastfeed.

'People who harm a baby with the eye are those with bad hearts, they see a nice healthy baby and say, "*Yu!*"' '*Yu!*' is the usual way women exclaim in surprise. I will find myself still doing it, years later.

'So one should say "*mashallah*"?' This, 'what Allah wills', is the standard expression, widespread in the Muslim world, to avert any harm and show good intentions.

'*Mashallah* is bad, you should say "*Gar'allah esh-sheitan*" – "Allah avert the devil" – that sends away devils at once,' Yahya's sister suggests.

'Do people with the eye know what they're doing?'

'Yes, a woman with an eye like this knows, she doesn't injure people by accident. My son was ill from something like this, he went to a *mubadbid* – there are none here, there used to be one in the village over there but he's dead now. The *mubadbid* got the *sheitan*, devil, out through his mouth and it ululated as it came. The treatment is with a *herz*, an amulet, he still wears one in his pocket, with *merr we hiltit*, myrrh and asafoetida, and a piece of donkey hoof in it – this sends away witches.'

She goes on: 'There's an illness, people die from it, it's caused by someone giving them ground-up human bones, from old graves, in their food or *gahwa*.'

'What about an *'ulla*, how does someone get that?' I'm keen to check what people say about this horrible creature. She says the same thing I've heard before: 'From *sagwa*, being given menstrual blood to drink in tea or *gahwa*. The blood stays inside, like a clot, and forms an *'ulla*, it has eyes. It comes out of a woman after she dies, and jumps about.' She makes vivid pulsing movements with her hands. 'Zohra Ahmed died after giving birth to Mohammed Hamadi, the baby was all right but after it came an *'ulla*, pulsing and trying to get back into her. It's *haram* to poison women like this – the dead one waits in the grave for her enemy, the killed one goes to heaven and the poisoner goes to hell.'

'Does this happen much?'

'A lot. Also poisoning with flea powder.'

'Don't people find out, send them to prison?' I'm thinking about the flea powder.

'But the dead person's dead.' Sa'adia shrugs.

'There are witches in Milhan,' she goes on. 'People die *besa'atu*, right away, without being ill, from them. No one knows who. Their blood agrees with the dead person's.'

She tells a tale we've heard before: 'A witch in Milhan turned a lad from near here into a bull.' She names the boy: 'It was the son of the *dowshan* who comes here sometimes, he travels round making money praising guests in gatherings.'

'How did she turn him into a bull?'

'What the witch does is make a person die, then she goes to their grave disguised as an animal and gets the person out and changes him into an animal. A *sayyid*, a descendant of the Prophet, saw him. He knew he was a man from his eyes; he was weeping like a man. He threatened the witch with burning, she blew on the bull and changed him back. Then she was burnt alive at the request of her family. The boy had been away for months, he was given up for dead. He was a bit deaf after that, his ears were *thagil*, heavy.'

Last time we heard the story, we were told the *sayyid* had passed his flip-flop seven times round the bull's head and then blown on him to change him back. And we were told that butchers often slaughter bulls which are really people.

'*How* does a witch change a person into an animal?'

The answer isn't clear. 'She has a *herz*, a charm, from *jinn*, a bad charm. Her blood agrees with his blood.'

We take our leave and go home puzzling. It's not the first time we've heard about the blood agreeing. Someone tells us it means the witch has to have the same blood group as her victim, but this seems like using a more modern idea to explain an older one. We are never to get to the bottom of it.

Photographs: a row with the sheikh

We take photographs of the scenery, the exhilarating vistas that surround us, the jagged rows of peaks and mountain crests, each silhouetted against a paler one behind it. It is only after rain that we can get close to capturing the magnificence that is always, except at times of mist, in front of us. After rain the air is clear and every peak stands out more sharply, ranged towards the coastal plain to the west.

We take pictures of the town, the many-storeyed stone houses with their tall windows on the top floor, decoration picked out in white paint, pots of green basil edging roofs and perched on ledges. I go up to the roof of the sheikh's house, at the top of the town, by arrangement with his schoolgirl daughter. From there the town is a jigsaw of intersecting flat rooftops at different heights, square and oblong, whitewashed, stone-edged, with little towers where the internal stairs come up. I can see container gardens, rugs spread out to air, clothing hung on lines and draped over parapets. We take pictures of any men and children who ask us. Hardly anyone in the town has a camera – perhaps a few Polaroids that take low-quality instant pictures, or one or two broken ones. Once, Tim saw a man attempting to repair a Polaroid camera that wasn't working by pouring in the valued cure-all *samn baladi*, local clarified butter. I've learnt that taking pictures of women is unacceptable or fraught with problems, but we photograph their children and babies at their request, and the children who run around and play in the streets. Sometimes people ask for a special picture to send to a relative abroad. Women ask for pictures of their children. 'Then if they die,' one says – a woman I don't know well, a neighbour of Hamda's – 'I can look at the pictures.'

A deaf boy who communicates in hand gestures asks us, as we cross him on a path outside the town, by miming taking a photograph. When he meets us afterwards, he mimes his enquiries as to when the prints will be ready.

At times we feel tired of the whole business of taking photographs of people. Sometimes we see the pictures getting crumpled and torn right away, snatched from hand to hand by children. Other people keep them carefully, and will get them out to show us years later when we come back on visits.

Women ask me secretly for photos. Sometimes there are repercussions later. One woman, Selma, and her sister-in-law ask me for pictures. They dress up specially in their newest and best clothes and I take several, and give them the prints when they arrive in the post. Later, when I offer to photograph Selma's new baby, she says, 'I'll ask my husband. I can't without asking him. There was lots of trouble over the pictures you took of me and my husband's sister. Her father was angry, he hit her. He's afraid they will appear on television. My pictures are gone from where I put them, I don't know who has taken them.'

Once, a whole household of women of all ages, married sisters-in-law and unmarried daughters, invite me, encourage me, to take pictures of them all. The men are away, or out for the day. Then I'm disconcerted, and terrified by the responsibility, when one girl says: 'You mustn't tell anyone. If anyone finds out, my engagement will be called off.'

Tim's friend Yahya, sitting in our room in the evening for an English lesson, instructs us: 'You shouldn't photograph any woman without permission from her father or husband.'

I try to work out the different attitudes. The male view is that men have the right to control images of their womenfolk, as they have the right to control their movements. However I follow the principle of going by what the woman says she wants, assuming it's up to her to assess any risk and decide for herself.

Photographs, and the struggle over control of photographs, are the cause of one of my worst moments in the town.

'I want a picture, take a picture of me for me to give my son.' It's the old woman we sometimes give water to, who lives alone in one room. I don't know her given name: everyone refers to her as *bint* Ma'rif, daughter of the village near the town that she originally came from. She's in our house when she asks me. She has come in with a group of neighbours and a swarm of children who are visiting, looking at our kitchen, criticising the state of it, the mess, the dirty gas burner. I try to defend myself by saying it's Tim's responsibility too, but they don't think so. I'd like to take a photo of this old woman's lined face, of her bent, neglected, but indomitable form; a woman whose children have gone, or who don't look after her, but who remains, hanging on, given charity, a regular presence in the street. But Tim has gone out with my camera, with the print film in, leaving his with slide film, which won't so easily make a print to give her. After the neighbours have left, and he has come back, I take the camera out to look for her. On the way I pass my downstairs neighbour Nuriya in the doorway.

'Go on,' she says. 'She's just out there, take a picture.'

'In the street?'

I've always been so careful, never taking any pictures of women where anyone could see.

'It doesn't matter.'

I assume she knows better than me.

I should have heeded my own misgivings. Just as I'm focusing my camera on the old woman, the sheikh passes on his way into the telephone office. He's immediately angry, shouting at me: 'Don't take pictures! All photography is forbidden!'

The sheikh has accepted photos from Tim, photos of men taken in his own *diwan*, his sitting room, but now he is defending the public face of the town. I'm taken aback. I don't get my picture, to my lasting regret. I am worried and badly shaken by the sheikh's displeasure.

Tim goes later to speak to him. He's still angry. No pictures of women, he repeats. And the children we photograph are dirty. Tim defends me: 'We've given people lots of photos at our own expense, only ever taken pictures of people who wanted them, and this woman asked for one to give her son.'

'You're making Yemen look bad, bringing discredit on the town. You take pictures of dirty children, sordid butchering, decrepit old hags. And you give people pictures, but not as many as you take, so some are staying in your country.'

I'm upset by this incident. It seems unfair, and also I am angry with myself after so many months of treading warily. A little boy comes and stands, gawping, in our house, watching me crying. It's all too much. Exhaustion with the whole process of trying to fit in, understand, behave appropriately, make sense of the bewildering, negotiate the unfamiliar, takes hold of me. I feel I've had enough, I'd like to leave the town.

Tim goes out and takes some pictures at once, especially of the hakim, who has asked him. Nuriya from downstairs comes up, very supportive.

'Pay no attention to the sheikh!'

A lot of others say the same. The sheikh's authority is not uncontested or automatically accepted. Our friend Yahya explains more carefully how he used to feel about tourists taking pictures of non-modern Yemen. But he also says I should have kept my dignity in front of the sheikh. I should have stood up to him, he says, I shouldn't have burst into tears. 'If the government makes an order, the best thing is to go against it right away, but not in a way to cause too much provocation. If someone gives in to tyranny, then anyone can push them around in the future.'

Bint Ma'rif's son tells Tim we have his permission to photograph her, though he can't see why we're bothering with an old woman like her.

Word spreads. Everybody asks us what happened. Most are sympathetic.

The rabble of kids in the street change their chant. Instead of the constant chorus of 'Photograph me! Photograph me!' which followed us everywhere before, they now have the cheek to shout at us instead: 'Don't take photographs!'

Big men

'Don't go to Sana'a on your own, the police abduct women. Abdullah should go with you. What do you want to go for?'

I went to Khadija's to return a bowl in which she had given me some *helba hamudh*. 'I made it specially for you, I only like it with *bagl*,' she said – the large white radishes that are served raw with their leaves. Now we're sitting, comfortable, in her room drinking *gahwa* and smoking the *mada'a* in turn, glancing at the street to see the cars that come.

'I want to get my post, and get my blood and urine checked because I'm always ill.' I'm tired. I have missed a lot of days, precious fieldwork time, because of headaches, flu-like illnesses and feeling simply, symptomlessly, unspecifically unwell.

'How can you go to a doctor without Abdullah? How will you know your way round the streets in Sana'a? If you get into a car, the driver might take you away. Aren't you afraid of the police?'

'No, I have papers.' I'm sure it isn't illegal for me, as a foreign woman, to walk around alone. Sana'a feels safe to walk in, probably safer than the streets of London. This is long before the days of kidnappings. 'Do you want anything from Sana'a?'

'No. I wanted a water filter, but I've ordered it from someone else.'

I go to Hamda's house to ask if she has any messages for her son, who works in Sana'a. I sit and drink *gahwa* with her and some neighbours. He hoped to get married last time he came to the town, but his bride's mother's husband was very ill, so the wedding had to be postponed.

'When's your son coming to be married?'

'I don't know,' Hamda answers.

'Shall I give him any message from you?'

'Give him my greetings, and don't ask from me when he's coming, only ask from yourself.'

'Why, would it be *'aib*?'

'Yes.' The women sitting round all explain together. 'It would be as if she was asking when he's coming with money and presents for her.'

Sana'a seems to me huge and crowded and noisy. I haven't been here for several months. A year ago I would walk around Sana'a in Western clothes, either trousers or a dress, head uncovered. Now I find I feel more comfortable wearing a skirt over trousers and a scarf on my head, as I do in Safaqayn. The more I cover, and the more confidently I speak Arabic, the lower the price of a taxi ride seems to be; now I'm charged 5 riyals a trip, where it used to be 10.

Tim is out when I get back, exhausted by the long, tiresome journey and the double change of altitude down from Sana'a to the wadi and up again, and stiff all over from the bumps in the road and from bracing my arm muscles while clinging on. Nuriya downstairs calls me in on my way up to our rooms and I am grateful to sit and be given tea. I am glad to be home.

In Sana'a I racked my brains for presents to bring back. I have vitamin pills for pregnant women which I give to three women I know who are pregnant, and whose nutrition is probably inadequate; but I don't think they'll take them. They are afraid the baby will get too big and cause problems at the birth.

'It's better for them to come out small, and get big afterwards,' one tells me.

I've brought packets of cardamom seeds from the spice market and frankincense, little lumps, both useful as presents because they're expensive; Tang orange juice powder; cloves and raisins; the resin chewing gum which looks like incense; and some nylon headscarves in bright colours and patterns. It's impossible to keep up with the constant small gifts, let alone the generosity of welcome, acceptance, time and patience in explaining that many women give me.

I find Thuraya on her roof washing clothes. I've come to her house with a brush and dustpan she asked for and some face cream, which is my idea. She wasn't in her living room when I mounted the stairs; she called from higher up, 'Come up, *ya* Mariam!'

I sit on the flat whitewashed expanse of the roof, smooth and warm to the touch in the welcome sun. The weather seems to have changed while I've been away, and now it's clear all day with no mist gathering.

I watch Thuraya vigorously pounding in a large, shallow metal bowl. 'You manage with less water than me, one wash and one rinse for each thing.'

'Except prayer clothes, they have to be rinsed till the water's clear.' Thuraya pours the water away through a drain hole at the corner of the roof.

In the enclosed yard below, on my way out, I see Khadija, in a small room off her courtyard, washing her hand mill. She's scraping and rinsing off the residue of runny sorghum paste. The mill has two round grindstones and a wooden handle to turn the top one round. There's a wide, shallow trough round the bottom. The grain is ground together with water, and the trough collects the thick liquid that results. It runs into a dish and will be kept for a day or two to ferment slightly before being made into *lehuh*.

'Come and sit by the door,' she suggests. 'Not on the stones, there was a snake there. I found it in Ramadan, it was curled round the grinding stone, I got a big fright from it.'

'What did you do?'

'I went to the mosque, and gave seventy riyals for a man to read the Quran.'

'Here in the house?'

'No, in the mosque, to make the snake go away. I haven't seen it since. Lots of people die from snakes.'

I ask about the sorghum she's grinding. 'Why don't you take it to the mill?'

'It isn't nice when it's ground at the mill, it's only good for a day and after that the *lehuh* falls apart. Ground by hand, it's OK for three or four days.'

'So it's not because of the money?'

'No, that's not the problem, it's only five. Sorghum flour for making *jehin* bread is all right from the mill.' I sit and look on and chat a little while longer.

Late that evening soldiers come to our house, at what seems to me an uncivilised time. They have come to summon us to the *mudir el amn*, the security director, a government employee who works alongside the *mudir el 'amm*, the general director or prefect. Tim has already been asked for his passport. He sat in the *mudir*'s office in the old government building outside the town, and explained I had taken it to Sana'a in order to try to renew his driving licence. The *mudir* was carrying out his usual work, dealing with a dispute. A farmer was trying to persuade him to send soldiers on his behalf: 'Someone has stolen 270 *ghusn*s of qat from my lands. I'm a poor man,' he said (although Tim noted he was smoking an expensive brand of cigarette), 'and the man who stole the qat is already rich.'

Now, in the office again, we show the *mudir*, a young man, all our papers. He is very nice and polite. He apologises to us for having to do this. I feel quite reassured.

Tim explains the stamps in his passport, where he's been, that there isn't a stamp from the time he spent in Palestine as it's in his Australian passport. The *mudir* seems to want to see this too, but Tim explains it's in London. One of his soldiers is a man we know, and he seems supportive and approving.

Finally the *mudir* asks to keep the passports overnight, saying he'll give them to us in the morning. It's all low-key, we are not alarmed. Perhaps they are bored and want something to read.

But the next morning, when Tim goes with his friend Yahya to get the passports, he's told they have been sent to Sana'a because our residence permits have expired. That is not true. It's early in the year and the permits are valid until August. I feel very shocked by this perfidy and lying. Tim appeals to witnesses: last night the *mudir* said all was in order.

'I'll give you ten thousand riyals if the residence permits have in fact expired,' Tim says to the *mudir*. Later, he recounts this to the group of men he's chewing with in the afternoon. It goes down very well. They congratulate Tim: 'You have really become one of the *qaba'il*.'

Meanwhile, anxiety takes hold of us. We spend tense hours trying to address the problem. We decide to phone the British Embassy, but the telephone office is locked. We go looking for our friend the communications representative, and on the way find our old friend Ahmed Ali, who helped us settle in when we first arrived. He immediately goes to the *mudir* with Tim. This time the *mudir* says Tim should go to Mahwit, the province capital, and tell the *muhafidh*, the province governor, about the problem. Yahya goes back to the *mudir*, this time without Tim, still to no avail.

We go to look for the communications representative again. On the way we tell the story to another friend, Mohammed Ahmed. We've known him from early days, but we've never spent much time with him, though Tim had *gheda* with him a few days ago. I've always found him irritating, bouncy and overbearing. 'Why didn't you tell me before?' he says, and he too goes to the *mudir*, also without success.

When we get into the communications office and try to phone the embassy, all possible numbers are either wrong or engaged. I tell Khadija about our problems. She is vehement about the general dishonesty and rapaciousness.

'The *mudir* wants money. All these officials "eat the people", extort their money. People are just out for themselves, you can't trust them,' she says.

'Should we give him some money?'

Khadija makes an emphatic gesture, twisting her hand downwards with the index and little fingers out. '*Walla buksha!*' Not a penny!

'Don't be afraid,' says Abdul Mughni, the post official with whom we have such an ambivalent relationship, as we pass him on our way up through the town. He is perhaps implying he will help us, but also laughing at our anxiety.

After lunchtime bouncy Mohammed Ahmed comes to our house. 'Don't worry, I'll get your passports, I had *gheda* with the *mudir*.'

He comes back later in the afternoon. 'You have to go to the *mudir*.'

He sets off with Tim. I am half sorry and half glad to be left out, not to see for myself, have a chance to persuade; not to be involved in the hassle. This is an example of Tim bearing the brunt of unpleasantness and the interface with officialdom, where I have an easier time. It wouldn't be impossible to be a lone female researcher, as others have been, but as we are a couple it falls to Tim to deal with some challenges, and I am partly sheltered.

I hear about it afterwards. They went into a small room with chairs – the only chairs in the town? – and a safe. The *mudir* kept protesting he couldn't return the passports as they had already been sent to Sana'a. Then he said he could return them if Tim gave proof of his other nationality. He took the point that Tim didn't have his

Australian passport with him, but wanted to see his ID, and it was impossible to convince him that there were countries where such a document didn't exist.

Eventually he seemed worn down by arguments. He asked if Mohammed Ahmed would be Tim's *dhamin*, guarantor. Mohammed Ahmed immediately rattled off an oath, which sounded like a set formula. The *mudir* wearily got up, opened the safe, and gave back the passports he had had all the time.

All the men who went to the *mudir* for us claim some credit for the result. We are warmed and touched, anyway, by the amount of support, the number of people who went to talk to him on our behalf. I tell Khadija we have the passports back and she seems relieved for us.

Tim's friend Yahya doesn't think the *mudir* was trying to get money out of us, but others do, and more than one asks us how much we had to pay.

It wasn't the Security Director but the *mudir el 'amm*, the general director or prefect, who at the end of our stay took Tim's mini clock radio and kept it, a nice gadget. He claimed he thought it was equipment for spying for Israel. He looked at it, agreed it was only a clock radio, but wanted to keep it overnight. Not to worry, he said, on his honour... When Tim went back the next morning, he said he had to keep it as Tim didn't have a receipt for it. After some argument Tim realised that he wanted it for himself, despite his tale of having to pass it on to National Security. He handed Tim 250 riyals for it, then rather gave himself away by asking exactly how it worked. Our old enemy Abdul Mughni was perhaps involved; Tim heard from Yahya that he had been going round saying it was a communication device. Abdul Mughni had been wanting to buy the clock radio, but Tim didn't want to sell it. He was attached to it, and, as he explained, it was a present from his mother. It would be *'aib*, Tim said, to sell it.

There is certainly gossip in the town about us being some sort of spies. Our friend the electrician says he's been asked about the strange thing we have on our roof. Are we using it to communicate with our country? Does he know what kind of signalling device it is? It's the makeshift TV aerial he constructed for us out of old tin lids. His wife, my friend Amina, says people told her we are reporting to the British government, and that we will cause problems between England and the Yemeni government. She says she told them this is not true. The sheikh tells Tim that many people in the town and beyond have warned him that we are spies, and he has stood up for us. And the German engineer who came to assess potential water projects: was it possible, as people had been saying, that he was communicating by radio with someone when he spoke into a small device in his hand? Tim had been careful to point out to people at the time that it was a tape recorder with mini cassettes, for taking notes.

But our problems with officials seem more to do with their personal gain than genuine suspicion. We notice again and again how nasty important men are, how badly they behave. To us they seem to be breaking the basic rules we think we've learnt here, behaviour we've internalised and now take for granted. Big men are rude. The norm is always to offer people food if you yourself are eating it. We pay a visit to the *muhafidh*, the province governor, in Mahwit, the province capital, and he eats a dish of choice morsels in front of us without offering us any. With hindsight, this begins to seem more like a pattern than an exception: important men enacting their status.

Big men hog the *mada'a*, or keep it close to them for long spells without actually smoking. They flout the convention of passing and sharing, flaunt their power by breaking the norms of politeness. Rereading Tim's field notes, I find that instances of important men being rude jump out at me. It has to be more than a coincidence.

Women of status seem to me to call on their privilege rather less. One day, early on, at an afternoon gathering, I'm puzzled to note the welcome given to a tall, gaunt woman I have seen once or twice. Women vacate a place for her, there's a flurry to arrange cushions and blankets, a sense of her being somehow special. I am left wondering if she's particularly liked and popular. But it is status being accorded to her. I realise later she is a descendant of the Prophet, one of only a handful in the town. (She is married, as in the past they never were, to the son of a prominent local 'tribesman'; that is, not a descendant of the Prophet.) However on this occasion she didn't accept the special attention, she demurred, protested, and sat somewhere else. In Tim's field notes, I am forcibly struck by the difference in ethos and atmosphere between the male gatherings he describes and the ones with women I spent my time in, the enormous and overt importance of status and hierarchy running through his account of socialising with men, the open exploitation and humiliation of 'butcher' men and the placing of some people in servile positions. Among women status seemed masked, to the extent that I didn't perceive it clearly till later.

I don't mean that the women were always nice. They gossiped, ran each other down, competed, were suspicious. But they did not often seem to publicly demonstrate privilege and contempt for underlings. Poorer women did complain that the 'big' people expected more in the way of a gift when they were visited after birth than the standard two tins of fruit. Women did use others for errands and for help – boys, girls, a woman who was said to be slightly feeble-minded – but somehow more tactfully or respectfully than the men Tim observed. With men status was a real concern, enacted daily. Men talked explicitly about a dog-eat-dog world, and the importance of not being seen to be weak. Women said themselves that they were intrinsically weak and powerless, that a woman was *terhim*, weak, pitiable.

There is law, mediation, traditional mechanisms of conflict resolution and redress, but also it is a matter of morality, of right behaviour, to stand up for your own advantage. A man can, and should, stand up for himself in the melee in front of the butcher's tripod and assert his claims. Being a man, even more so being a powerful man, is linked to imposing on others – demonstrating power, behaving badly because you can, showing off – not as a character flaw but as a necessary display.

Abdul Mughni the postmaster tells Tim: 'There's chaos in Yemen, Yemenis are like beasts of prey. The large prey on the small, it's hunt or be hunted.'

Our old friend Ahmed Ali says the same thing: 'You have to be a beast of prey like the others to survive here.'

He talks about a family land dispute: honour is the important thing. 'You mustn't be seen to be the loser. If people don't stand up for themselves, assert themselves when it's necessary, if they aren't prepared to use their weapons – then they will be pushed around no end.'

A shopkeeper friend complains to Tim about one man who bought goods and didn't pay. 'It's no use making a complaint about such a powerful man, I just have to forget their debt. Big men run up debts everywhere even if they have lots of money in their pocket, they oppress the small people.' He adds, 'You have to be like other people here, trick people, make money and survive.'

Big men are hospitable too, giving feasts and gaining prestige through generosity. This is at the cost of trouble for their wives. It is hard work being the wife of a big man, cooking for his guests, and women say so.

An afternoon's talk

'Sit down and drink some tea.'

I've come to the qat seller's house to buy a supply for the afternoon, and now I'm chatting to his wife. '*Mishqor* for you,' she says, and hands me a big bunch of basil, green with tufted purple bracts. I admire it, inhale the uplifting smell, then tuck it into my headscarf to hang by my cheek.

The qat is grown on land that is mostly hers. 'My land is from my dead husband,' she says. 'It's with my husband.' Her current husband, her second.

'You don't keep it separate?'

'He's the father of my children.' She is expressing a level of trust, a perception of common interests that not all women here feel. It is usual for women to keep their own property separate. 'And the house is both of ours, we built it together.' Though she then points out a particular room as hers.

'How many children do you have?'

'Four died with my first husband, none survived. Three died with this husband, and then four lived.' So there are no children from the first marriage to have inherited, to be in competition with the second husband. She would have liked more than four. She speaks sadly of the dead ones, but she seems content with her situation, that some children survived in the end, and with the joint enterprise with her second husband.

I take my qat the same afternoon to Na'ma and her daughter-in-law Fatima, whose company I enjoy because they explain things, and because Na'ma, with her shining dark eyes in her high-cheekboned face, acts out so brilliantly what she is explaining. I am aware that this is a family with poor standing in the town, and I'm not quite sure why. They say themselves that other people gossip about them, make imputations – here Na'ma makes an unmistakably sexual gesture with her elbow – about how they got the money for their new house. Other friends warn me about them. 'They only want things from you, when you go.' But even if they did, it still wouldn't repay my debt to them for their patience, their willingness to explain, and the entertainment of Na'ma's miming.

This time my downstairs neighbour Nuriya is *rabakh*ing there too, with her little daughter. They told me she didn't *rabakh* with them, so perhaps this is a new development.

I leave my flip-flops at the door, kiss hands, settle into the corner and sip my *gahwa*. I realise how much I am enjoying this, how it is good to be able to sit down and take part, talk and understand, feel comfortable in this room and in the language. I can follow the gossip now.

'Zohra Mohammed's baby died today,' Na'ma says. 'It hadn't suckled properly for days.' Zohra Mohammed is the worn-out, exhausted woman I saw recently who gave birth in hospital in Hodeida after being in labour for four days here, and who complained about having a baby every year, relentlessly. Though in that, she isn't alone.

'She'll soon be pregnant again, her husband doesn't wait till the *wafe*'.'

'But she looks so tired,' I say, 'she needs a break.' They all agree.

'Hamid's wife had her *wafe* yesterday,' says Nuriya, my downstairs neighbour. She describes the celebration: 'Henna, *nugash*' – extra decoration, made on the back of the hand with a sort of black ink. One afternoon, three weeks ago, I went downstairs with my qat to Nuriya and she said she was going to visit Hamid's wife, at a house close to ours.

'Is the baby dead?' I asked her then. 'I heard some women saying so. I heard they were taking it to Hodeida to the hospital when it died.'

Nuriya hadn't heard. She said: 'And she was happy to have a girl, after four boys. The baby was ill, something with its throat.'

'Which is better, girls or boys?' I took the opportunity to ask her.

'Girls are *haba'ib*,' she said: sweet, beloved, darlings; like her own little daughter.

My neighbour and I left the house together, and I went to buy two tins of fruit to give the *walida*, the woman whose childbirth was being celebrated. I was expecting to go with Nuriya, but when I came out of the shop I couldn't see her. I went to Khadija's to check if she might be there, and the old woman Shu'iya sitting with Khadija said she'd gone to the *walida* already.

I gave Khadija some qat and she pressed me to stay and *rabakh*. 'We'll go to the *walida* together tomorrow morning on the way, on a *dowra*.'

'No, I must go, I told Nuriya I'd go with her.'

'What are you going to give the *walida*?' Khadija asked me.

'Tins.'

'Give her money instead,' Khadija and Shu'iya both instructed me, 'she's poor.'

'How much?'

'Ten.'

I got 10 riyals out of my purse and ready in my sleeve. When I arrived at the *walida*'s, a small room with grubby cushions round the walls, Nuriya was already sitting there, with several women, and two men: the *walida*'s husband and his father. The older man sat in the middle of the women, and the husband over on the other side of the room. I pressed the money on the *walida*. She first tried to refuse it, then accepted.

A woman I didn't know asked a lot of questions about me. 'Does she sleep alone when her husband is away? Does she *semer* alone? Have they got furnishings? A *mada'a*?' Nuriya answered all the questions before I could.

The conversation was cheerful with laughter, but towards the end the women talked about babies and children they and other women had lost, and they told the mother, again and again, that her dead baby was a daughter of paradise. That was three weeks ago. Now I ask Na'ma about the *walida*: 'Is she still sad about the baby?'

'She's already pregnant,' Na'ma says. Is she joking or guessing? She's asserting something she can hardly know. 'Already thinking about the next one.' Na'ma passes me the *mada'a* and I take the mouthpiece, wipe it with my hand and inhale smoke.

'Mohammed Ahmed Saleh is really getting married this week. Zubeida's going to be *muzayyina* at the wedding.'

'Why not Zohra?' I ask. 'Isn't Zohra angry?'

'Yes, she is, the new one's taking her place. But anyway, there was a quarrel between her and the bride's father, a while back, he wanted to marry her, she said no.'

'Why didn't she want to marry him?'

'*Teramil 'ala juhalha*, she's remaining a widow for the sake of her children.'

The reason for not remarrying, they both explain, is care for her children, to avoid making problems for them by giving them a stepfather. 'Widows with children marry again or not as they please, but it's better not, for their children.'

'So then who provides for the children?'

'Zohra gets one thousand riyals per wedding.'

'But other widows?'

'They eat from people, get given their livelihood.'

Which *muzayyina* do you think is better?'

'Zohra, she plays and sings better.'

I think so too; to me, the beat of her drum is stronger, more compelling, the rhythm easier to follow with the small steps of a dance, as I've had to do when women have dragged me up to dance with them in front of a crowd. But later, I find myself sitting next to Zohra one afternoon, and she tells me, 'I've stopped doing weddings in town. They can have a young woman instead. I'm only doing outside.'

I throw sprigs of qat to each of the women in turn. They give me the ritual thanks, with a sprig held to the forehead: '*Akramish Allah.*'

I reply, '*Akram man akram.*'

'Ah, she knows now,' they say. Knowing the right phrases for specific occasions is seen as great progress in speaking their language.

The room is close and cosy, and smells of tobacco smoke and the sharp tang of qat. I pick up my sprigs, stroke them, stuff them in my mouth. Na'ma repeats to my neighbour the story she told me before of the nocturnal prowler and the spittoon poured on his head. Nuriya laughs, but I think she looks a bit disapproving. Then, lively and miming, raising her hand with a sprig of qat in it to mark the dramatic moments, Na'ma tells another story.

'The wife of my aunt's son had a man in the house while her husband wasn't there. Her mother-in-law came back and she couldn't think where to put him' – Na'ma mimes shock, perplexity – 'so she hid him under the bed. The mother-in-law went to get flour from where it was stored under the bed, and...' – climax, amazement – 'felt the man there!'

Everyone laughs, but I ask, 'What did she say to her daughter-in-law?'

This is rather off the point of the story, which was told, clearly, for the shock and comedy of the older woman finding a man under the bed when she went for flour.

'Her daughter-in-law asked her to say nothing, and she said nothing; she had eight children, her son would have divorced her... She knew anyway what her daughter-in-law was up to.'

Nuriya's little daughter Sabah is whiny, bored by the afternoon. She wants to go home. 'Can't she go out and play?' I ask. There are always children playing in the street.

'She can't go out in the street alone because of boys, they'd deflower her.'

'Youths?'

'Small boys, they'd do it, even girls, with a finger, to make her bleed.'

'A girl as small as her?' I'm shocked. She's four.

'Yes.' They mime how the boys would cover her mouth, and make perfectly clear entering gestures. They give me two words for what they'd do, one which I'm allowed to write down, and one which I'm not, because it's 'aib.

I wonder, horrified, if they really would. And later I wonder if all little girls would be equally at risk, or whether the fear has to do with what people told us, that our neighbours are weak. Would a girl from a powerful family be safer? Are the pioneer schoolgirls, disproportionately from prominent families, protected by their status? I think about people saying they're afraid to send their girls to school. I hadn't thought the dangers were so real.

Nuriya gives the little girl her breast to soothe her, and presently she falls asleep and the afternoon becomes more tranquil. I ask Fatima how many children she wants.

'Four, five like my mother-in-law,' she says, snuggling ingratiatingly against her. (She will in fact have seven.)

'And you?' I ask my neighbour.

'I don't want any more, that's why I'm still breastfeeding my daughter. If I stop I'll get pregnant.'

I ask about the older woman and mother of many who often *rabakh*s with them, and who said she is *mubazi* her baby. They explained then that it means breastfeeding her baby and not having sexual relations with her husband. This is possible because he has another younger, newer wife. 'Otherwise,' Na'ma said, 'the husband is waiting for when the wife reaches her *wafe*', he's ready waiting for as soon as she does.'

Now she says, 'Yes, it's so as not to get pregnant again. Breast milk when the mother is pregnant makes the baby ill, it gets thin and sick. As soon as she knows she weans the baby at once, but meanwhile the baby is drinking *wesikh* – dirt, contamination – from when she conceives to when she realises.'

'But surely most women sleep with their husbands and breastfeed?'

'We feed for a month or two, then we get pregnant again.'

My neighbour adds: 'Because she's *mubazi* her milk is clean, it makes the baby thrive, he's better for it.'

'So otherwise her milk wouldn't be clean?'

'The mother should wash after sex, and only then feed the baby,' Na'ma says. 'Before, I didn't have a bowl to keep near the bed to wash in at night. I had to go downstairs, and I got frightened – the door rattled, I felt something plucking at my clothes, I didn't know what. So I fed the baby anyway without washing, and washed in the morning, and the baby didn't get ill.'

'Would some women give a bottle, rather than wash at night?'

'Yes, but that's not good because once the baby starts on a bottle, the mother's more likely to get pregnant again.'

The conversation leads, then, to their telling me a proverb, a saying, that I will always remember as a bleak summing up of how women see their lot. It starts with Na'ma saying: 'My son went today with the man who's going to marry the new *muzayyina*, he's her father's brother's son.'

'What about his first wife?'

'He'll wait till she's given birth, then divorce her.'

'Won't she be unhappy?'

'Yes, she loves him a lot. He loves her, but a little.'

'Why doesn't he keep both?'

'Only big men keep more than one.'

'What would you do if your husband married another wife?'

'I'd be divorced.' She seemed to think it was better to be divorced than stay when all the attention was going to his new wife.

'Who will keep the children from the man's first marriage?'

'The woman till they're big, then the man.'

'Isn't the woman sad to give them up?'

'For a bit, then she turns to the new ones from her remarriage. A man has lots of children from his wife till she's worn out, then divorces her and gets a new one, and she leaves with nothing.'

Then they say: 'The mother of ten leaves and in her hand a stalk.' A straw, a sorghum stalk, a discarded, worthless thing – the word rhymes with 'ten'. 'He's done with her, he doesn't think about her any more.'

'Like a car,' I say, 'wearing it out and getting a new one.'

'True!' they say. Later I check the phrase 'The mother of ten leaves and in her hand a stalk' with Tim's friend Yahya. He shakes his head and says, 'Men would never use this saying.'

We stroke our qat sprigs one by one, put the tender leaves in our mouths, chew, push them into our swelling cheeks; the familiar rhythm of an afternoon, pacing the conversation.

I ask if there must be blood on the wedding night – what if the girl is afraid, or the man can't?

'Then the next night. People won't talk straight away. When the bride bleeds, the husband must fire a rifle.'

'Isn't rifle fire forbidden in the town?'

'He must fire, otherwise people will think the bride wasn't a virgin.'

'What if she's divorced, or widowed?'

'Then none of this.'

'When I get married, I'll fire a rifle,' says Na'ma's ten-year-old son. I think how, after all the weddings in the town, I've only once heard a shot sounding through the night, fired by the bride's father, and wonder if I've missed others.

Fatima, the daughter-in-law, tells us about her first marriage. 'I was fifteen, I hadn't reached puberty, I was still thin and not developed. I loved him before, but on the wedding night I bled so much I was frightened. I bled for a fortnight. Then I refused to sleep with him again, I slept with my mother-in-law for five months. After six months my mother-in-law said I must sleep with my husband, but

I ran away. My father sent me back once, but then he was kind and kept me.'

'So he's good, he loves you? Some fathers would make their daughters go back, by force?'

'Yes, they would. My father went to prison for five months. My husband wanted me back. After nearly two years I was divorced. I kept the *mahr*.'

She kept the bride's portion, they all explain, for the defloration and the blood.

'My father had to give back fifteen thousand out of the 35,000 bride price, that was the judgement. He married me to Mehelli, and paid from the 25,000 he got as bride price from that. I had met Mehelli once, he came to my village and I saw him, I decided he was all right.'

'Where will you give birth?' I ask her.

'Here, in the house.'

'Who will help you?'

'My mother-in-law.'

The ten-year-old boy describes with relish how Fatima will shout and cry out.

'Lutfiya Mohammed has given birth again,' Fatima says.

'She has a baby every year. If you give birth every year you can only breastfeed a little, it's not good,' says Na'ma. Many years later, I will hear of the fate that eventually came to poor Lutfiya.

'I breastfed Ahmed two years,' Na'ma goes on, 'and then two more, my husband had had an operation. Ahmed was very fat, plump and beautiful, I kept him in so no one would see him.'

'Why?'

'If women see a nice fat baby, he can get ill and die from eyes.'

'Who especially?'

'An old woman, or a young woman with a baby that was born at the same time but isn't thriving.'

'They're envious?'

'Yes. The Prophet said the eye and sorcery are true. The dangerous time is when a baby is four or five months old and plump. Later, a year or so, it's not dangerous.'

'What about twins?'

'People exclaim a lot, women say "*Yu!*", so they die.' The danger seems to be in the exclaiming, the amazement expressed, or envy. Twins were born in the town earlier in our stay, and named after the male and female lead of the current soap opera. Someone told us, 'They don't show them to anybody.' I feel bad because, in ignorance, I asked to see them. At that point I hadn't heard anything about the dangers of the eye and people looking at babies. Other people had happily shown me babies without being asked, and the family of the twins didn't seem to mind. Perhaps I don't count, am not part of the pattern of danger. I hope it's not that they were too polite to refuse.

There's so much I don't understand.

Endings

'Shall I come to your country and burn the women there?' says Khadija, laughing, as we sit in her *mafraj* one day sipping *gahwa*.

She's been telling me more about curative burns, *misam*s. Burns are made in different places on the body to treat different problems. Everybody does them; especially older women, perhaps, but I know one little girl who has several small white scars at the very top of her forehead which she says she did herself, with a lit cigarette, because she had been frightened by a dog. When I asked Warda if she had any, she showed me one on the back of her neck, large and irregular, from when she was weak after giving birth, and one on her head under the hair at the front, from after she had a fright involving a car.

Khadija says, 'I must have about twenty on my head for fright. Mild fright needs a burn on the head, severe fright on the stomach. If you get a fright and don't have a burn, it's bad for your liver, it makes you weak.'

Her daughter shows me a scar on her head, under the hair. 'That was for the fright after I was bitten by a donkey, I cried and cried.' And Thuraya has two scars on the back of her head above the neck, seared deep into the scalp, for a problem she had with her ear.

Another time, up in Thuraya's room, we look at a more recent treatment.

'It's come out really well, better than with a *sherim*.' Around and above her navel Thuraya has twenty or thirty tiny new blisters. Khadija is admiring, with slight surprise, the effect of the new method used to make them. She herself would have used a heated sickle.

'Ali Abdu's wife did it.' This is my friend Amina. 'She heated the ends of a broom till they were burning, and applied them.' I don't understand at first, till they show me the broom, a bundle of twigs with its ends now charred.

Thuraya has been ill for twenty-four hours. In this time, she has had two sets of burns administered by different people: the cluster on her stomach, and one on the sole of each foot. One foot has a cross shape of two burns made with a heated sickle. The other has only one bar.

'I couldn't stand to have the other line done, it hurt too much.'

'Doctors are better,' Khadija says. 'Going to a doctor is what people do, who can.'

'*You* wanted to do my stomach and legs with a hot *sherim* last night,' Thuraya retorts.

As well as the burns she has had a total of three injections from the Sudanese health worker and local pharmacists, and four lots of pills. Friends and neighbours visit, bringing thermoses, and sit and chat while she lies on a high bed, groaning.

Thuraya turns to me. 'Can you go to the hakim's daughters, and ask them to finish off a dress each, that I can't do? It's just setting the skirt on to the bodice.'

I find the dresses in the room upstairs where Thuraya's sewing machine is sitting idle, and take them round to the house nearby with the message. The hakim's wife welcomes me in.

'Sit and have some *gahwa*.'

I sit with the girls' mother while they finish off the dresses. She is the elder of the hakim's two wives, and lives in one room within the house, with a charcoal burner she can cook on and something I've seen nowhere else, a gas fridge.

After another day I am sent late in the evening to fetch the 'doktur', a local pharmacist, and he and the Sudanese health worker decide together that Thuraya must go to Mahwit, where there are facilities for blood and urine testing and X-ray machines, and relatives she can stay with. Our time in the town comes to an end before she returns, and I don't see her again till I come back on a visit four years later, and stay in the house with her and Khadija.

'When are you going?' Hamda wipes tears from her eyes when I tell her.

'We haven't got to know each other! You must come every day till you go.' She gives me some bread.

People keep saying they don't want us to leave. It's painful dismantling our home and existence in the town. I am having the most interesting time I've had since we arrived, now that I understand what people say, and know so much more about who everyone is and how things work. I feel I haven't finished, haven't understood everything, there is still so much I don't know. But, after a year and a half, I am exhausted.

'I hope you'll get money for your stuff,' Khadija says. 'You have too much, tourists don't buy so much, you're not *muwattenin*,' citizens. We have tried to be *muwattenin*, but now our attempts to be a part of the town seem invalidated by our departure.

Zeinab, the one who seems happily married with no children, wants to buy our TV. I go to see her and she bargains hard to bring the price down from 550 riyals to 500, but I stand firm. Then she comes round to our house to try to get Tim to agree to a lower price. We say we can't come down, we need the money towards our plane fare, but we agree to throw in the cord and clips for the battery. Then, after all the haggling, when she gives us the money she adds 10 riyals extra: 'For you, from me.'

When I say goodbye to Khadija, she tries to give me money for the journey, folded notes. I refuse it vehemently, so don't find out how much she was trying to give me.

We arrange transport to Sana'a and drive away, bumping over the rough road. Our last contact with the town, on arrival in Sana'a, is a nasty argument with the driver about how much extra we have to pay for the transport of our luggage.

IV
GOING BACK

1987

Karima breathes just slightly heavily with concentration and effort as she mounts the stairs with a large *barmil* of water on her head. It's for me to wash – far more than I need, heated, and very welcome.

It's 1987, four years since we left. Tim is working for a development charity down on the Tihama plain, and I am visiting. Already at the airport, between the plane and the terminal, my heart beat faster at the smell of the bus: already, it smelt of Yemen. Something like dust mixed with fenugreek and chilli powder and incense. Now I'm in Safaqayn for a week and, as Tim isn't staying, I have been taken in by the women who were our neighbours.

'It's best if you stay with me, there are no men, no problems,' Thuraya said. They are very sorry, though, not to have seen Tim when he dropped me off. 'It would have been all right for him to come in briefly, and drink tea,' they say. I sleep in Thuraya's *mafraj*, and eat with Khadija, Karima and Mohammed. Nabila is gone, married to a second cousin in another area.

'But she wanted to study,' I say.

'*Zowaj min Allah*,' Khadija says, marriage is from God. Just one of those things.

Karima doesn't study any more. The family would no longer let her. She's regretful; she would have liked to continue, she only got to fifth elementary. Her little brother is now in sixth, further than she ever reached. Now she sews for merchants in the market.

When I say I still haven't got children, some women respond, '*Beridu!*', leave it, forget it. Some time before, Tim visited the town on a break from his work. As he walked in so many people asked him, 'Has Mariam had a baby?' that he kept count and, he says, made it forty-two times.

Down by the cistern, a woman in a *sharshaf* rushes up to me and enfolds me in a warm, tight hug. She is veiled to the eyes, and I can't recognise her. Both Selma Yahya and Fatima Abdu tell me that they approached tourists who came to the town, asking if they were me or had news of me.

I walk around the town, get called in, visit as many of my old friends as I can. I feel anew how being here, doing fieldwork, is tough on my own sense of identity – always worrying, waiting to be told what to do, in the position of a child. But sometimes it works the other way. I remember who everyone is, and when someone is mentioned, I say, 'Oh yes, the son of Fulan.' The women I'm sitting with remark, 'She knows better than us!'

Our downstairs neighbours welcome us when Tim drops me off. The Qadi pours out blessings and a small bottle of rose oil all over our hands. We are grieved to hear of the death of their beloved daughter, the little girl we had grown fond of, who used to come up on her own and sit quietly in our room.

'She had pains in her stomach. We took her in a car to the hospital in Hodeida, but she died on the way.' Nuriya's top teeth are all gone. She looks old and broken with grief and loss.

'What's the use of life?' she says, *en el fa'ida?*

2000

Thirteen years after our last visit, years when we were busy with work and small children, we return to Safaqayn with our three children. We want to show them Yemen, and to show our friends in Yemen the children.

'Look, I did have children, in the end, after all!' I say, quite proud of myself for having, at last, joined them as a mother. People in the town are unimpressed. One after another, they say, 'What, only three?' Women I know have had nine in this time. Nobody seems to think that three really counts.

We stay with Ahmed Ali, the English speaker who helped us when we first arrived. He has a clean, spacious new villa with a garden around it in the overspill area outside the town, a space that's fast filling up.

I am struck by the number of warm, serious greetings from older men we used to know, which contrast with the rallying cries of 'Mariam!' from young men. We pay a courtesy visit to the sheikh.

Already in Sana'a I have met people I used to know as children. Ahmed Ali's son took me to a house with a big family of twenty-one people. One is Muna, who as a small girl took my hand and gravely led me around the town, right at the beginning of our time there. Her husband and his three brothers live in the house. The four *salifa*s, their wives, each cook for three days, clean for three days, and have six days off. I enjoy being able to talk about breastfeeding and pregnancies with the women.

'How long did you breastfeed?' Muna asks me. 'Good!' Everyone is very interested in my childbirth history and the operation for appendicitis that ended the suckling of my last child.

To my undying gratitude, Tim takes the children off donkey trekking in Manakha, an area more developed for tourists. It was boring for them sitting while I talked to women, and hard to find things they would eat, further complicated by it being Ramadan. They enjoyed Sana'a, the fabulous buildings of the old town. One Ramadan night we stood and watched the blacksmiths in the *suq*, fires flaming against the darkness, striking sparks off the metal they were shaping, and had fun guessing what each piece was going to be, as it was hammered and bent: an agricultural tool, a pair of tongs for picking up coals. The stay in Safaqayn was, for them, the least enjoyable part of their trip.

While they are away I stay, again, with Khadija and Thuraya. Khadija tells me about her daughters' marriages. Nabila is *murtah*, relaxed and happy, flourishing. 'Her husband's father has two wives; she only has to clean three *mafraj*es,' Khadija says. Karima's husband entertains a lot and so her life is *ta'ab*.

Mohammed, who was a cheeky small boy, is now a young man who wears the best jambiya in town, inherited from his grandfather, worth, I am told, the equivalent of £80,000. He is married to a second cousin. Khadija is no more happy as a mother-in-law than she expected. Her daughter-in-law, she says, doesn't do much work. 'It all still falls to me,' she complains.

Khadija tells me she went on the Hajj with the money from Nabila's marriage. 'Half went on that, and half in gold to Nabila. The Saudis take too much money for the Hajj, it's wicked.'

Many more girls are in school now. Khadija says UNICEF paid start-up salaries for women teachers, and paid sacks of grain and other foodstuffs to families whose daughters studied. That did the trick.

I try to avoid Khadija making breakfast in the morning, in daylight, just for me, by getting up to eat with them at 4am. My strategy fails completely; she brings me breakfast before I can stop her. I have to eat it as well as the 4am breakfast.

I make my rounds of visits and catch up with as many people as possible. Women call me in, beckon from windows, greet me in the street. A large number greet me whom I can't recognise. Veiling seems much increased. There are no more *sharshaf*s, though Thuraya says she wears one in Sana'a. Here women are wearing the more convenient *balto*, a long, straight black overdress, to go out, with a black scarf round the face, and perhaps a *saramiya*, black with a red stripe, thrown over the head and shoulders.

The clinic has two doctors who come from nearby villages. Local, home-grown doctors! One remembers me. He says he was in fourth class when I was here. He studied in Sana'a.

Fatima, the daughter-in-law of Na'ma, who I used to *rabakh* with, has had six children with a seventh on the way, and two dead. Adiba, whom I remember as young and cheerful, looks much aged after nine children and an operation so as to have no more, after years of *nazif*, haemorrhage. Once she was the young wife, with an older, sidelined co-wife. Now her husband has married another new wife.

On this visit I hear what happened to Lutfiya Mohammed. I didn't know her well, but I often saw her because she was the *salifa*, husband's brother's wife, of Selma, whom I often visited. 'Lutfiya died,' women tell me, 'after giving birth to her seventeenth child. She didn't have a haemorrhage, she had diarrhoea before she gave birth, a pain in her back after, and just died. She had a baby every year. We cried a lot for her, ah, she was good.'

Eleven of Lutfiya's seventeen children survive. Her husband has married again and they are now looked after by the new wife, who is herself already pregnant with her second.

I'm asked in by a young woman. She tells me who she is, the names of her parents. She shows me, on the wall, the picture I took of her mother's kitchen. 'That kitchen's been turned into a sitting room, there's a new kitchen upstairs.' She is now a salaried teacher. Six of her contemporaries, those who followed the first pioneers in girls' education, are now teaching girls in the six classes of preparatory school.

I come back up to the town at 9 o'clock from a visit in the next village. Safaqayn looks beautiful, lit up on the skyline. I check in with Khadija and Thuraya then go to *semer* with Selma Yahya till after midnight. Thuraya has kept her window open to hear me knock, over the noise of her sewing machine and the gas lamp. She pulls on the rope from three storeys up to lift the latch and let me in.

On our last morning, back at Ahmed Ali's with Tim and the children, busy packing up, I am unexpectedly called to the door. There is someone to see me. Standing there is Warda come from her village an hour away. I wanted to go there, but didn't manage it. We embrace. I'm enormously touched that she came.

2009

My daughter and her friend are spending two months of their gap year studying Arabic in Sana'a. They learn to good effect: more, it turns out, in two months than in the whole of a first-year university Arabic course. I take the opportunity to visit, and then go with them both to Safaqayn.

It's wonderful to be in Sana'a again, to feel its extraordinary atmosphere and bustle. Already, before we even get to Safaqayn, we get a massive welcome from people we used to know there, now in Sana'a for the further education of their children. I meet a new generation of educated young women, whom I knew as little girls. The older women of the household remember how I used to write down words in notebooks. 'What about the bad words?' ask the ones who didn't know me – the same old concern.

In the 1980s people knew nothing of where we came from, or where it might be. Now they ask me about the economic crisis in the UK: 'How are things there, are you all right?' And about

English attitudes towards grown-up children. 'Is it true you say to your children, "Go!"?' they ask, flinging an arm out to point at the door.

And they ask me, 'Have you written a book?'

Only an unpublished thesis, I explain, but I'd like to write about Safaqayn, what life was like then.

'You should,' they say.

Finally, I see Katiba again, at an afternoon gathering with primped young Sana'ani women at the bedside of a new mother, the wife of one of the toddlers who used to come to our place with Katiba. The new mother on the bed is hanging over her firstborn, moving the baby around and rearranging her, interacting with her, obviously besotted. I never remember, during all those many visits to women lying in after childbirth, seeing a mother paying any attention to the baby beyond feeding it if necessary. I wonder if this was to do with fear of the evil eye, but I don't know.

The young Sana'ani women wear shoulderless dresses and have very pale face powder which looks white on their olive skin. Their hair has blondish or copper streaks and is sprayed stiff in high waves over their heads. It seems like an exaggeratedly artificial ideal of beauty. They shock me by saying they want to have as many children as they possibly can. I remember women always complaining about having to have so many, desperate for the means to prevent it. I assumed, as more survived, people might want fewer.

When Katiba comes in, she's instantly recognisable. The scarf round her face hides the added plumpness and frames her features as they used to be. When she takes the scarf off to reveal a much broader, fatter face, and takes off her outside clothes, she is transformed into a stout middle-aged woman.

I am very moved to see her. We embrace warmly. We both wipe our eyes, then Katiba goes to sit down on the other side of the small room and immerses herself in conversation with the other women. This feels exactly right, an acknowledgement of the time we shared, briefly but intensely, long ago; then moving on. Sitting with the other women, she's jolly and laughs a lot.

In Safaqayn

'What's the point of education?' the old man says. 'Who is going to cultivate the land? People used to grow almost everything they needed, fruit, grain, vegetables... Nobody wants to do that now, they all want to go and live in the city. And the educated young people – there are no posts for them.'

His eldest daughter was one of the small group of pioneering schoolgirls – Muna, who took me by the hand when we first arrived and led us around. All his nine daughters have been educated. Now some of them are at home, helping to run the household, looking after the children of their cousin and one sister who do have posts in the girls' school.

The girls run cheerfully up and down the many stairs of the old house, getting things, making lunch. Their mother presides. Her lined face, after fourteen children (two died), still has a faded, serene beauty. One of the daughters stands in the doorway, beating up the *helba* in a bowl. She is using a small, thick, shaped stick. I've always seen it done with a bare hand (and tried not to think how likely it was that the same hand was supporting the uncovered bottom of a baby on the woman's hip just before).

Here I am again, one leg bent up and one down, having more difficulty folding my knees than thirty years ago, holding the still-warm round of bread with its aromatic little black seeds, tearing off a piece, soft inside, and dipping it into the bubbling bitter green froth. After the dishes of Sana'a restaurants, delicious in their way but still for me not quite the real thing, it tastes right, just like I remember, the mix of bitter and meaty and peppery and spicy flavours in rich, perfect balance.

The old man presses me to eat, and again, after I've refused with thanks to Allah. I'm really full. One of the girls looks at him and says, quietly but firmly, 'Enough!' To my amazement, he desists.

'Ah, *kan ayem*, those were days!' he says later, as we sit chatting after the meal. Looking back, the early 1980s when we lived in the town seem like a sort of golden age. There was money, from men's earnings in Saudi Arabia. People were emerging from poverty and ignorance, there was hope. Now, a generation of educated young people are adrift.

It is more wonderful and extraordinary to be back in Safaqayn than I can express.

I sit down on the foam mattress in the house of a woman who was born while we were first in the town. She was the baby her mother was carrying when I saw her, young, strong, and nine months pregnant, bringing a full load of water on her head back to her house with apparent ease. Now she has a toddler of her own. Also, she's an educated professional. Everything is familiar, everything is different. I have carried this place with me while I lived my English life, worked, had and brought up my children. It seemed as much another world as somewhere entered by magic through the back of a wardrobe or a hole cut in the air. The sense of stitching together and making whole my own life, the sheer joy of being back, are overwhelming. The full ease I had with the language thirty years ago is not there, but I can still understand and speak more than I had expected. Also, I feel more at home listening to and speaking the dialect of Safaqayn than in Sana'a, feel '*This* is what I speak', rather than Arabic or even Yemeni Arabic; a homecoming in the language.

Perhaps, however fluent I was, I would still struggle, fumble for words to articulate what I'm feeling, my wonder and thankfulness. My hostess is confident and self-possessed, bossy even, a teacher. She turns towards me the helpful face of someone who knows the answer, and tells me what to say: '*Sobhan Allah*' – praise God, glorious is God.

I repeat it. That will do. I am content to have words to express my sense of gratitude and awe.

My daughter and her friend and I reckon that there are a hundred women crammed into the room, hot and sweaty, the windows steamed up and water running down inside. It's a post-wedding party, *wafe' el arus*. The bride looks extraordinary. She has a huge, flouncy white dress. Her hair is streaked with highlights and put up high and stiff, with sparkly little flower spangles stuck in it. She is wearing masses of make-up; various strange colours on her eyes extend in points out towards her temples. Other women too are wearing lipstick with a black outline, an inordinate amount of eyeshadow, and pale face powder which makes them look ill and ghostly. A local girl, the little sister of a woman I knew, does the bride's face and hair 'for dollar money', we're told.

A handful of women have removed their black outer layer and are wearing sparkly clothes, but most have not taken off their *balto*s and headscarves. They are sitting there all in black, overheated, fanning themselves with ends of scarf as best they can.

'It's the custom, unmarried girls keep their *balto*s on,' someone tells me when I ask. But there are some married women covered up too. Customs have changed. I only remember once seeing a young girl keeping her outer clothes on, in a gathering where no one else did.

The music is recorded, not as pleasing, I think, as Zohra's playing in the old days. She stopped doing weddings ten years ago, and now there is no local *muzayyina*. Sometimes people hire wedding singers from further afield. As we watch women dancing, the music is described as Egyptian and Algerian. It seems to me a loss of local skill and richness, local production of art and culture. For me, a local girl who can put the bride's hair up in streaked, sprayed hoops, and paint her eyelids in many colours, doesn't compensate.

The bride stands up. The dance she performs – sexy, crisp, accomplished – is like nothing I remember seeing before. Then my daughter and her friend are dragged up to dance in turn, despite their cringing reluctance, and women ululate for them.

I produce from my bag a small album full of my old photos. People look at them and pass them on for a long time, group after group in turn giving them full attention, pointing things out to each other. They are hugely interested in the old pictures of the town as it used to be.

Towards the end of the party my daughter and her friend are decorated on the backs of their hands with something red, like henna, 'from Hodeida', an elaborate curving and spreading feathery-flowery design up their arms, at once free and intricate, done very skilfully by a couple of young women. It smells chemical and they say it burns slightly, but the result is lovely.

To my relief and joy, people are really, unmistakably pleased to see me. Khadija brings out an old padded envelope, addressed by me to her son as propriety requires, full of old photos from us. There is quite a bundle of them, an extraordinary assortment, all carefully kept: me skating in furry coat, hat and gloves, to try to show what the cold weather is like in England; my new baby when I finally had one, and later, our children.

Khadija's house has new tiling at the entrances to rooms and in the bathroom, new paint on the doors, redecorated by her son. Her son took her to visit her birthplace, which she so missed, more accessible now that the road is asphalt all the way. Her father is dead, but she saw her brother, and stayed a month.

She tells me with pride about her granddaughter's education: 'Nabila's daughter is studying at university. Nabila paid the fees with her own money.' This is the fruit, I reflect, of Khadija's determination, which got her daughters part way through their education. Now their daughters complete the process, as if it took three generations to get there.

The son of the house we first lived in, Ahmed, who was impatient to get a new wife, is now a bearded patriarch. He and Selma welcome me into the house they moved into and show me where their married sons and their children live in rooms scooped out under the ground floor. So she succeeded in moving out, leaving her in-laws' house to set up independently with her husband, but now has her own daughters-in-law under her roof.

I don't see Hamda, who worked so hard looking after her cow because her husband wanted milk and butter. I hear she is living with her sons in Sana'a. Her husband is here, has married again, has children by his new wife despite being, as people tell us critically, an old man. The new wife is a village woman, and keeps a cow for him.

In Sana'a, where she lives now, I see Warda. I spend half an afternoon with her and some of her daughters; she has had nine children. She reminds me once again how I first appeared in Safaqayn, *kashif*, indecent, wearing no trousers.

I look at gardens with a new and better-informed interest, because I now have a garden and an allotment myself. Fatima, the daughter-in-law in the house where I *rabakh*ed so often, shows me with pride the narrow garden that borders her house. Peppers, tomatoes, chillis, herbs, and small apples and peach trees. Another garden I'm taken round proudly has potatoes, beans, qat, coffee and a small banana shoot. Did people grow a smaller variety of things before, or was I just not so interested? I examine it all. I look at the worked earth, smell the coriander and mint, avoid smelling the rue, admire the little shiny developing peppers, marvel at the apples and peaches. I feel the bridge that gardens make, a connection across cultures and distance between people who grow things. I tell them what I produce in my allotment, show pictures. They can make sense of me growing vegetables on a plot of land rented from the local government. Do I sell them, they ask, but I explain it's just to feed the family. When we go, I take back seeds of Yemeni flat onion greens and Yemeni basil, green and purple, and a yellow fluffy flower from our hostess, and rocket and parsley in little paper twists from Fatima.

Mixed with the pleasure of being back is the anguish of change, of what's irrecoverably gone. It seems to me, from what I see in Sana'a and Safaqayn, that the fashions have become part of a wider global, or Middle Eastern, scheme. Before, they were local: even areas quite close to each other had distinctive clothing for women. In Milhan, an older style of smock dress, black velvet with coloured metallic stripes, and yellow and black striped trousers with a web at the knee that formed a decency-preserving panel when the wearer sat with legs apart. In Jebel Mushriq, less than ten kilometres away as the crow flies, everything overdyed in a turmeric shade of yellow, with the original pattern and colour showing through, so that I saw women spread over a hillside all in a striking, co-ordinated red-orange-yellow colour scheme. I asked about it and they showed me a tin box of powder dye labelled 'Metanil Yellow', imported from India. And in Safaqayn the bright coloured nylon dresses with tight bodices and full skirts to just below the knee, with flared trousers below. In each region the women used a distinctive, different scarf or shawl, associated with that area even though it might be imported from India or the Far East. One woman I knew visited her family in Adhra, seven kilometres away if one were a crow and didn't have the steep descent into the wadi and the climb back up. Afterwards she wore the yellow-and-black-and-red headscarf of that area for a few days, and gave me one; but when I wore it people commented unfavourably. Even *sharshaf*s seemed Yemeni, a different cover-up from adjoining countries. Now, only a few older women still wear *zenna*s like before; most are in waistless, long dresses, bought rather than hand-sewn. The long, straight black nylon *balto* looks as if it could be worn anywhere in the Middle East. Instead of the bright-coloured *lithma*s – pink, green, red, yellow – worn around the face, with a *saramiya* or *sharshaf* veil on top, women are wearing black veils with small eye slits, which again have to me a generic Middle-Eastern look.

There is more covering up. I wonder if what I always used to wear – skirt over trousers, sleeves to wrists, or nearly; small scarf over my hair, with some showing – is enough now. I start to wear a longer scarf over my head and wound round my neck, to hide all my hair. In Sana'a I buy a *balto*. I hate the slimy black nylon. My daughter and her friend wear theirs daily, going to their lessons and about the old town, always together. Several people tell them they would make good wives for brothers, because they get on so well; or, one suggests, co-wives for the same husband.

Men's clothes have changed too. Gone are the *futa*s, simple skirts gathered at the waist, in grey and white, pink, sky-blue and primrose. In Sana'a our friends' sons wear trousers. In Safaqayn everyone is wearing Saudi-type robes, white, like a collared shirt extended to the ankles, but still with a jacket.

The town doesn't smell of woodsmoke, that most characteristic and evocative smell of the morning that used to hang in the air as women lit their bread ovens. Now everyone has ovens which are still cylindrical, for sticking bread on the inside, but gas-fired. No more thin, curling columns of smoke, rising at intervals, all over the town. This is progress, I should not regret it. Women don't have to buy or carry firewood and kindling; the end of another task that was *ta'ab*. Most people say the bread tastes the same.

Houses also now have piped water, though it often doesn't run. It comes up from the wadi far below. In the house where we stay, our hostess offers to do our washing: she has a washing machine, as well as running water from taps. Even a fitful supply must make a huge difference to women's daily work; getting water was the most tiring task they still had to do. At the same time, the absence of a regular, legitimate reason to range further than the neighbouring houses must make a difference to women's lives and constrict their world. But nobody says they would rather have the work. Leisure was always valued. The usual way of saying someone is happy, *murtah*, derives from words rooted in rest: to be relaxed was to be content.

Almost worst of all is the loss of the stars. I told my daughter and her friend about the sky at night, after the generator was switched off: the unimaginable number and density of its crowding, dazzling stars, more than you would ever dream of from nights at home. I hoped there would be a clear night, but this time the nights are cloudy: rain is expected, though it doesn't come. But worse, there are street lights. The household electricity supply is unreliable, with long power cuts, but the street lights aren't cut and stay relentlessly on all night. There are no more stars visible than in urban England. I wonder how far we would have to go away from the town, into a clear night, to see those skies again.

The greetings have changed. When women enter a gathering, they still go round the people already assembled, but I don't often see the old alternate-hand-kissing that seemed such a fixed and characteristic ritual. They either embrace or shake hands – like people in large parts of the globe – and don't always kiss their hands afterwards. Older women still kiss hands, or more anyway than the younger ones do. I miss the charm and measured, patterned warmth, the elaborate politeness of the hand-kissing, like a miniature dance, the few moments of contact and exchange it gave with each woman in turn.

It's at least a couple of days before I'm offered any *gahwa*, which, together with spiced tea, was the old staple, automatic offering of hospitality. People often buy cold fruit drinks instead, more than before. The hospitality is costing money. *Gahwa* didn't, as people often had coffee from their own lands; friend after friend still gives me whole dried coffee berries to take home with me. Every shop sells bottled water. I wonder if anyone goes to Hasib any more.

Am I imagining it, or is the hospitality more unpleasantly pressing? Before, it was easy, effective and not, as far as I understood, rude to say bluntly, 'I don't want it,' when offered something. Certainly women did to each other. Now we are definitely having to drink more fruit drinks than we want. At a meal, saying *alhamdulillah*, praise be to God, meant you were full and usually you weren't urged further, or not much, in contrast to other Middle Eastern countries where the pressure to eat was more intense. Now we are feeling that pressure, as if customs have fallen in line with a wider Middle Eastern norm.

There are new, separate, lower and upper school buildings for boys and girls. Our teacher hostess shows me round the girls' building with appropriate pride. The girls' classrooms are full. I take pictures of the little girls, neat and clean, sitting at desks in sober rows, long scarves – white, coloured, patterned, leopard print – wound and tucked and pinned around their faces and falling over their shoulders, and the older ones in black veils with slits for their eyes. I speak to the class, congratulate them on being there, on their education. When I first came here, I say, the school was outside under a tree. But there is still no electricity or computer in the girls' school. The teachers are home-grown, Yemenis from the town. The school directors, sitting in an office with maps and posters on the walls and flowers in a vase on the table, are men I knew as very small boys. They give us cold drinks.

The girls are being educated, but what for? Female education has resulted in a pool of unemployed young women, as well as young men. I still can't feel it's a bad thing. I feel moved by the classroom full of girls. I remember all the girls who for various reasons didn't go to school before, and Khadija's struggle to get her daughters educated.

The town is much more built up, and the population said to be three thousand – at least twice what it was when we were there. And the population of the mountain, at forty thousand, has doubled. We're invited into houses which are new buildings, fine and imposing, with interiors much cleaner than any I saw before, slick, amazingly elaborately decorated with shiny coloured walls and lurid plaster mouldings. But the rubbish is if anything worse, a still unsorted problem, with an added piling of plastic water bottles on a rubbish heap on one side of the town.

Women wear henna in patterns now, flowery stencilled designs. I remember bringing Indian stencils back from Sana'a before, but no one was interested: it wasn't how they did it then. Babies and small children wear nappies. Qat is sold in little plastic bags with the tender leaves preselected, and women carry these little packets of qat in handbags, instead of long, wrapped *rubta*s tucked under a corner of their headcloths.

Older women used to be thin and screechy, now they're stout and screechy. Middle-aged women are really much fatter. One, whom I thought hauntingly, wistfully lovely as a girl, has thickened, in contrast to her mother whose beauty still shows in her thin, worn face.

And there is a new horror: mobile phones. Everyone has them. I dread phone calls, I find it almost impossible to understand fast Arabic on the phone. I am amazed, shocked, that when Tim visits, later that year, with our younger son, when I am back in the UK, he describes talking to a young woman – one we knew as a baby – on a phone from the next room, rather than face to face. Is she extreme in her observances? It's very different from the days when roomfuls of women called him in so they could have a look at him, and seemed to feel that as a non-Yemeni he didn't quite count as a man.

From the tallies of children that women have had in the intervening years, it seems that far fewer babies are dying than in the past. But there has been one particularly poignant death recently. It was the common old scenario, a woman in labour for hours, days, with the baby stuck, eventually taken on the three-hour drive to Mahwit too late to save it. But this woman – I knew her as an infant – had seen her baby on a scan, in Sana'a. Technology was there to intensify her loss, but not at her time of need, to prevent it. The state has cracked down on the unqualified pharmacists in town. But the new polyclinic built while we were there still lacks the equipment or the personnel to deal with the pressing needs of women in difficult childbirths.

Keen young men have set up a computer office in a house in the town. They have developed a website, with pictures of the landscapes and villages of the mountain, hoping to encourage tourism. I have brought lots of old prints of the town, photos we took nearly thirty years ago. Whole roomfuls of people pore over them, pass them from hand to hand, point the houses out to each other.

'That was Ali Fulan's. That's been pulled down now. Look, that's before they built on there.'

'Look how the town's grown. And how small the next village was before, hardly any houses!'

When I get back to the UK, and before Tim visits, he rounds up every photo and slide of men, children, landscapes and the town that we had taken, several hundred, and scans them on to disks. He has prints made of the pictures of people. On his trip he takes the disks and prints to give. People are fascinated.

'Look, that's your uncle!' men point out to a younger generation. Men and women ask for old pictures of themselves – 'You photographed me when I was a baby!' He hunts among innumerable, hard-to-distinguish pictures of small children, and I look for more at home.

'Is the town on fire?' one boy asks, looking at a picture of the smoke from the wood fires in the old bread-baking ovens, rising among the buildings of the town as it did every morning.

There's a special women's showing of the pictures on the disk, fed into a TV in someone's house, for women to crowd in and see. I can hardly bear the frustration of being in England and not there, of missing this occasion. The young men who created the website are now delighted to add scenes from the past. In the early 1980s nobody else photographed the town and the people and now they are glad to have this record, to be able to see what is gone or changed, to remember people who are dead. Tim gives a disk to the sheikh.

When Tim visits I send some packets of seeds from a garden centre with him as presents. When he returns he brings a small bundle. 'Fatima gave me this for you.'

A black plastic bag. I fumble, untie it with eager fingers. Inside I find six or eight little knotted twists of thin, rustling plastic, fragments torn from plastic bags. I can see through the thin plastic: each one is knotted around a little heap of seeds. I sit at my kitchen table and carefully pull apart the knots with my fingernails. Each twist of plastic has a scrap of paper inside, with blue lines on – torn from a school exercise book? They are labels, naming the seeds. *Bay'ah, ward 'anbar, jirjiri*. Onion greens, a yellow flower, rocket. There is also a handwritten note, and I see with excitement that it's a letter! It's written as if from Fatima, but the letter explains at the end that all the writing has been done by Fatima's daughters. They – the baby she was pregnant with when I left, and her successors – went to school, part of the first literate generation of girls.

The *bay'ah*, especially, flourish in my garden, produce their strap-shaped leaves and pretty, round pinkish flowering heads on long stalks.

The phone rings in our house in Oxford. I hear Yemeni Arabic, 'Ya Mariam!' This is surreal, it's unbelievable, two realities brought into an impossible conjunction: one should make the other dissolve, crumble away. It is Warda, bright, vivacious Warda. I saw her so briefly, a quick catch-up at the end of my visit, and wished there was more time.

All the time on my last trip I was plagued by phones and phone conversations. People who felt responsible for us would ring once, twice a day to check we were all right. I could never understand. I depended on sitting with my interlocutor, watching them, willing them to speak slowly and clearly. Phones became my bugbear. Now, the most intensely frustrating of all: I can hardly understand a word. I can't even make out if she's ringing for a particular reason, or simply to bridge the gap, keep in contact. Dislocated, head spinning, appalled at what is slipping from my grasp, I stammer what I can, and give up. I gather only that when I come back, I'm to let her know at once, come and see her. I nearly missed her this time and the last time, only caught up with her when I was about to leave.

The only thing I can do is hope to go back soon, and I decide that I will try never again to leave longer than two or three years between visits.

But my plans fail. There are incidents of foreigners being kidnapped, and then it's not only the east, the south, the north that are risky, where there are long-standing conflicts, but everywhere. In Safaqayn, in the west, people kept telling us with pride how safe their area was. Now everywhere is dangerous. Travel permits to leave the capital are unobtainable. I think about going just to Sana'a, where after all there are plenty of people I'd love to see. Then foreigners are kidnapped in Sana'a, in the centre, in broad daylight. Even before the later onset of war, the risks are serious. I long to go back, and I can't.

The experience, the life of the women of the town settles in my head. I try to hold the contradictions: the enviable close support of women, the visits at critical junctures, childbirth, sickness; the gossip and criticism and watching by which women control other women and social norms are enforced; the tight relationships with in-laws and brothers' wives that can be happy or intolerable. The marginality of men, their posturing and bluster on their stage while the women keep the show going behind the scenes. The cruelty of the conditions women live in, the so-frequent deaths of babies and children, never forgotten, always numbered along with the survivors. The lack of medical care and the work to safeguard health which they pursue by all available means. I think about the general constraints, on movement and independence, and the specific women I knew, their individuality and spirit.

In children's stories the characters go into other worlds, by a sudden instant transfer, through rabbit holes or wardrobes or holes in the fabric of this one, or through the frame of a picture. Within the conventions of children's literature, they mostly cope unfazed, and return again as if it had all been a dream; in the Narnia books, for example, they return to the instant of their departure, even when years have passed and they have grown older in Narnia. But when I returned from my long stay in Safaqayn I felt as if I had been to another world and was changed and dislocated by it, and coming back to my own was not simple. Re-entry was hard. I didn't know how to cross the road at home any more, having adapted to a technique of weaving through traffic making eye contact. I couldn't believe it was really all right to hand over money in my left hand. These are trivial examples. I was deeply dislocated in who I was. I felt as if I had been to the moon. Nobody was interested – or not as interested as I was. Yemen, my experiences, were a separate part of my life; yet they were an integral part.

Over the next years I thought about Yemen as I wrote my thesis, slowly, interrupted by the arrival of my children. I made those brief return visits and each time got hennaed so I could wear the evocative hand and nail colour home and bridge the gap. My daughter did an Arabic course in Sana'a.

And at the same time they, the people of the place I knew, are coming closer; the world is becoming more unified, globalised. Mobile phones, even the fashions, children of people I knew learning English and going to university. And Warda's phone call, that I couldn't understand.

The only answer is to go back again – but it's never a permanent answer. It's as if there is a crack in me that I can never quite close.

Was my time in Yemen all for me, an enriched self, greedily living extra lives? I wish I could do, or have done, something more useful: be a midwife, a doctor, help in some way. I wasn't useful to the pressing needs people had then. And now, when to love Yemen is to feel pain (and how much more, and how much more again, since I first wrote those words in earlier drafts of this book) – I am helpless. If only I could do something.

'I want to know all about your lives, want to understand everything...' This is what I said to the women of Safaqayn. But of course theirs was an impenetrable world of interconnected lives and inconsistent customs I could never really know. There would always be surprises, shocks, puzzles.

But I do know quite a lot... And what I know is a world that's gone, that was changing then and has changed even more in the intervening years.

What does it mean, what does it do to us, to go somewhere else, be somewhere else, experience something so different? Nothing is ever the same again. It is right that it should not be the same again. It's important to know that there is an other, to know that there isn't only one point of view or way of being. As the world becomes more uniform, how do we hold on to this? I am writing not about how it felt to be them, nor even only about how their society worked, but about that experience of otherness, connecting with others across a gulf of assumptions; to celebrate the existence of difference before it's swallowed up by a monolithic – or polarised – world.

Things that have seemed one way can seem another way. It's the most banal realisation, ordinary, but it is important. To try and understand what is different, like learning a new language, affects the self and shakes the taken-for-granted. This is painful, and a privilege.

It is always there inside me. But what is? The possibility of difference. The importance of experiencing otherness. A change forever in my relation to reality. My journey has been from the outside to the inside, from observing to feeling, from admiring a landscape and a picturesque world around me to absorbing it. What was once the exotic and the unfamiliar has become incorporated into me – literally, in my body, as I say 'Allah!' when I stumble, beckon with my palm held downwards, give change with my right hand; but also in my mind. The other that was outside me is now inside.

GLOSSARY

This glossary contains words not immediately glossed in the text, and recurring words.

'aib shame, shameful, not done
'andinna with us, at our place
'asha prayer time, after *maghreb*
'asr afternoon prayer time
'athek species of the sandalwood family, used for tanning hides
'uzzab species of oregano
ajr reward
balto full-length, narrow, black outer gown
balugh post-pubertal
barmil round metal water container
beit house; *beit Mohammed* Mohammed's house
beit el ma 'house of water'; bathroom, latrine
bilad country
bint daughter, girl; *bint Mohammed* Mohammed's daughter; *bint* (or *bint es-sahn*) 'daughter of the dish', layered pastry dish with butter and honey
dabba plastic jerrycan
dafi bread heated up into a sort of porridge with milk and *samn*
diwan reception room
dowra outing, walk or drive for pleasure, excursion
dunni! (imperative, f) duck, bend down!
efter to have the evening meal that breaks the fast in Ramadan
feter evening meal that breaks the fast in Ramadan

futa skirt or sarong worn by Yemeni men

gafu'a flat bread enriched with oil and eggs

gahba whore, prostitute

gahwa coffee, but in Safaqayn used for *gishr*, a drink made from coffee husks and spices

gheda midday meal

ghusn sprig of qat

gumi! (imperative, f) get up!

gushab a herb, *Picridium tingitanum*

hakim judge

haniq angry, used particularly when a woman leaves her husband's house in protest

haraban (dialect) she has run away

haram wicked, sinful, religiously prohibited

helba fenugreek; also stew of meat broth and vegetables topped with beaten fenugreek froth (called *selta* in Sana'a)

helba hamudh sour *helba*, beaten up with sugar and vinegar substitute

herz talisman, charm, amulet to protect against evil

heynan decorative herb, a species of *Lavandula*

ibn son; *ibn* Mohammed, son of Mohammed

inshallah Allah willing

itfaddalu 'andinna (pl); *itfaddali* (sing, f) come in

jazzar butchers; in wider sense, a status group

jehin bread made with millet, sorghum or barley flour

jinn (pl), *jinni* (m), *jinniya* (f) spirit, demon, being of a different kind from humans

kak small glossy buns made of dough enriched with egg and oil

kashif uncovered, exposed

khadhab black substance used to paint decorative patterns on arms and hands

khobz flat rounds of wheat bread

khazzan storage tank

kohl eye cosmetic of ground antimony

ku'ub breasts, of a young girl

lehuh thin, spongy pancake-style bread made with fermented sorghum batter

lithma thin nylon scarf wound round the face as a veil

ma'shara tray

mabruk (reply: *Allah yebarak*) congratulations

mada'a tall water pipe for smoking tobacco

mafraj top-floor reception room

maghreb sunset

mahr the portion of the money paid by the groom to the bride's family that goes to the bride

merkez administrative centre

misam curative burn

mishqor herbs or flowers worn as decoration

mubadbid practitioner who treats possession by devils

mudir manager, head, chief

muzayyina wedding attendant, musician and decorator of the bride

qaba'il 'tribespeople', a social status, to which about three-quarters of the town belong; adj. *qabili*

qat (often spelt 'khat' in an East African context); a bush of which the mildly stimulant leaves are chewed

rabakh (verb)/ *rabkha* (noun) to relax in the afternoon/afternoon's relaxation *rubta* bundle of qat, made up of long shoots and twigs, including some older leaves

sadiq male friend

salifa husband's brother's wife

samn clarified butter

saramiya headcloth or thin shawl

seil in this area, a spring in the side of the mountain

semer to sit up and chat in the evening or at night

shahi tea

sharshaf black outdoor covering with full skirt, cape and veil

sheikh tribal leader

sherim small sickle used for cutting fodder

shfut dish of *lehuh* soaked in buttermilk

suq market; street of shops or weekly market

sura picture, photo

ta'ab tiring, exhausting, hard work

tafrita word used in Sana'a to describe sitting and relaxing in the afternoon, equivalent of *rabkha*

tannur cylindrical clay oven

wafe' completion, e.g. of confinement after a birth

walida woman who has given birth

we and

yu! women's exclamation of surprise

zahaweq relish made with ground tomatoes, chillies, herbs and spices

zebb penis

zenna dress with close-fitting top and full skirt